THE OLD BAILEY

The Old Bailey

*Eight Centuries of
Crime, Cruelty and Corruption*

Theresa Murphy

MAINSTREAM
PUBLISHING
EDINBURGH AND LONDON

First published in Great Britain in 1999 by
MAINSTREAM PUBLISHING COMPANY (EDINBURGH) LTD
7 Albany Street
Edinburgh EH1 3UG

ISBN 1 84018 762 X

This edition, 2003

A catalogue record for this book is available from the British Library

Typeset in Berkeley Book
Printed and bound in Great Britain by Cox & Wyman Ltd

CONTENTS

PREFACE

There is little unique about any of us. We take our opinions from the media, our religion from the church, our history from the schoolroom and our laws from the Romans. Each has landmarks that we use to guide us through life – such as the date 1066 in history, the birth of Christ in religion and the Old Bailey to epitomise justice. The world-famous Central Criminal Court is fundamental to our belief that Britain is a democracy rooted in the rule of law. But today what was long regarded as an absolute is being seriously questioned. A succession of revealed blunders, with innocent men being released after many years in prison, has it that either British justice ain't what it used to be, or that good old Abraham Lincoln had it wrong, and you can fool all of the people all of the time. Stewart Steven, a columnist for the *Mail on Sunday,* once wrote: 'We are all in contempt of court. How can we be otherwise in the face of the Stephen Lawrence case or the Hanratty miscarriage of justice?'

We once could measure our temporal and spiritual progress by the yardstick of comparison between the barbarity of the original Old Bailey and the humane procedures of today's fine and stately building. Yet where is the difference between sentencing a boy to death in the first half of the nineteenth century for the theft of twopennyworth of hard paint, and the hanging of a young man in the second half of the twentieth century for a murder that he did not commit? Can we take pride in any advancement in our criminal justice system, or have we gone round in a circle of delusion?

Maybe Rose Bertin, dressmaker for Marie-Antoinette, was right when she declared: 'Nothing is new, only forgotten.'

If, as Stewart Steven says, we are all in contempt of court – and events in recent years make it impossible to argue with him – then our system of criminal law is truly in crisis. In the rejoicing when an innocent man is freed from prison, it is easy to overlook the fact that whoever is guilty of the crime for which he was wrongly convicted has gone free. Any search for a solution to this problem, which is so fundamental to our society that it could soon lead to vigilantes forming lynch mobs as they did in the old Wild West, is sure to be stymied by the present system and those who preserve it. Yet possibly a clue can be found in the following study of the history of the Old Bailey and a look at a selection of its trials from the 'bad old days' up to the present time.

In the pages that follow the reader will rub shoulders with many of the most notorious criminals known to the records, cringe from the hangmen, pity the jurymen who in the old days shared the trepidation of the accused, and hear the voices of famous judges. The reader will meet the bad and the ugly. The good are there, too, perhaps most often on the 'wrong' side of the law. To read on is to enter an arena of crime and degradation, of infamy and human anguish.

Executions outside of the Old Bailey attracted huge and unruly crowds. Windows were rented out at a high charge in nearby houses. The mob was delirious. Gathering excitedly on the evening of an execution, the people would spend the long night singing and dancing. Some strange connection between sex and death, violent death in particular, resulted in drunken fornication on the streets.

The wealthy spectators who hired rooms overlooking the gallows drank champagne and engaged in rampant immorality. The writhing bodies of the hanged prisoners enjoyably boosted the entertainment.

Often the judges passing sentences were under the influence of drink, and even the chaplain frequently had difficulty in staying upright. The appetite is the second most powerful instinct, and this, aroused in the high officials of the Old Bailey and Newgate Gaol by the legal killings, was satisfied by lavish feasts that were known as 'hanging breakfasts'. After the sumptuous meal, the dignitaries, one hand holding a delicate lace napkin to wipe their mouths, a glass of wine in the other hand, would look for the next big thrill in the proceedings – the cutting down of the bodies.

Even some of the condemned prisoners enjoyed a tasty last supper, and perhaps more. The highwaymen, who seemed to regard both life and death as some huge joke, would have women brought into their cells on their last night on earth.

Included here is Sir Crisp Gascoyne, Lord Mayor of London, who sat in No. 1 Court, clad in his richest robes of office, wearing a medallion of a thousand glittering gems, his plumed cocked hat on his knees, ready to judge an old gypsy woman accused of abducting a young girl. Gascoyne set the hag free, not because she had been proven not guilty, but due to the fact that he was bedding her lovely daughter. The young girl who had been abducted, a simple creature, was accused of perjury. Sir Crisp presided at the trial, while his son, Bamber Gascoyne, acted as junior counsel. The unfortunate girl was found guilty and deported to America.

Although this preface began with the contention that little has changed through the years, this book couldn't have been written in the 'bad old days'. Anyone in that era, writer or publisher, daring to tell the truth about the evil conditions obtaining, was imprisoned. An additional punishment usually inflicted was for the right hand of the offender to be cut off.

Acting out of the best intentions as a staunch royalist and patriot was no defence. When John Stubbs, a writer and scholar who had graduated a Cambridge BA, and had studied law at Lincoln's Inn, vehemently opposed by means of a pamphlet the negotiations to marry Queen Elizabeth I to the Catholic Duke of Anjou, he found himself in trouble. Though his attack was aimed at the Duke, and he wrote in loving terms of the Queen, Stubbs had somehow angered her. Elizabeth I ordered that both Stubbs and his publisher, a man named Page, have their right hands cut off. What followed makes Stubbs' courage admirable, but suggests his loyalty was misguided, to say the least.

The moment after his right hand had been severed, he plucked off his hat with his left hand and shouted, 'God save the Queen!'

Even though gruesome episodes such as this conceal the fact, some progress was made through the years. According to the records, torture ceased in 1640, but long after that Edward I's *Peine Forte et Dure*, commonly known as pressing to death, continued for many years. This was an agonising and often fatal practice applied to force prisoners to plead guilty as charged.

Capital offences were gradually reduced through the years. In 1861 only four – treason, piracy, mutiny and murder – remained as hanging crimes. By the time 1908 arrived, the law decided that those under sixteen years of age should not be hanged, and when 1933 was reached, this concession was extended to the under eighteen-year-olds.

No one can read this book without many of the stories invoking a very real sense of horror. It doesn't seem possible that our kind can be capable of such barbaric acts. The only hope for all of us, and for future generations, is that the terrible things recorded in these pages never again happen. But what of the future? Is the past really a 'foreign country' as L.P. Hartley opined in the prologue to his *The Go-Between*? It is likely that people don't change, therefore the growing crime rate, the increase in violence, and the burgeoning dissatisfaction with life may one day soon swing the arrow of public opinion back in favour of the return of capital punishment.

Weighed against the contents of this book, and with the fragile 'civilisation' at this beginning of a new millennium in mind, that would be a despairingly retrograde move.

1. THE OLD AND THE NEW

The 'old' Old Bailey adjoined Newgate Gaol, and for close on a thousand years inflicted cruel punishment and unmerited death. Felons and bawds were branded on the thumb, with the odour of burned flesh acting like some kind of riotous aphrodisiac for unruly Londoners as it carried the few hundred yards down the narrow thoroughfare called the Old Bailey into Ludgate Hill.

Now that the grim old building has passed from living memory, the imagination won't stretch to compare it with the stately Central Criminal Court of today. Over the portico of the main entrance of the Old Bailey is a fine sculpture depicting the Recording Angel supported by the figures of Fortitude and Truth. What an awesome task the Recording Angel had in the days when batches of prisoners were hanged just outside the door, amid the clamour of eager spectators. Those poor wretches kept Fortitude fully occupied, but there has been little veneration for Truth in those days, or since, as recent injustices illustrate. The gloomy atmosphere of yesteryear has gone, but it takes more than a new building to bring about any substantive change.

The old Central Criminal Court was a depressingly grey place with a narrow door through which, to the joyous shouts of the waiting mob, condemned men and women were dragged for mass executions in public. Inside the entrance was a dingy square hall flanked by offices lurking in semi-darkness behind half-glass partitions. To the left of the entrance was a twisting wooden staircase leading up to a landing on which there was a choice of a dark, uninviting passageway and a brightly pleasant corridor. The passageway was for witnesses, and it led into Court No. 1, where the principal judge sat to try the most serious cases. Not that there was much deliberation, as most of the accused were presumed guilty without the opportunity to protest their innocence.

Those permitted to use the not unpleasant corridor were the officials such as the prosecuting counsel and the defending counsel, together with their minions.

In the courtroom itself it was necessary for a gaslight to burn continuously, for what daylight did filter in was too feeble to be of use. There was just one window in the court. Situated above the jury-box, it had a reflector affixed outside in the failed hope of boosting the minimal amount of daylight coming in. Although reached by a considerable climb up stairs, the gloomy well of the court gave the impression of being a basement. Rising up from it in a position facing the sole window was a tier of seats known for some forgotten reason as 'City Lands', destined to occupy a similar location in the new court. The bench took up the whole length of one wall, and was packed by judges determined to secure a verdict of guilty at all costs. Sitting at one end of the bench was a terrifying black-draped figure, truly a personification of death. This was the chaplain, who played no part in the proceedings until he would move up beside the judge to say 'Amen!' at the end of the death sentence. To the left was the dock which was overlooked by a small public gallery that, on the demolition of the old building, was fittingly moved to the Chamber of Horrors at Madame Tussaud's.

The court and the adjacent prison had a conveyor-belt system that was as self-contained and efficient as any modern turkey-packing plant. With the prison, courts, gallows and burial ground all under one roof, the prisoners were processed with the maximum speed and the minimum effort. Brought in at one end of the 'hate factory', he or she would be tried, condemned, held in the death cells for a specified time, then hanged and buried. It was an inhumane, endless cycle of human brutality and distress.

Trials at the Old Bailey attracted vast crowds, and until 1860 there was an entrance fee to the gallery. This was pocketed by the

Keeper of the Court. However macabre are those who today queue outside the courts in which the fate of a fellow human being is to be decided, they are orderly and civilised in contrast to the drunken, rowdy mobs attending the Old Bailey hearings of long ago.

If dissatisfied with the verdict, the judge, a member of the jury, or a witness, the mob would exact its own form of vengeance. When presiding over a case in 1753, Sir Crisp Gascoyne, a knight and Lord Mayor of London, paid more attention to a beautiful young gypsy-girl witness than he did the defendant, who was a favourite with the mob. They were waiting for the knight when he stepped grandly out into the sessions yard. When the howling crowd went for him, Sir Crisp fled, gold chain swinging this way and that around his neck as he went. Mud and stones were thrown at him while women screamed foul insults. Even with the help of his minders, the Mayor could only make it to the nearest tavern. Dirtied and bleeding, his fine clothes ruined, he cowered there in fear. It was fortunate for him that the mob lost interest and didn't follow him into the tavern.

Reprehensible though it was, the behaviour of the mob was understandable in the light of the example set by officials of the court. Until 1834, all prisoners found guilty of any one of the two hundred or so capital offences then in existence, were herded together into the dock on the final day of each sessions to receive the death sentence. That saw the start of the episode in the legal system that was most enjoyed by court officials and the people alike – the executions outside the Old Bailey.

House-owners in the vicinity charged as much as ten pounds for a seat at a window overlooking the gallows. They, and the perverted people willing to pay to witness so horrible a scene, were in no way as bad as the officials of the day who put on 'hanging breakfasts' that were attended on the invitation of the prison governor and city officials. The privileged guests were afforded seats on the actual gallows, while the also-rans of the social hierarchy of the day were accommodated on a nearby platform. One governor who promoted these events regularly used his daughter as hostess. She would usher the guests to their seats, then go and prepare herself for the rest of the programme that was to follow.

After the hangings, when the grotesque dancing on the end of a rope ceased and the bodies swung, lifeless and uninteresting, the dignitaries retired to the special dining hall in the prison for a lavish feast at which no expense was spared.

As their 'betters' ate and drank to excess, the mob outside had their fun by jeering as they stoned the bodies of the recently dead, or pelted them with rotten fruit and vegetables.

In what has to be some ironic kind of justice, many of those who gloated over the poor wretches on the gallows were crushed to death in the excitedly milling crowd. Twenty-eight people died in this way around the scaffold in 1807.

When the mammoth feast, paid for by the Corporation, was over, the belching, drunken gluttons, having satisfied one perverted appetite, were keen to gratify another. What came next was a treat, the thought of which they had been savouring throughout the meal: the cutting down of the bodies.

This vile behaviour boded ill for those yet to be tried, as W. Eden Cooper revealed in his book *History of Newgate and the Old Bailey*: 'It was no uncommon thing for judges to return to the bench and pass sentence of death while under the influence of wine, the chaplain, or "ordinary" as he was then called, standing by in the same condition. When persons of distinction visited the court to listen to the death sentence, or view a notorious highwayman, they were invited to partake of the feasts. In 1807–8 the dinners for three sessions (nineteen days) cost Sheriff Philips £35 per day, the total figures given being £665.' During this period '145 dozen bottles of wine were consumed at an additional cost of £450'.

Yet this dreadfully sinister place was not without humorous 'characters' who occasionally lightened proceedings. One such person was a wit named William Davy, a former grocer from Exeter who had seen the law from both sides, having been in a debtor's prison before becoming a lawyer. Unorthodox and anti-establishment, the clever Davy was in demand as a defender of London's criminals.

At a trial where he was defending counsel, Davy made a point of law that was dismissed contemptuously by the judge, Lord Mansfield. He scoffed, 'If this is the law, I must burn all my books, I see.'

'Your Lordship had better read them first,' Davy advised dryly.

Another flash of humour came from an unexpected source at an unlikely moment. This was when four people were brought out of Newgate to be executed. First was Mrs Amelia Dyer of Reading, who had murdered many infants, while the second was a brutal killer called Seaman. Third and fourth were the Muswell Hill burglars Fowler and Milsom, former partners in crime who had fallen out. In the Old Bailey dock, Fowler, a formidable-looking man of powerful physique and with a hard, ugly face that was a caricature of the criminal type, waited until the warder in the dock was preoccupied before violently attacking Milsom, who was ferret-faced and of slight build. It was with difficulty that warders were able to pull the muscular Fowler off Milsom, thereby preventing murder from being done in the dock of the Old Bailey.

Planning to hang the Muswell Hill burglars together, but fearing yet more trouble between them, the authorities decided to make it a triple execution by placing Seaman, a callous killer, between them. Not surprisingly, Seaman protested, for there was likely to be a collision of bodies when the lever was pulled, and he would die a slow, agonising death instead of having his neck instantly broken by the rope. If Seaman had any rights in his miserable life, they had been sacrificed when he had slaughtered a man and a woman who were old and defenceless. His objection was overruled, and as the cap was placed over his head, he was heard to mutter wryly: 'Well, this is the first time I have ever played the part of a bloody peacemaker!'

The four hanged on that occasion were, like all those executed at Newgate, placed in crude shrouds and buried under the stone pavement that was appropriately known as 'Dead Men's Walk', and sometimes referred to as the 'Birdcage', presumably because the roof of open ironwork resembled a cage in which birds are kept.

This burial-ground was under a long corridor which connected the prison and the adjoining courts. The ironwork was rusty and the stone flooring blackened with the malignant grime that London produces through the years. So it was that when a prisoner accused of a capital offence walked to the court for trial, he was treading on his own grave.

Following an execution, the flagstones would be lifted yet again, the body put underneath, and the paving lowered on top of it. A meagre epitaph consisted of just one letter, the initial of the dead person's surname, carved in the wall facing the grave. For a short time this letter would show up bright and white as the stone showed through. But then deposits of dirt swiftly wiped out all that remained in this world of some poor creature who would probably have preferred not to have been born rather than live a sordid life that ended in a ghastly death at the Old Bailey.

The wait for three clear Sundays to pass between a sentence of death and the actual execution – to allow a condemned man to make his peace with God – was in itself an extreme punishment. Hargrave Lee Adam, in his book *Old Days at the Old Bailey*, recalls a hardened criminal remarking to him: 'It isn't being 'ung wot would worry me, but it's the thought of that f***ing waiting in the cells for weeks wot gives me such a funny feeling in the Darby Kelly [belly].'

Half-dark at all times, the condemned cells were sparsely furnished, low-ceilinged, horrible places. The walls were plastered with religious messages intended to allow the condemned man or woman to prepare for the next world, but mostly succeeded in amusing the hardened criminal and terrifying others who were more sensitive.

At midnight before an execution, a bell-man, paid £1 6s 8d a year to ring a hand bell giving 'twelve solemn tolls with double strokes' outside of the prison gate, would recite:

> All you that in the condemned hole do lie
>> Prepare you for tomorrow you shall die
> Watch all, and pray: the hour is drawing near
>> That you before the Almighty must appear.
> Examine well yourself; in time repent

> That you may not to eternal flames be sent.
> And when St Sepulchre's bell in the morning tolls
> The Lord above have mercy on your souls.
>
> > Past twelve o'clock.

This melancholy chant certainly wouldn't have cheered those inside the gaol trying to come to terms with this being their last night on earth. But the bell-man earned his money by going on to recite the following admonition:

> You prisoners that are within
> Who for wickedness and sin,
> After many mercies shown you, are now appointed to die tomorrow in the forenoon, give ear and under-stand that tomorrow morning the greatest bell of St Sepulchre's shall toll for you in form and manner of a passing bell as used to be tolled for those at point of death; to the end that all Godly people hearing that bell, and knowing that it is for you going to your deaths, may be stirred up heartily to pray to God to bestow his grace and mercy upon you while you live. I beseech you for Jesus Christ's sake to keep this night in watching and prayer for the salvation of your own souls . . .

In the morning when the solemn procession to the scaffold began, a single bell in the church of St Sepulchre's was rung. This fine old church, standing opposite the Old Bailey, fronting Holborn Viaduct, was built in 1178 and founded, together with St Bartholomew's Hospital, by minstrel Rahere, a favourite of Henry I. If all mention of St Sepulchre's was removed, the annals of the Old Bailey and Newgate would be sorely depleted.

There was extra work for the bell-man if the condemned were to be taken to Tyburn for execution. The gallows at Tyburn were on a site occupied by Marble Arch to the west of what is now Oxford Street. On the traffic island where Oxford Street joins the Bayswater and Edgware Roads, is a circular commemoration plaque of the approximate spot. The gallows were known as 'Jack Ketch's Tree', as he was the hangman who executed more than 200 Monmouth rebels here. The name Tyburn comes from two streams, the Tye and the Bourne, that met here. In 1571 the first permanent gallows were erected here in the form of a tall tripod with long beams that made it possible for several men to be hanged at the same time.

As they went by the church on a cart, the prisoners were passed a nosegay. That was when the bell-man came up over the church wall to exhort the prisoners and onlookers to pray:

> All people pray heartily unto God for these poor sinners who are now going to their death, for whom this great bell doth toll.
>
> You that are condemned to die, repent with lamentable tears; ask mercy of the Lord for the salvation of your souls through the merits, death and passion of Jesus Christ who now sits on the right hand of God, to make intercession for as many of you who penitently return unto him.
>
> Lord have mercy upon you Christ have mercy upon you
> Lord have mercy upon you
> Christ have mercy upon you.

John Foxe, the English Puritan teacher and author of the *Book of Martyrs*, tells of how the bell-man had what for him must have been the sorrowful and confusing duty of giving his over-the-church-wall exhortation to John Rogers, his own vicar, who had been held in Newgate, tried on a charge of heresy, and condemned to death by the Catholic Bishop of Winchester. First degraded, Rogers then suffered the fate of all the heretics of his day, by being taken to Smithfield and burned at the stake. Whatever his failings, John Rogers was a good Catholic in one respect, as Foxe's description of his doomed last journey attests: 'His wife and children, eleven in number, ten able to go and one at the breast, met him as he passed. This sorrowful sight of his own flesh and blood could nothing move him, but that he constantly and cheerfully took his death with wonderful patience in the defence and quarrel of Christ's Gospel.'

It was unlikely that the entreaties of the bell-man had any effect, for his voice couldn't compete with the noise from the jostling, jeering, cheering crowd following the prisoners on their final journey from the Old Bailey to Tyburn.

Everything about the original Old Bailey, which was often described as an arena of human drama (it was attended by the actors of the day eager to learn new techniques) but was more the scene of many a grim tragedy, cried out for change. Charles Dickens sat through the sensational trial of a woman named Maria Manning, who was tried with her husband for the murder of her lover, Patrick O'Connor. Both received the death sentence. Dickens witnessed the worst of both sides of the case, with Maria going into a hysterical rage when the jury returned their verdict. When the judge donned the black cap she was still angry enough to pluck some of the little posies of rue that decorated the ledge of the dock, and throw them at the judge. Judges hoped that the strong-smelling rue, for long a symbol of repentance, would be an antiseptic defence against unwashed and diseased prisoners.

She was hanged on a scaffold outside the Horsemonger Lane Gaol. Dickens was among the crowd that Maria Manning treated with contemptuous scorn. She wore a dress of black satin, and although she was mocked for wearing such a fine garment, it is curious that from that day black satin went out of fashion for some three decades.

In what must have been a great act of courage for a sensitive man, Dickens forced himself to watch Maria Manning put to death. Horrified by the proceedings and the behaviour of the people around him, he immediately wrote the following letter to *The Times*:

> I believe that a sight so inconceivably awful as the wickedness and levity of the crowd collected at the execution this morning, could be imagined by no man, and could be presented in no heathen land under the sun . . . When I came upon the scene at midnight, the shrilling of the cries and howls which were raised from time to time, denoting that they came from boys and girls assembled in the best

places, made my blood run cold . . . When the day dawned, thieves, low prostitutes, ruffians and vagabonds of every kind, flocked to the ground with every variety of offensive and foul behaviour. Fightings, fainting, imitations of Punch, brutal jokes, tumultuous demonstrations of indecent delight, when swooning women were dragged out of the crowd by the police with their dresses disordered, gave a new zest to the general entertainment . . . When the two miserable creatures [Mr and Mrs Manning] who attracted all this ghastly sight about them were turned quivering into the air, there was no more emotion, no more pity, no more thought that two immortal souls had gone to judgement, no more restraint of any of the previous obscenities, than if the name of Christ had never been heard in this world, and there were no belief among men but that they perished like beasts . . .

I am solemnly convinced that nothing that ingenuity could devise to be done in this city, in the same compass of time, could work such ruin as one public execution, and I stand astounded and appalled by the wickedness it exhibits.

Sharing his father's views, Sir Henry Fielding Dickens did his utmost as Common Serjeant at the Old Bailey to administer more humane justice, but one man cannot bring about change when the establishment of that era, just as today, is primarily concerned in maintaining the status quo.

Yet it wasn't only outsiders who were sickened by public executions, which went on for another twenty years after Dickens made his protest in *The Times*. William Field, for many long years chief usher at the Old Bailey, was determined never to attend the execution of those he saw tried and condemned, and lived in dread of being officially ordered to do so.

Field was spared the distressing experience but, as a young man, shortly after his arrival in London and starting a live-in job as 'plate butler' at the Mansion House, official residence of the Lord Mayor of London, he had suffered when hearing the sounds leading up to the hanging of Franz Muller, a German. With rail travel in its infancy, Muller committed the first murder, the first of many, on English railways. His victim was an old man named Briggs, and the killing was done on the North London Railway on the evening of 9 July 1864.

The body of Mr Briggs was found on the track after he had been visiting relations at Peckham. Making his way home from Fenchurch Street to Hackney by train, he was robbed and murdered in one of the carriages.

Muller was not at first a suspect, and he was safely on a sailing vessel to America when the police investigation pointed a finger of something more than suspicion at him. Policemen boarded a steamer to chase after the sailing ship, catching up with the German to bring him back. Standing trial at the Old Bailey for the murder of Briggs, he was convicted and condemned.

Everything possible was done to obtain a reprieve for Muller, but to no avail. These efforts went on until the very last moment, as a frightened William Field was to discover. First, however, he was awoken at the Mansion House at midnight, prior to the morning of the execution, by the noises made by the crowd as it wound its way to Newgate for the hanging.

'I shall never forget that crowd,' Field, who had lain in his bed in an upper room of the Mansion House listening to the sounds of human degradation, said later. 'It was a terrible crowd, shouting, yelling, shrieking, uttering ribaldry and obscenity; men drinking from bottles and women smoking. It was more than enough for me. I covered my head with the bedclothes to shut out the hideous noise.'

Field's attempt at shutting out the noises of the crowd awaiting Muller's execution were thwarted by the arrival at the Mansion House of some Germans who believed Muller to be innocent. 'On the night in question,' he later recounted, 'in the early hours of the morning, when the stream of pedestrians had somewhat subsided, there came a sudden and loud knocking on the door below. I started up. Who could it be at such an hour as this? Hastily throwing on a few clothes I hurried downstairs, opened the door cautiously and saw two men standing outside. I asked them what they wanted and they replied in a breathless tone that they wanted to see the Sheriff, that they had an important communication to make to him on behalf of Muller. They were Germans, and I told them that they could not see the Sheriff, that he did not live at the Mansion House, that, in fact, he lived some distance from London, and therefore could not be got at in the time which yet remained prior to the hour fixed for the execution to take place. So at last they with reluctance withdrew and I returned to my bed.'

Could Franz Muller have been spared had those two Germans been able to reach the Sheriff in time? The answer is no. Like all condemned persons, Muller was encouraged to seek God, and he passed a few hours in the gloomy, depressing chapel that aspired to being the house of God in Newgate. Upon his last Sunday on earth, Muller was placed in a special pew for those awaiting execution. It was so constructed that he couldn't see the other prisoners at the service, and they couldn't see him. On these occasions the sermons were always appropriate to the hanging that would take place in a couple of days' time.

This service seemed to have a profound effect on Muller, and he responded to a last-minute question as he stepped onto the gallows trap door. His spiritual consoler, Dr Cappel, perturbed by all the protestations of Muller's innocence, and fearing that a grave miscarriage of justice was about to be carried out, asked the condemned man if he had murdered Briggs.

Franz Muller replied: '*Ja, ich habe es getan.*' ('Yes, I have done it.')

Arguably the most baffling case heard at the 'old' Old Bailey was that of Elizabeth Canning in 1753. Presided over by the already mentioned Sir Crisp Gascoyne, those involved had names that would make a writer of fiction envious – Fortune Natus, Virtue Hall, Francis Gladman, Ezra Whiffin, Sarah Star, James Angel and Loomworth Dane.

Eighteen-year-old Elizabeth was the shy maidservant of a carpenter named Lyon, who lived in Aldermanbury. On New Year's Day 1753 Mrs Lyon gave Elizabeth the day off to visit an aunt and uncle, Alice and Thomas Colley, at Saltpetre Bank. Elizabeth took what was the shortest route, through Moorfield, just at the rear of

Bedlam Hospital, through a pretty park and then along Hounds-ditch into Rosemary Lane, from where it was just a short distance to the Colley home near Wellclose Square.

Spending the afternoon watching her glass-blower uncle at work, Elizabeth then had supper with her relatives. The Lyons were expecting her to be home by nine, but Elizabeth didn't leave until that time, and the Colleys walked with her as far as the corner of Houndsditch, going past the pastry cook's shop and nearly to the Blue Ball tavern before taking leave of their niece and watching her disappear into the darkness.

No one in that area saw Elizabeth Canning again until ten o'clock on the night of 29 January, when she walked into the family home in a condition that her mother described as 'pale, tottering, emaciated, livid, bent almost double, with no clothes but her shift, a wretched petticoat, a filthy bed gown, a rag tied over her head, and blood from a wound on her ear.'

Too weak to say anything for some time, Elizabeth then told a truly amazing story. After leaving the Colleys, the girl said she was attacked by two men who robbed her of the little money she had, took her gown, then knocked her unconscious. When she recovered she was being dragged along a road and then taken into a house at Enfield Wash. Elizabeth had passed out once more, and when she came round she was in the kitchen of what she soon learned was a brothel. With her was Mary Squires, a gypsy, aged, tall and bent, who would have been a frightening figure without a huge lower lip that was deformed by scrofula. Also there was the 'lady' of the house, Suzannah Wells, and an unpleasant-looking young woman, a whore who was inaptly named Virtue Hall.

As soon as she saw that Elizabeth was conscious, the old gypsy woman grabbed her. Recalling this, Elizabeth told her mother: 'The old woman took my hand and asked if I would go their way, saying if I would I should have fine clothes. I answered no, and then the old woman went to a dresser, fetched a knife, and cut the lace of my stays and took them from me.'

The story was so extraordinary that it would have been thought a lie had the girl's physical condition not supported it. Though she had passed water during the time she had been held at Enfield Wash, she had not once had a bowel movement in the whole four weeks. She was so blocked that a number of glysters (the equivalent of an enema in those days) had to be administered before relief was obtained.

Mary Squires and Suzannah Wells were arrested when the authorities were told how Elizabeth had been held against her will. Virtue Hall backed Elizabeth's story. At Bow Street the ugly prostitute made a statement to Justice Henry Fielding, in which she said she had been at Mother Wells's house when Elizabeth had been brought in, and even confirmed that Mary Squires had cut the girl's stays off her.

What had the appearance of a straightforward case was complicated by twenty-five witnesses swearing that Mary Squires had been at Enfield during the period in which Elizabeth Canning was missing from home, while thirty-five witnesses swore that the old gypsy woman had been one hundred and twenty miles away at the time – down at Abbotsbury in Dorset.

Strangely, when no one gave a damn what happened to a gruesome-looking old gypsy woman, and there was much sympathy for Elizabeth, who was still very sick from the ordeal she had been through, things started to go against the girl. First Virtue Hall, after a visit to the Mayor of London, Sir Crisp Gascoyne, changed her story completely, making a second statement in which she denied ever having seen Elizabeth Canning before, and certainly not at Mother Wells's house.

None of this worried Elizabeth's supporters, because Virtue Hall was a whore, Suzannah Wells ran a brothel and Mary Squires travelled the country on foot with her family, including beautiful daughter Lucy, selling smuggled goods. In contrast, Elizabeth Canning had led a God-fearing and blameless life. They were in no doubt as to whose word would be believed.

It was as they thought. In due course Mary Squires and Suzannah Wells were tried by Sir Crisp Gascoyne, found guilty and sentenced to death. But then Crisp Gascoyne did a sudden about-turn and expressed his opinion to the King that public prejudice against the two women before the trial deprived them of material evidence, and neither was guilty. It was insinuated, but never substantiated, that Sir Crisp was at that time bedding the lovely Lucy Squires. Whatever, the girl's mother, Mary Squires, was granted a free pardon by the King.

That was by no means the end of it. Elizabeth Canning was tried at the Old Bailey on a charge of perjury. Sir Crisp Gascoyne presided, and Bamber Gascoyne, his eldest son, was junior counsel. After a long, convoluted trial, the jury went out to consider their verdict at twenty minutes past midnight. Time dragged on, the bell of St Sepulchre's marked off the quarters and the hours, and still the jury was out.

When two o'clock had come and gone, impatient court officials sent a bailiff to get the jury moving. They filed back in at fifteen minutes past two, and a calm Elizabeth Canning looked the foreman straight in the eye as he read out the verdict: 'Guilty of perjury, but not wilful and corrupt.'

It sounded like an acquittal, and Elizabeth caught her breath, but her relief was short-lived.

'I cannot accept your verdict,' the Recorder told the jury flatly, 'because it is partial; you must either find her guilty of the whole indictment, or else acquit her.'

Going out once more, the jury returned some half an hour later to give the final verdict: 'Guilty of wilful and corrupt perjury; recommended to mercy.'

An already defeated democracy was replaced by hypocrisy when Elizabeth Canning was told by the Recorder: 'It is your particular happiness that you are in a country where severe and sanguinary laws are not so familiar; and though many expect, and the court could in this case justify, the most severe and exemplary punishment which the law can inflict; yet you will soon be convinced that your sentence is in no degree adequate to the greatness of your offence. The judgment therefore of this court is, that you shall be imprisoned in the gaol of Newgate for one month; and after the expiration of your imprisonment, you shall be transported to some of His Majesty's colonies or plantations in America for the term of seven years; and if within that term you return, and are found at large in any of His Majesty's dominions of Great Britain or Ireland, you shall suffer death as a felon without the benefit of clergy.'

Elizabeth Canning, a young girl who had never sinned, was sinned against by the Central Criminal Court. Of the sixty witnesses in the case, either the twenty-five who had said on oath that they had seen Mary Squires in Enfield, or the thirty-five who swore that at that time they had seen the old gypsy woman in Dorset, were most certainly more guilty of perjury than Elizabeth, but no action was taken against them. From that time onwards there have been many theories as to her month-long disappearance, with possibly the most plausible being that a neighbour and further employer of Elizabeth had arranged for her to be abducted and taken to the house at Enfield for his use. Her refusal to obey the 'house rules' to become a prostitute, and eventual escape, foiled the plan this man, a publican, had for her.

So it is that the puzzle of Elizabeth Canning lives on as one of the most remarkable judicial mysteries of the legal history of this country.

Reaching America, she went into service for a Methodist minister at Wethersfield, Connecticut. She married John Treat, a wealthy but wild young fellow, and they had a family. Her seven-year banishment from England was up in August 1761, and there was a report that she returned to this country in November of that year. This wouldn't seem to be so. In the 22–29 June 1773 issue of the *Connecticut Courant* a brief story read: 'Hartford, June 22nd. Last week died very suddenly, at Wethersfield, Mrs Elizabeth Treat, wife of Mr Treat, formerly the famous Elizabeth Canning.'

One of the most momentous trials in the long history of the Old Bailey led to what is known as the McNaughton Rules. Daniel McNaughton was a Glasgow wood-turner with a grievance, apparently an imaginary one, against Robert Peel, who was then prime minister. One night in 1843, an armed McNaughton lay in wait outside 10 Downing Street. Edward Drummond, the Premier's secretary, came out through the door and McNaughton, believing him to be Peel, shot him dead.

At the trial of McNaughton, he was obviously mentally unstable.

This prompted the question of whether, due to his mental condition, he could be legally held responsible for his actions. Lord Chief Justice Tindal directed the jury that if the accused was incapable of determining between right and wrong, he must be held non-culpable. Obeying this direction, the jury brought in a verdict of not guilty. At that time there were no institutions such as Broadmoor for the criminally insane, and Daniel McNaughton, who beyond any doubt had killed Edward Drummond, walked free.

A public outcry resulted at a murderer being freed. In the unprecedented circumstances the House of Lords was forced into taking the unusual step of asking the judges to consider the decision taken by the Lord Chief Justice at the trial of Daniel McNaughton. The McNaughton Rules were initially promulgated in a memorandum agreed by all but one judge, and presented, in what would be a contradiction in any other walk of life, but not in the legal profession, by Tindal himself. The judges' decision was to the following effect:

> That no act is a crime if committed by a person who is, at the time, prevented by any disease of the mind from:
> 1. being aware of the nature and quality of his act;
> 2. knowing that the act is wrong; or
> 3. controlling his own conduct, unless the absence of control has been produced by his own default.

Although accepted then and still valid today, the McNaughton Rules are insufficient in the light of modern psychology telling us that the man who knows what he is doing but is unable to stop himself from doing it, is just as insane as the person covered by rules one hundred and fifty years old. The statute that brought the concept of diminished responsibility into the criminal law of this country, though welcome, does not redress the flaws in the McNaughton Rules. Most remarkable of all about the McNaughton case is the fact that the Old Bailey permitted a murderer to walk free, yet refused to allow adequate defence to any accused person who might well have been able to prove his innocence.

In those days there were frequent but not strident calls for reform. In 1810, the House of Lords was asked to consider that the death sentence be abolished as a punishment for thefts to the value of five shillings. This was opposed by Lord Ellenborough, the Lord Chief Justice, who vehemently pointed out that those who have property must be protected against those who haven't, saying: 'I trust that your Lordships will pause before you assent to an experiment pregnant with danger to the security of property, and before you repeal a statute which has so long been held necessary for public security. I am convinced with the rest of the judges, public expediency requires that there should be no remission of the terror denounced against this description of offenders. Such will be the consequence of the repeal of this statute that I am certain depredations to an unlimited extent would be immediately committed.'

This sparked off a lively debate that concealed the fundamental question as to whether a human life could be valued at five shillings or less.

Further on in the debate, Ellenborough spoke again: 'My Lords, if we suffer this bill to pass, we shall not know where we stand: we shall not know whether we are on our heads or our feet. Repeal this law and see the contrast – no man can trust himself for an hour out of doors without the most alarming apprehensions that on his return, every vestige of his property will be swept off by the hardened robber.'

The legal system was every bit as much a 'closed shop' then as it is today. The priority of the establishment and the faceless men behind it is to resist change, and when at one time there was a call for a Criminal Court of Appeal, Sir Charles Darling (later Lord Darling) was of the opinion that the existing courts were sufficient, saying: 'I do not think it at all necessary. There is an appeal on the points of law, and as matters now stand a prisoner has every possible opportunity of establishing his innocence, if he be innocent. Independent of the coroner's inquisition, there are two public investigations, the magisterial inquiry and the trial by jury. There is still the higher though informal appeal to the Home Office, where a most exhaustive enquiry is held by officials who are eminently competent for the task. Here the judge's notes are perused, and the judge himself often consulted; and, in fact, everything that can be said or done in favour of the prisoner is considered. No public form of appeal could possibly go so far, or be so favourable to the prisoner, as is the present Home Office inquiry.'

As Wellington once said in an entirely different set of circumstances: 'If you believe that, you'll believe anything.'

A man dubbed 'the wit of the King's Bench', Sir Justice Darling had a sense of humour that was admired greatly, but none of the accused who came up before him could find anything to laugh about. With a grand house, Lady Cross Lodge, in the New Forest, and having served many years as Conservative Member of Parliament for Deptford, he lacked both the experience and the imagination to put himself in the place of those faced with the choice of either abject poverty or a life of crime. With no interest in sport, he described the House of Commons as 'a very good public school, with the advantage over the ordinary public school that you had not to play games'.

Another reform, long overdue, being demanded was that a prisoner be given at least a fighting chance of justice by being allowed to go into the witness box to give evidence in his own defence.

On this, Darling said: 'Speaking generally, I do not see why a prisoner should not make a good witness in his own favour. There may be, of course, certain things upon which it were better that a prisoner remain silent. Cross-examination? Well, my experience is that cross-examination strengthens the evidence of an honest witness. I will admit, however, that in the case of a nervous witness with a bad memory, it is possible for cross-examination to create an erroneous impression, but the judge takes care to correct this.'

Subsequent statistics proved Sir Justice Darling was mistaken, for the number of thefts fell after the death sentence for thieving had been abolished. The theory that people are brutalised by the knowledge that someone has been deliberately hanged in cold blood, that the savage in them is roused so that those who are easily unbalanced may be incited to commit a similar act of callousness, may well be as right as Darling was wrong.

As a later chapter in this book will reveal, some kind of rough justice decreed that most hangmen suffered, sooner or later, due to their grisly occupation. Insanity plagued the legal killer. Many executioners carried out unlawful killings, others committed suicide, and a few ended their lives on the gallows. Those who abuse the legal system also often bring terrible punishments upon themselves. Mr Justice Hawkins, a particularly cold man nicknamed 'the hanging judge', went insane and spent his time sitting on an imaginary bench sentencing imaginary prisoners to death, until he himself died.

Perhaps faring better in later life, although suffering terribly when sitting on the bench at the Old Bailey, were sensitive judges such as Mr Justice Bucknill, who was referred to by court officials and prisoners alike, both with affection, as 'Tommy Bucknill'. When he had to say those dreadful words 'to be hanged by the neck until you are dead', Bucknill would be in a distressed state. This display of sympathy for and empathy with the prisoner often backfired on the kind Bucknill, for the accused man would himself crack up on witnessing how upset was the man sentencing him.

If anything, the Old Bailey of up to the turn of the twentieth century evinces that though the reformers have made some inroads on the worst horrors of judicial wrong-doings and mistakes, our criminal justice system, probably even we ourselves, can never evolve to a higher form of civilisation in which discovering why a criminal has committed a crime takes precedence over punishing him.

Newgate Gaol was demolished before the Old Bailey itself. As the grey stones of the old prison fell, the courts continued. Both the jurors and the prisoners in the dock could watch the workmen wielding pickaxes and sledgehammers, destroying the building while the ghosts and the place's reputation escaped to live on into eternity. It must have been disconcerting, if not bewildering, for those waiting to be found guilty and sentenced to see the prison disappearing before their eyes.

In March 1907 the new Old Bailey building was opened on a dark and gloomy morning that belonged to winter rather than the threshold of spring. King Edward VII performed the opening ceremony of a stately building surmounted by a copper dome on which stood a bronze statue of Justice, sixteen feet high and looking out over London from a height of two hundred and twelve feet.

Because the Corporation of London needed to give the Old Bailey an image of fairness, this statue of Justice was not blind-folded, which made it unique in the world. This was an exercise in propaganda that relied upon memories being short, for less than thirty years before people were being hanged in the street on a spot almost immediately outside the new main entrance.

The new courts were most certainly an improvement on the old. The walls, floors and staircases were marbled in various colours. There were stained-glass windows, impressive frescoes and beautiful azure mosaic arches studded with stars that glittered like precious gems. The spacious main hall was tall and had an Eastern appearance with its pendant beaten brass spheres.

Compared to the gloomy, ever-present twilight of the old building, to enter the new was to step into the brightness of sunlight. It was a sign that all had changed, that the old black era could be forgotten as British justice entered a fresh and wholesome domain. It seemed a good omen when the last case heard in the old building, that of a woman accused of arson, was dismissed for lack of evidence.

Whether or not the contemporary euphoria was justified is for the reader to decide on reaching the final page in this book. Something that hadn't changed was the sense of humour of Lord Darling, as anti-hanging campaigner Mrs Violet Van der Elst writes in her book *On the Gallows*. Referring to a trial at the Old Bailey in the First World War, she says: 'I had never been in the Old Bailey, and I arrived just in time to hear the Counsel make their speeches, and Mr Justice Darling sum up the case and condemn the man [Louis Voisin] to death. I could not sleep for many nights after that, because of the horror of knowing that a man had been sent to his death by a judge who had made a joke only five minutes previously.'

2. THE HISTORY

'Give me a child up to the age of seven and I will make him anything you like,' wrote a Jesuit. This is an empty boast, for a Jesuit can only make Jesuits. In the same way, as the history of Newgate and the Old Bailey reveals, the judiciary is capable only of producing judges who, through the ages, have differed little from each other. They come from similar educational backgrounds, and all attain their position after years of toil in the narrow and hardening atmosphere of the courts. A judge is appointed for his ability as an administrator of the law, never for possessing a quality of humanism. This shows through in the pages that follow.

As a man, a judge is as vulnerable, weak and fallible as the rest of us, but he is vested as a judge with an absolutism that has his counsel sought on subjects unconnected with the law. The government still has a judge conduct an inquiry to placate angry public opinion on some issue, yet an ever-growing number of people don't believe that justice is obtainable through the courts today.

How different it might be had a philosopher, an artist or a poet been long ago appointed to the bench! Such a suggestion might make the materialist sneer, but it is not entirely without precedent. Men of eminence sought the opinion of Voltaire; and Milton, although his *Paradise Lost* might suggest otherwise, was never regarded as a helpless dreamer.

Now it is too late. Simone Weil, the religious visionary,

confirmed this when she said: 'The apparatus of penal justice has been so contaminated with evil, after all the centuries during which it has, without any compensatory purification, been in contact with evil-doers, that a condemnation is very often a transference of evil from the penal apparatus itself to the condemned man; and that is possible even when he is guilty and the punishment is not out of proportion. Hardened criminals are the only people to whom the penal apparatus can do no harm. It does terrible harm to the innocent.'

In the story of the Old Bailey we meet judges of all kinds. There are those similar to the judge depicted in a play by Dryden who desires to decide a cause after hearing only one side. When compelled to listen to the statement of the defendant, he flies into a terrible rage, exclaiming: 'There now, sir, see what you have done! The case was quite clear a moment ago, and you must come and puzzle it.'

Then there is the vindictive, vicious type epitomised by the notorious Judge George Jeffreys, of whom Macauley wrote in his *History of England*: 'The depravity of this man has passed into proverb.' A man with a handsome face but a black soul, Jeffreys at his most malignant could give an impression of being benevolent and angelic. When trying Titus Oates, a success-ful agitator who was a thorn in many sides of the establishment, at the Old Bailey for perjury, for example, Jeffreys sentenced him to be pilloried in New Palace Yard, led round Westminster Hall with a placard over his head that described his crime, pilloried again in front of the Royal Exchange, tied to a cart and whipped from Aldgate to Newgate, then, after two days, whipped from Newgate to Tyburn.

When Oates was in the pillory he was pelted with refuse, stones, anything the people could lay their hands on. His first flogging took place before a large crowd. Though it was severe from the start, Oates taunted Jack Ketch, the hangman, who with his assistants was carrying out the punishment, telling him that they would need to do better if they wanted to make an impression on him. He fell quiet then, enduring his punishment bravely and without a murmur, but he eventually broke and his screams are recorded as having been terrible to hear.

Oates fainted, but still the punishment went on without any mercy being shown. When his bonds were untied he flopped as loosely as a corpse, and most watchers believed that he was dead.

Another huge crowd had assembled at Newgate two days later when he was dragged out and, because he was unable to stand, pulled to Tyburn on a sledge, where he received hundreds more lashes even though he was unconscious. Taken back to Newgate he was clapped in irons and held in a dark dungeon.

Whatever Titus Oates was, and history often depicts him as a blackguard equal to Judge Jeffreys, his endurance has to be admired. In the wake of being flogged with a whip of six thongs, and said to have received in all over 2,250 lashes, he got a Newgate bed-maker pregnant.

In the pages that follow are innumerable instances of the corrupting influence of power over the lives of others; a power that has turned men into savage monsters.

Judges who are the opposite of Dryden's ultra-simplistic dispenser of justice use legal jargon and unnecessary points of law to sidetrack the real issue, diversions under which are concealed the extreme difficulties of the truth. With vested interests they concentrate on practical, administrative tasks that block their view of the wider meditation. The tragedy isn't so much in the wrong answers being given as that the right questions are not asked. The essence of humanism is to ask questions governing the relationship of reality to appearances and of truth to half-truth. To seek a selfless, uncorrupt man in the history of a divided-mind institution such as the Old Bailey is to search in vain.

The situation was not improved by many criminal laws being mutations of the 'impure thoughts' offences in the old ecclesiastical courts. They punished a man caught masturbating not so much for committing the act, but because he was a masturbator. Analogous in criminal courts is the tendency to judge an accused on what he or she is, and the status of the persons they have harmed. Those convicted of the 1963 Great Train Robbery received severe sentences that seem disproportionate to their crime. A terrorist convicted of planning some act is likely to receive a much longer sentence than a child killer who has carried out his heinous crime.

Because the Church had so much influence on public opinion, the secular courts began to support and reinforce the ecclesiastical courts and embody some extraordinary prohibitions in law. Fortunately, the procedure evolved in 1308 by Archbishop Winchesley didn't become law. This attempted to use marriage as a punishment for fornication. A couple caught in a first offence had to sign a contract to agree to being considered as man and wife since the time of the first offence, if caught at it a third time. The legal difficulties in having a present situation entirely dependent on a future event kept this off the statute books.

Law was, and still is, an immense problem. There is no public system that will effectively regulate the private doings of men and women and their very thoughts. All that could be devised was a crude system of psychological control based on terror. The offender had to be induced, of his own accord, to confess his own sin.

This leftover from the Church courts lives on today with the police encouraging a suspect to make a statement. Confession is undoubtedly good for the soul, but it destroys all hope of a defence in court.

Balthasar Cossa, who was elected pope to end the Great Schism, showed what confession was all about in an ecclesiastical court when he made a statement to the Council of Constance saying he was guilty of 'notorious incest, adultery, defilement, homicide and atheism'. With a cv like that it's amazing that he got the job in the first place.

The practices of the Church courts were unified with civil jurisdiction by another lecher, Henry VIII, who was syphilitic. Until that time adult homosexuality had not been a crime. The Romans put those they considered to be perverts to death out of court, as it were, but tolerated Emperor Hadrian's well-known preferences. A marked increase in homosexuality in the twelfth century was, without justification, attributed to the Norman invasion. When King Rufus died in a New Forest hunting accident he was refused burial in consecrated ground due to the fact that he was homosexual. It was so common by the time of the straight but oversexed Henry VIII that it became a criminal offence.

Suicide, a religious sin, was outlawed under Henry, as were sodomy and bestiality. Bigamy, something which Henry wasn't likely to mess with, subsequently became a felony under James I. Eventually it was Charles II who completely removed criminal jurisdiction from the ecclesiastical courts by abolishing the *ex officio* oath.

This outline makes a useful prelude to the history of Newgate Gaol and the Old Bailey, together with a selection of the trials held at the Central Criminal Court. The origins of both owe more to speculation than fact. London was once, of course, a walled city, and most antiquarians agree that the site of the present-day Old Bailey was the West Gate of Saxon London, referred to as 'Westgetum' in a charter of Burhed of Mercia dated 857. The Domesday Book tells us that William the Chamberlain, the City Treasurer and a King's officer, paid six shillings a year for his vineyard at Holborn in 1086. This suggests that the later name of Chamberlain's Gate came from the Chamberlain owning property outside the City gate, and in his *The Old Bailey and its Trials*, Bernard O'Donnell writes: 'In the City he [the Chamberlain] had his own court in which he heard and gave judgement in disputes between masters and apprentices. What is more likely, then, than this gate should be known as Chamberlain's Gate because that officer had his court there? And what is more likely than when this gate fell into ruins, making necessary the building of a new gate, the new structure should be named New Gate?'

A second opinion on how the name of Newgate originated can be had from the *Survey of London and Westminster* (1598), the monumental work of John Stow, who states:

> This gate was first erected about the reign of Henry I or King Stephen, upon this occasion: the cathedral church of St Paul being burnt about the year 1086 in the reign of William the Conqueror, Mauritius, then Bishop of London, repaired not the old church, as some have supposed, but began a new work such as men then judged would never have been performed . . . After Mauritius, Richard Beamore did

wonderfully advance the work of the said church,
purchasing the large streets and lanes about, wherein were
wont to dwell lay people, which grounds he began to
compass about with a strong wall of stone and gates.

By means of this increase of church territory, but more by
enclosing ground for so large a cemetery or churchyard, the
high and large street stretching from Aldgate in the east until
Ludgate in the west, was in this place so crossed and
stopped up that the carriage through the city westward was
forced to pass without the said churchyard wall on the north
side through Paternoster Row to Ludgate . . . which passage
by reason of so often turning was very cumbersome and
dangerous, both for horse and man; for remedy whereof a
new gate was made and so called, by which men and cattle
with all manner of carriages might pass more directly (as
afore) from Aldgate through West Cheap by St Paul's on the
north side; through St Nicholas Shambles and Newgate
market to Newgate, and from thence to any part westward
over Oldbourne Bridge, or turning without the gate into
Smithfield and through Isledon to any part north and by
west.

Stow's 'Isledon' is Islington, and if we read between his lines it
appears that the New Gate was constructed, or reconstructed, where
the city wall turned sharply at the northern end of the street of Old
Bailey. It was needed to relieve the traffic jams caused by the building
of St Paul's, which inconvenienced the knights, merchants and
pilgrims travelling up from Canterbury towards Middle England.

That the original dispute court of the Chamberlain had both
altered and extended its scope is revealed by Stow as he continues:
'This gate hath of long time been a gaol or prison where felons and
trespassers, as appeareth by records in the reign of King John and
of other kings . . . '

There are references to the committal of prisoners to Newgate
from the year 1218, in the records of the City Corporation. From
the very beginning it must have been a terrible place, a fetid, filthy

establishment in which the laws of the country were administered with horrifying cruelty. It was to become worse, much worse, when those charged with guarding the prisoners became corrupt with an avarice that added greatly to the distress of the miserable wretches they were paid to look after.

The rot had already set in in 1241, when some rich Jews were persecuted by the law. In modern parlance they were 'fitted-up', and faced the prospect of being kept prisoners indefinitely or paying 20,000 marks (more than £13,500). Everyone was out to make a fast buck at that time, in what was on a parallel with a newspaper columnist's recent comment on lawyers: 'Richer now than they've ever been in their history, and greedier too, I tell you that the robbers in the dock are seldom as pernicious as the robbers at the Bar.'

Nothing changes. Crime has always paid off for somebody, and in those early days the beneficiaries were those supposedly on the right side of the law. The suffering of prisoners in a disgustingly filthy and fever-ridden prison is unimaginable. With no media to watch out for, or give publicity to, injustice, the authorities had it all their own way. The 'sessions', as they were called, were held only once a year. So a prisoner, with nothing to look forward to but a trial followed by the sentence of death, could lie in that stinking prison for anything up to twelve months.

Before 1426, prisoners who refused to plead were starved to death. The fact that by refusing to plead a man stopped his property from being confiscated, and so was able to leave it to his dependants, saw many brave men prefer to die rather than to plead. So the punishment was changed. A prisoner refusing to plead was put on his back in a low, dark room. Naked apart from a dirty loin-cloth, he had very heavy weights placed upon his body. On the first day he was given a small quantity of stale, often maggot-ridden bread, while on the second day he would get a small drink of foul water. This diet continued until he died, and this form of punishment went on until 1828.

With the origin of the name Newgate at least tentatively established, considerable speculation has to be involved in finding how a narrow little street running from Ludgate Hill to the corner of Newgate Street became Old Bailey. Equally as intriguing is how the name came to be applied to the Sessions House that was eventually built in the street, and is now world-famous.

Is the historian Frederic Maitland correct in his theory that it derived from Bail Hill, a high place where the bail or sheriff dwelt and held his court, or should we go back to John Stow and his suggestion that it came from the Ballium, or space outside the city wall? Perhaps the strongest clue comes with baileys having been part of the old city fortifications. Their locations had these fortifications referred to as inner and outer baileys. It is probable that the site of the Old Bailey may well have been part of one of these fortifications that enclosed open spaces.

These varied opinions and conjecture are a direct result of the records of Newgate Gaol and the Old Bailey being so scanty; 1334 is the date of one of the first recorded trials, but there is nothing to say whether the hearing was held in the gate-house prison or one of the special buildings in Old Bailey that were hired by the sheriffs, with the City Corporation picking up the bill.

Although records of Newgate Gaol for the thirteenth and fourteenth centuries are extremely scarce, it can be gleaned that it was a grim place that was overcrowded and had inadequate, practically non-existent sanitation. There were reformers and people who cared in those days, but there was little that they could do to bring about a change for the better. One, Thomas Knoles, who was at one time Mayor of London and a grocer by trade, 'caused sweet water to be conveyed to the gates of Newgate and Ludgate for reliefe of the prisoners there', and once more it is the historian Stow who tells us that in 1385 Sir William Walworth 'gave somewhat to relieve the prisoners in Newgate, so have many other since'.

Welcome though these kind actions must have been, they were made insignificant by the increasing degradation that was to last for centuries at Newgate. There was no separation of prisoners. Men, women and children waited for months to be brought before the king's justices. At first fornication brought about by desperation was rife, but then the governor of the prison and the gaolers lined their pockets by organising the inmates, taking charge of everything including vice. Food, alcohol, sex and just about anything else, including better accommodation, was available to the prisoners – but it all came at a price. There was even an early version of the protection racket that has for so long been a part of modern life in London. Prisoners paid to avoid being assaulted or tortured, mainly by the people to whom they passed their money. It was a lucrative business that had men eager and willing to pay big money to get into Newgate Gaol as keepers. One man who held this post, Captain Richardson, sold his position for three thousand pounds, a veritable fortune in those days. But Lord Clarendon did better than this when he charged a man named John Huggins five thousand pounds to make him keeper at Fleet.

Nepotism crept in, and in the fourteenth century even the king was manipulating the Newgate staffing situation so as to secure the office of keeper for his relatives.

All of this corruption went on as the prisoners, the guilty and the innocent, the young and the old of both sexes, were forced into contact with vicious and depraved men and women. All sense of decency deserted those who had nothing to lose because they were sentenced for life. Shame was a luxury that no one held in Newgate could afford, as wild scenes and indescribable orgies of lust and depravity raged continuously.

The rot began at the top, with the governor adding to his regular income, quite legally, by permitting unlimited drinking in his prison and pocketing the profit from the sale of alcohol. Babies were born, some of them dying and the filthy rags being instantly torn from one little body to clothe another, possibly less fortunate, child that still lived.

England's criminal justice system bypassed civilisation on a route to brutal torture. Condemned mothers were dragged from Newgate to the gallows, often with a child at the breast and two or three more clinging to her skirts, bewildered and screaming in terror. An estimated 72,000 people were executed in the reign of Henry VIII, with even small children taken to be hanged.

This was in the days when the Old Testament with all its barbarity and eye-for-an-eye-tooth-for-a-tooth vengeance was firmly believed in. Serious men, highly educated and much respected, sat on the bench, religion hiding their own insanity from them as they condemned to death boys of nine or ten years of age.

Boiling to death was made a legal method of execution, while burning at the stake or drowning was the terrible fate of women accused of being witches or of murdering their husband. In burning a rope was tied around the victim's neck when she was tied to the stake so that, if she was lucky, her own struggling would strangle her before the flames reached her. A woman named Catherine Hayes was literally burnt alive at Tyburn in 1726. The flames reached the hands of the executioner first, causing him to release the rope sooner than usual. With flames leaping fiercely around her, Catherine, to the delight of a host of spectators, filled the air with her screams as she tried to push the burning faggots from her. She was fighting a losing battle, for other flaming faggots were thrown at her. Even so, her death was a gruesomely protracted one, and more than three hours of horror continued until her body was at last completely reduced to ashes.

The nauseous institution of Newgate was the unofficial epicentre of all these atrocities. Although records prove that some aldermen made attempts to ban the practice, the keeper would charge the prisoners a fee for water, with those who couldn't pay going without, just as those who couldn't afford the price of having their irons struck off were manacled day and night. The prisoners were subjected to the greedy demands of the prison officers, from the keeper down to the lowest hireling. The sighs of relief of the minority of prisoners brought up to the Old Bailey and acquitted were scarcely uttered when they were being dragged back down to the prison again if unable to pay the keeper's illegal fees.

Despicable though the gaolers were, they were not alone in their wicked extortion. The 'cellarman', a trustee, the equivalent of today's prison 'red band', was permitted to sell candles to his fellow-prisoners, and name his own price. Also, in a kind of lower echelon of the protection racket worked by the prison officers, old lags charged newcomers what was known as 'chummage', which allowed the new arrivals a place somewhere close to the fire, and guarded them from the persecution of the other prisoners. Newcomers who couldn't pay, or were foolish enough to refuse to do so, were often stripped and beaten.

The wildest, drunken carousing was done by men and women waiting to be hanged. Aware that there would be no tomorrow for them, they made the most of being able to mix freely with, and use and abuse, other prisoners. A great source of callous amusement came from baiting lunatic prisoners who raved up and down the wards spouting gibberish. Another form of entertainment came with the one-shilling-a-trick prostitutes whom the gaolers allowed into the prison in return for a share of their takings.

A form of class distinction provided a much more lucrative set of arrangements for the head keeper of Newgate Gaol. This involved what was known as the Press Yard or Castle, which provided luxurious accommodation for felons and prisoners of state who had the means to pay for the comforts and diversions they desired.

For a figure that could go as high as five hundred pounds, the keeper would provide a veritable suite in the Castle where the prisoner could indulge his whims and vices without interference or restriction. They were allowed to entertain their friends, or invite women to their pseudo-cells. A further payment to the keeper, far in excess of the one shilling the underprivileged in the main part of the prison paid to satisfy their carnality, would have him arrange a visiting prostitute.

Even marriages, some of them farces rather than recognised ceremonies, were carried out here in the Castle. A Major Bernhardi was married in Newgate, and as he was held for forty years without trial, it was a lasting arrangement during which his wife bore him ten children. Bernhardi died in Newgate at the age of eighty-two.

Tortures and mutilations went on up to and throughout the reigns of Charles I and Charles II. Yet although the iniquity of Newgate Gaol would continue through more centuries, the worst of the punishments ceased at the time of the Commonwealth. These two kings brought trouble upon themselves by dunning the people for payment of taxes, bringing about the revolution. The mob became incensed by kings with massive fortunes of their own having fun at fabulous expense to the country. The rapacious Charles II was in the habit of making his mistresses duchesses, with each requiring a fortune of her own.

It was during the reign of Charles II that events turned a small circle, and the judges who had condemned Charles I were themselves put to death in a series of ten executions that began on 13 October 1660 and went on daily until 18 October. First to suffer was Colonel Harrison. Dragged along on a sledge past Whitehall – where Charles I was executed – to Charing Cross, he was hanged in the presence of the King himself and many ladies of the Court. Cut down while still alive, his intestines were drawn out and thrown into a furnace before his quivering body was quartered.

Each day the executions became more horrific. What had happened to Harrison was terrible, but there was worse in store for two well-known parliamentarians, Cook and Peters, who were being held at Newgate. Peters was tied to the rails of the scaffold and forced to watch shocking atrocities carried out on Cook, and then it was his turn to suffer the same awesome fate.

While these public obscenities were going on, the same old corrupt régime continued in Newgate. An improvement had come about after Common Serjeant John Westone's complaint to the Committee of the Common Council in 1406 resulted in a tower being built on the site of a house next door to Newgate Gaol. Westone made this tower into a women's prison that lasted until 1422, when the executors of Dick Whittington's will reconstructed the prison.

This was Dick Whittington, he of the cat, who was thrice Lord Mayor of London. A new prison was a strange monument to a well-liked man, and it wouldn't have brought the name of Whittington through to today in the way his pantomime has.

Little is known of the building, which for a time had Newgate called 'Whittington's Palace', the only trace found during the excavations of 1903 being a watercourse.

Whittington's posthumous act did provide a new prison, but it in no way altered the harsh régime and poor conditions that had become part of the Newgate Gaol system. Even when Whittington's building was replaced by a larger and healthier prison, the bad old ways continued.

As the city and its trading built up, and crime increased so that three or four sessions a year were being held, accommodation in which the trials could be held became more difficult to find. In 1539, a resolution was passed first by the Court of Aldermen, and then by the Court of Common Council, which resulted in the first purpose-built Sessions House – the very first Old Bailey, as it were – being erected in 1550. At least some of the reason behind this new building was to avoid the actual prison that in 1419 had been devastated by a rampant fever that killed a total of sixty-four prisoners and gaolers. In addition it provided a place for the privileged to enjoy feasts.

In appearance it was a pleasant building surrounded by gardens in which it was a delight for the Lord Mayor and King's Justices to stroll. Yet in reality the law was administered inside with every bit as much barbarity as before. When the building was damaged, but not completely destroyed as often believed, in the Great Fire of London, more improvements were made, including the construction of a large dining room over the court, for 'feasting'. Once again, the lot of the prisoners was ignored.

In 1750 fever returned to Newgate Gaol with such virulence that, in what some saw as the first justice ever witnessed in the Old Bailey, two judges, the Lord Mayor of London, a number of aldermen, several jurors and members of the public who had attended trials as spectators, were stricken and died.

The death of the dignitaries was a shock. Nobody had been concerned that the death rate of prisoners had been high for years, due to the insanitary conditions in Newgate, but now that two of His Majesty's judges and other important men had died, something had to be done.

An investigation discovered that the infection had permeated the courtroom from the prison cells below. The solution decided upon was a massive, clumsy windmill ventilator, a giant extractor fan, which was placed atop one of the gateway towers to pull the infectious air away from the court and the prison. This ugly contraption caused great alarm in the neighbourhood, with people logically deducing that if it was carrying germs away from the Sessions House and Newgate Gaol, it must be putting the locals at risk.

The protests were ignored, and then, with the stench coming up from the prison into the courtroom being really atrocious, the judges and all those attending them on the bench were given further protection in the form of sweet-smelling herbs to carry. Other herbs were strewn about the dock, and strong vinegars sprinkled around.

This custom continued down the years in the Old Bailey, with the judges, recorder or common serjeant carrying a nosegay of flowers with them to their places on the bench. A pretty tradition in later years, but neither that measure nor the Heath Robinson-like fan was of any use then. In 1772 another serious outbreak of fever hit a number of officers of the court. Three years later, with Newgate in a terrible state of disrepair, the Common Council reported to the City Corporation that the gaol was 'incapable of improvement or tolerable repair', and that 'it is overcrowded with victims of public justice, under the complicated distresses of poverty, nastiness and disease'.

'An abominable sink of beastliness and corruption' is how Sir Stephen Jansen described Newgate in 1767, and in 1770, by Act of Parliament, the construction of a 'new and commodious Jail' commenced.

Included in the rebuilding of Newgate was the reconstruction of the Sessions House. This was the oppressive, dark and dingy, unhygienic building detailed in Chapter 1, and which lasted until the new Old Bailey was opened in 1907, although it suffered some perilous incidents.

The rebuilt Newgate satisfied even John Howard, a man who had lived an insular life until he was made High Sheriff of Bedford in 1773, at the age of forty-seven, when he became active in prison reform after being shocked by a visit to Bedford Prison. Visiting Newgate Gaol, Howard wrote, albeit five years later: 'At my visit in 1779 the gaol was clean and free from offensive scents. On the felons' side there were only three sick in one of the upper wards . . . Of the 141 felons, there were 91 convicts and fines who had only the prison allowance of a penny loaf a day. Mr Akerman [a keeper who was humane and a cut above his predecessors and successors] generously contributed towards their relief. In the Felons' court the table of fees, painted on a board, was hung up.'

In between Howard's visit and his penning of a report, Newgate was damaged in the Gordon Riots, led by young Lord George Gordon, who had overdosed on religion. The son of the Duke of Gordon, George was a particularly fevered Protestant who was President of the Protestant Association. The aim of this organisation was to get a repeal of an Act of William III, which had relieved much of the suffering of Catholics.

As was later to be proved in court, Lord George was more than a few sheets short of a hymn book, and when in the summer of 1780 he marched on the House of Commons, the 60,000 he led had been infiltrated by criminals and hoodlums who incited the others to riot so that they could take advantage of the violent disorder to go on a rampage of looting.

First Roman Catholic churches were damaged and robbed, then the violence escalated so that public buildings, including the Bank of England, were attacked, and prisons broken open. The Old Bailey came under attack just after six o'clock in the evening of 6 June. Mr Akerman, the keeper, was aware of the mob surging down Holborn, those in front bearing three flags bearing Protestant mottoes, and he had locked the door of his quarters before barricading it with furniture.

In what was a polite, civilised action for a man heading a mob, the ringleader knocked on Akerman's door. On receiving no reply, he gestured to his henchmen, some thirty of whom marched up abreast, armed with crowbars and other instruments. They broke open Mr Akerman's door, as well as the debtors' and felons' doors, while the eager mob came on behind them, carrying bludgeons and the spokes of cart wheels. It was soon obvious that Lord George wasn't the only madman involved in the riots. A crazy Quaker, son of a wealthy corn merchant, smashed all of Akerman's windows with a scaffold pole. As if it was a lunacy contest, a boy sitting on the Quaker's shoulders used his head to smash in the shutters. Akerman's possessions and furniture were thrown out into the street and set ablaze.

London was lawless. The Catholic Chapel in Lincoln's Inn Fields was burned to the ground, the Leicester Square house of Sir George Saville was gutted, and the Fleet and King's Bench prisons burnt.

With the keeper's house wrecked and his belongings burnt to ashes, the mob turned its attention to Newgate Gaol itself. Armed with sledgehammers and pickaxes taken from the Drury Lane premises of coachmakers and blacksmiths, they pushed Akerman's blazing furniture up against the door, setting it on fire. A courageous turnkey inside prodded through the back with a broomstick, trying to poke the burning furniture away, as well as pouring water on it. But he didn't have a hope of success. The rioters came crashing into the prison past gates wrecked by the use of crowbars. Breaking the roof and tearing away rafters, they grabbed ladders and descended to release bewildered prisoners who were weighed down by chains.

Troops had been ordered in, and although they were expected at any moment, the mob wasn't worried. Men and women were released, including a trio due to be hanged in three days' time, and were led to escape through the streets in their chains. Some of them were taken away on horseback, their chains clanking. It was reported that most of the white-faced prisoners were in greater terror at being released by the rioters than they had been when imprisoned.

Amid all the violence and confusion, the young hero of the mob, Lord George Gordon, was brought up to survey the scene in a coach drawn by his own mobsters.

Yet the recently rebuilt Newgate Gaol was made of stern stuff. Although damaged, its thick stone walls survived the ravages of flames, sledgehammers and pickaxes. Dr Johnson visited the scene on the morning after, as it were, and later wrote of what he had witnessed: 'On Wednesday I walked with Dr Scott to look at Newgate and found it in ruins, with the fire yet glowing. As I went by the Protestants were plundering the Sessions House at the Old Bailey. There were not, I believe, a hundred; but they did their work at leisure, in full security, without sentinels, without trepidation, as men lawfully employed in full day.'

It was all to no avail. Extensive rebuilding of Newgate Gaol saw the previous plan adhered to so that the old sinister building rose out of the ashes to house prisoners again, and the Old Bailey was restored. As for Lord George Gordon, the instigator, he was brought to trial on charges of causing the riots. Represented by Thomas Erskine, a brilliant Scottish lawyer who was for a time Lord Chancellor, Lord George seemed to be in with a chance of acquittal when his counsel made a great speech on his behalf. Erskine went on talking until after midnight, delaying the jury from retiring. They filed back in at five in the morning with a verdict of guilty but insane.

At least a veneer of reform was taking place at Newgate, with it being decided that the grisly procession of the condemned prisoners to Tyburn was to cease. This meant an end to around six hundred years of tradition, and the shutting off of a much enjoyed public entertainment. There was much protest, and among the objectors to what was said to be a humane advance was Dr Johnson. For a supposed intellectual he had a nasty mind, as he revealed when complaining of too much change too soon: 'The age is running mad after innovation. All the business of the world is to be done in a new way. Tyburn itself is not safe from the fury of innovation. No, Sir! It is not an improvement; they object that the old method drew together a number of spectators. Sir, executions are intended to draw spectators. If they do not draw spectators, they don't answer their purposes. The old method was most satisfactory to all parties; the public was gratified by a procession; the criminal was supported by it. Why is all this to be swept away?'

Dr Johnson and the other complainants were completely ignorant of the reason the trek from Newgate to Tyburn was being dropped. The City had become increasingly overcrowded where building was concerned, which resulted in grand homes being built for the rich and influential towards Tyburn. It was their dislike of having condemned persons and rowdy crowds traipsing past their properties that brought about the change. Despite John Howard's efforts to prod the public's conscience, nobody else really gave a damn about the prisoners.

All future executions were to take place in the road outside the Debtor's Door of Newgate Gaol. The morning of 7 November 1783 saw the last procession from Newgate to Tyburn. The subject to take an unenviable place in history was John Austin, who had been convicted at the Old Bailey of robbing and wounding one John Spicer.

When the chaplain had completed his duties, a calm, brave John Austin addressed the crowd with: 'Good people, I request your prayers for the salvation of my departing soul; let my example teach you to shun the bad ways I have followed; keep good company, and mind the word of God.'

As he spoke those words, Austin was spared the knowledge of what was to come. Tyburn tends to conjure up in the imagination a lofty gallows with steps that most of the condemned, especially romantic highwaymen, climbed with courage and stood in dignified silence as the noose was placed around their necks. There were none of these refinements, if that word can be used in the circumstances, at Tyburn.

The method of execution usually had the doomed person standing on a cart, noose in place, dropping as the cart was suddenly pulled away. This was the system used in the case of John Austin, and the rope slipped up round the back of his neck. As a consequence, he died a slow, agonised death.

Another method was to have the condemned person, the noose in place, climb a ladder. When the prisoner least expected it, the hangman would give the ladder a sharp twist, causing the climber to fall off and be strangled by the rope.

The cart was done away with when, on 9 December 1783, the street outside the Old Bailey became the official place of execution. There were three crossbars, which meant that a number of prisoners could be executed together. They were stood on a large trap door that was hinged and held by a sturdy pin at the loose end.

The prisoner or prisoners would have the knot of the noose placed in the right position under and slightly behind the left ear. The bolt was then pulled so that the trap fell and the doomed person or persons plunged into a pit below.

On that first morning ten poor wretches were hanged on the new gallows, watched by an appreciative crowd. It was the start of a bad time for prisoners, and a period of frustration for reformer John Howard. The War of Independence had ended in America; British soldiers, once resplendent in red tunics, and praised highly by their king and country, now wandered in rags, totally abandoned by the monarch and people who had formerly supported them. Penniless and starving, they had no choice but to go into crime, using the violence of the battlefield.

There was a crimewave, and the Home Secretary advised the King that judges must apply the law harshly and cruelly. The judges needed no second bidding. In the December 1783 Sessions at the Old Bailey, twenty-four people were sentenced to death and ninety were transported. None of these was a hardened criminal, but men and women who had committed their first offence.

Just over a year later, twenty men were hanged in one group outside the Old Bailey, several of them having been convicted of stealing items valued at only a few pence. Around that time, in 1785, hundreds of people awaiting transportation were crowded into Newgate, while the section where the condemned were held was packed by forty-nine prisoners awaiting a date with the hangman.

Time went by, but the lot of the prisoners in Newgate Gaol did not improve. Elizabeth Fry, who devoted her life to penal reform, was greatly moved by a visit to the prison, where she saw half-naked women fighting to get to the rails to hold out long sticks with spoons attached, pleading with passers-by to give them alms.

These dehumanised prisoners were described by W. Eden Hooper in his detailed work on Newgate: 'Many of them were mad drunk, others sat about the stones, squalid and ferocious. They all dragged heavy leg-irons about with them, riveted to the knees and again to the ankles, being unable to pay for "easement". In the wards they slept on the floor, many nearly naked; weak from want of food, savage from drink, unsexed and hopeless.'

Hooper referred to the magnificent work done for these women by Elizabeth Fry and her Ladies' Prison Visiting Association, saying: 'Steadily persisting in the task she had set out to perform, this humane woman quickly brought about an entire change in the habits and persons of her fallen sisters . . . she wooed the women through their offspring . . . In 1817 she formed a school for the children and the younger criminals.'

These changes for the better achieved at Newgate by Elizabeth Fry and others like her were brought about not with the help, but in spite, of the City Corporation. When she had requested to have the prison cleaned up, Elizabeth Fry was told by the Corporation: 'It is useless to attempt to reform such untamed and turbulent spirits except by punishment.'

The establishment did make progress with the appointment of a Commission on Capital Punishment in 1864. The press of the day was very active on this front, and Charles Dickens played a significant role in a campaign that resulted in the abolition of public executions in 1868.

The first execution to take place inside Newgate Gaol was the hanging of Alexander Mackay, who had used a rolling pin and furnace rake to beat his mistress to death. The unhappy distinction of being the last man to hang in Newgate goes to murderer George Woolfe, who went to the gallows in May 1902.

The beginning of the end of the Newgate Gaol came about indirectly in 1877 when a fire in the Sessions House caused so much damage that the City Lands Committee returned a report which said that to provide adequate accommodation for the proper holding of prisoners awaiting trial, and for the despatching of the increased business of the courts, the old Sessions House should be pulled down and new courts and offices built on its site and adjoining premises.

This report came out in 1878, the same year as the Prisons Act came into operation. Newgate was no longer used as a prison for debtors, and under this Act the Male Wing was taken over by the government. Sir William Harcourt, Home Secretary at the time, ordered that it should cease to be used as a regular prison 'except as a place of confinement for prisoners convicted of capital offences at the Old Bailey, and awaiting execution'.

Yet more than twenty years slipped by before it was agreed to erect a more modern and enlarged Old Bailey Sessions House on the site of the disused Newgate Prison. In the autumn of 1901, designs were invited for the proposed new building, and the plans selected were those of Mr E.W. Mountford, FRIBA.

Lord Alverstone was the Lord Chief Justice at the 1907 opening of the 'new' Old Bailey, which meant that he presided at the first sessions held there, and he also presided over the first big murder trial in the new building.

Newgate Gaol was gone, but it left behind the question of whether the Old Bailey would be any more just and fair without it. The study of a cross-section of old and new trials is the best way to reach a conclusion.

Democracy was absent in the Old Bailey on 24 July 1935, when the authorities, irritated by her animated campaign to end capital punishment, refused Mrs Violet Van der Elst admission to a murder trial. The media in general at that time had little sympathy with the Van der Elst cause, so there was no complaint against this minor, but important, injustice. As will be gathered later in this book, the Old Bailey wasn't always so lucky with the press.

3. THE TRADITION

Apart from individual societies, covert and overt, only the Church and the judiciary have carried ritual through from ancient times into today. Church ritual is employed to have the congregation march in mental step, chanting liturgies and chorusing canticles. It is an attempt at conditioning the human spirit, and it is voluntary. That is what separates it from legal ritualism – no one is forced to go to church, but anyone charged with a criminal offence is compelled to attend court. The accused and witnesses for and against, normal people accustomed to modern life, suddenly find themselves among men and women who wear ludicrous, ill-fitting wigs and speak an archaic language peppered with hypocrisy – such as counsel's toadying 'I am grateful to m'Lud', after being rebuked and put down by a supercilious judge.

Is this ritualism mere foolishness, or are the processions and the symbols really a mnemonic guide to constitutional functions that are a part of complicated convention into which fit conveniently most of the legislative and judicial activities of Parliament? Is it likely that anachronism is contributory to the crisis in the courts today? The legal profession is probably unique in attempting to operate in the modern world using archaic instruments. It could well be that ritual inevitably has the judiciary interpret the cases of today in the light of events of yesterday. The hue of the legal system's present is always coloured by its past.

The trickiness of the procedure protects it from rewriting, and it isn't likely that it will ever be changed. It would require a radical government to alter it, certainly not one made up of any of the political parties in existence today.

A look at the Old Bailey tradition will reveal only modest change through the years, and suggest that future transition is unlikely.

An ancient honour of the Corporation of the City of London is that the whole cost of the Old Bailey – the building as well as its maintenance – comes out of the private funds of the Corporation. By gladly and proudly bearing this financial burden, the city charges the ratepayer and taxpayer not a penny.

Before William the Conqueror stormed ashore, the City of London authorities had a body of civic law known as the *Judicia Civitatis Lundonie*, which performed judicial functions in criminal matters. When the Norman became king he agreed that, in return for the surrender of England's capital, the city should retain all its legal privileges and customs.

A Henry I charter of 1132 authorised the people of London to elect their own justiciar for 'keeping the Pleas of the Crown'. In 1461 another charter gave the lord mayor great powers and extensive rights, and the title of Justice of Gaol Delivery for Newgate, a name that continued after the prison itself was no more. With the Old Bailey policed by the City Constabulary and not the Metropolitan Police, the lord mayor, invested with the right to 'try, hear and determine' all offences coming within jurisdiction of the Old Bailey, was king within city bounds. By right he could at any time seek private audience with the reigning monarch as an *ex officio* member of the Privy Council, and his rank is that of an earl. The mayor is also Admiral of the Port of London, with jurisdiction over the tidal waterway between Havengore Creek in Essex, and Teddington.

Enjoying right of entry to the Tower of London at any hour of the night or day, the mayor, when Newgate Gaol was in existence, had a duplicate set of keys to all the gates and cells of the prison.

Nearly four hundred years after the Charter of 1461 it was disputed whether it was that charter which had the lord mayor sit as First Commissioner at the Old Bailey, or whether it was simply by virtue of the annual commissions which proclaim his office. Any doubt was ended by the Central Criminal Court Act, which was passed by Parliament in 1834, and confirmed the ancient privilege of the lord mayor. In addition, this Act extended the jurisdiction of the Old Bailey beyond being the Criminal Court for London and Middlesex. The Court was empowered to try criminal cases for parts of Essex, Kent and Surrey, as well as trying indictments for murder, piracy and felonies on the high seas. That was how the word Central came to prefix the previous Criminal Court.

The lord mayor headed the list when the same Act set out that the judges at the Old Bailey be the Lord Mayor, the Lord Chancellor, the Lord Keeper of the Great Seal, the Lord Chief Justice and the existing Judges of the Court of the King's Bench, the Dean of Arches, the Aldermen of the City of London, the Judges of the Sheriff's Court (which was to become the Mayor's and City of London Court held at the Guildhall) and any person who had been Lord Chancellor or a Judge of the High Court.

Three judges sat at a trial prior to the Act of 1834, which laid down that the presence of two commissioners was sufficient to constitute a court. This brought about a rule that one judge could sit providing another commissioner was somewhere in the precincts of the court. The Act removed the guard against bias and prejudice, no matter how flimsy it was, when three judges were required.

In the wake of that Act, the official position of the mayor was emphasised by all prisoners, despite having been tried by one of His Majesty's Judges, being sentenced by the Recorder of London in his capacity as the representative of the lord mayor. This show of strength lasted for three years until the accession of Queen Victoria in 1837, when the practice of the recorder reporting all convictions for murder to the monarch, and instructing that the sentences should or should not be carried out, was abolished.

On the opening day of each sessions of the 'old' Old Bailey, which invariably fell upon a Monday or Tuesday, the lord mayor would be there together with sheriffs, aldermen, the City Marshal (an imposing figure on horseback), the Recorder of the City of London (whose office is almost as ancient as that of the lord mayor), and the

Common Serjeant. A procession was formed to visit each court in turn, thus constituting the 'opening'. All the ushers would be in attendance, with the Grand and Petty juries also present. With the public opening taking place at 10.30 a.m., the ushers, who in addition to their demanding job also answered, unofficially, inquiries from all quarters, would have been busy for hours. All kinds of documents had to be produced and laid upon the table in the well of the court, including the list of cases to be tried that day, or which, at all events, were down for hearing, and the printed register of the sessions. Jurymen also had to be mustered and got into their places ready to be called. Should a required document not be to hand, or a juryman have gone missing, then it was the usher who had to answer to the judge.

In the old days the lot of a juryman was not a happy one, for there was no remuneration, and no expenses were allowed, even though, as often happened in the case of the assizes, it was necessary to travel long distances to the court. Neither were they very highly regarded. In one particular case in the 1870s, tried by Sir Thomas Chambers, a lone juryman held out against an otherwise unanimous verdict. Annoyed by this, the judge sent the jury back to their deliberations, telling them: 'Try and pummel it into him somehow.' As the jury left he tried to moderate his remark by calling after them: 'I don't mean with your fists!'

He didn't explain what other ways there are to 'pummel' anyone, and the jury ignored him anyway. Failing to reach a verdict, they were discharged.

During an adjournment for lunch in another trial of the same period, the members of the jury were eating a free meal consisting of cold meat, pickles, bread and cheese and beer, when there was panic at the discovery that one juryman was missing. There was immense relief when he returned to the jury box just minutes before the court resumed. His reason for being absent was astonishing. As a very poor man who had spent his last penny getting to the court, he had caught sight of the meal laid out for his fellow-jurymen and himself, and concluded that he would be asked to pay for it. Without any knowledge of his having to be 'exclusive' until the case had ended, he had gone out and walked up and down in the street to avoid the food.

The Recorder usually presided in Court No. 1, where hangs the Sword of Justice, unless the senior judge was presiding in a different courtroom. This sword, as fabled as Excalibur, has been variously described as golden or jewelled, and of immense value. Apart from being priceless in tradition, the sixteenth-century sword isn't worth much. It was given to the city in 1563 by Richard Matthew, a cutler. The haft of the sword needed repairing in 1806, and this was carried out in nearby Clerkenwell Close by William Summer, who perpetuated something of himself by engraving his intitials on the sword.

The weapon seemed to be in danger during the trial of swindler Horatio Bottomley. At the end of his trial for the Victory Bond frauds, Bottomley pointed at the sword while protesting his innocence to the jury, claiming in a loud voice that if he was found guilty the Sword of Justice would fall from its place on the wall.

Bottomley, a politician, journalist and financier, and for many years one of England's most notorious characters, specialised in defrauding small investors. In court many times, he was a brilliant speaker who conducted his own defence, often baffling famous KCs. In this case he was found guilty of selling bogus bonds and sentenced to seven years' penal servitude. Although millions of pounds had passed through his hands, he died in poverty after his release from prison.

4. THE HANGMEN

The accession of Queen Victoria to the throne was a blow to the low types who got their enjoyment from observing the suffering of fellow human beings. They were robbed of one of their most regular pleasures when one of the first Acts passed in her reign saw the abolition of the pillory. The mob's fear that public executions would be banned was unfounded, but in the first year of her reign the new Queen abolished the death penalty for stealing, and this reduced the number of hangings by almost two-thirds. Gone forever was the horrific spectacle of young people hanged for such modest offences as stealing more than five pounds. No longer did the death sentence apply for forgery, rioting, inciting to mutiny, armed smuggling, and aiding the escape of criminals. This humane reconsideration of the laws pointed to Victoria being a rare monarch indeed. But none of it was due to her. She was too young at that time to have such things concern her, and the changes for the better were due to Sir Samuel Romilly, an enlightened, active and fearless reformer.

Even so, the death penalty remained and the post of public executioner still existed. Names such as Ellis, Billington and Pierrepoint have come and gone, while that of Jack Ketch (d.1686) has lived on to become synonymous with the term hangman. Ketch carried out the orders of the notorious Judge Jeffreys with both diligence and a callous brutality. Although he obviously enjoyed his work, Ketch was something of a temperamental artiste, and, as there was considerable labour involved in hanging those sentenced to death for high treason, with the subsequent dissection, boiling and distributing of the culprit's quarters throughout the neighbourhood for display, he took a firm stance when Judge Jeffreys churned out a batch of twenty-nine rebels for execution on the first day of his 'Bloody Assizes', at Dorchester on 5 September 1685.

Ketch stated that he and his assistant, a butcher named Pascha Rose, could only handle thirteen executions a day. In 1682 he went on strike for more money – the only hangman ever to have done so.

When Lord William Russell and the Duke of Monmouth were sentenced to death for levying war against Charles II, Jack Ketch the hard man was for the first time seen to be fallible, possibly even weak. Lord Russell's father, the Earl of Bedford, offered the King £50,000 to pardon his son. Charles, who seemed to be surrounded by rebels and beset by plots against him, not surprisingly turned down the offer with 'If I do not take his life, then he will soon have mine.' So the death sentences stood, and both Russell and Monmouth were to suffer horrendous deaths at the hands of Jack Ketch.

Begging his wife to stay a little longer in his cell with him on the eve of his execution, Russell said: 'Stay and sup with me. Let us eat our last earthly food together'; and when she was leaving him he took her hand, saying: 'This flesh you feel now, in a few hours must be cold.'

The following morning, Lord Russell left Newgate in his own coach and was driven past his own house to a specially erected scaffold in Lincoln's Inn Fields. It was raining heavily and Russell, thoughtful for others to the last, was concerned that those riding with him in the coach would get wet once the destination was reached. Then, surprised by the size of the watching crowd, he mounted the scaffold, his lips moving in whispered prayer.

Jack Ketch barbarously botched the execution, and when news of how horribly Lord Russell had died reached the Duke of Monmouth, he took six guineas to his own execution at Tower Hill, handing the money to Ketch as a bribe to have the executioner concentrate and do a better job on him than he had Russell.

The payment for a speedy death was probably unnecessary, for Jack Ketch took pride in his work. He was adept at branding with a hot iron, nose-splitting, ear-cropping, whipping at the cart-tail and other cruel punishments. He had obeyed when Judge Jeffreys had ordered him to whip a woman with the words: 'Hangman, I charge you pay particular attention to this lady. Scourge her soundly, man; scourge her till the blood runs down. It is Christmas – a cold time for madam to strip. See that you warm her shoulders thoroughly.'

Yet the Duke of Monmouth wasted his six guineas, for Ketch made an even worse mess of the beheading. It was so bad that the executioner cracked up, with Monmouth still alive but terribly injured.

'I cannot do it. My heart fails me,' Jack Ketch wailed, but the sheriff, as unnerved as the executioner and all those watching, induced him to have another go.

Again Ketch failed, and the beheading had to be finished off with the help of someone else. The man who had made a name for himself as a hangman was a failure at other types of execution.

As well as working hard, Jack Ketch played hard, spending money at such a rate that one day on his way back from Tyburn he was arrested in Holborn for debt. He was immediately released when he paid with the few pence he had in his pocket, plus the proceeds from the sale of three suits of clothing he had pulled off the bodies of those he had hanged that morning.

The next time his luck had run out, and he was locked up in Marshalsea Prison as a debtor. While inside, Ketch pre-empted Oscar Wilde by writing a ballad with the clumsy title *The Man of Destinies Hard Fortune, whereby his hopeful harvest is like to be Blasted*. This told the story of the money his victims had paid him for a swift despatch from the world. He also penned another little epic while in gaol. This had the more easily handled title of *An apologie of John Ketch Esq.*, in which he tried to blame his bungling in the Lord William Russell execution on Russell himself, and someone said to have interrupted Ketch at the crucial moment.

Unbeknown to Ketch, his books would, when two more

centuries had gone by, inspire an American known as George, who was a butcher's assistant in Washington Market, New York. George was convinced that his destiny was to emulate the historically renowned high-executioner of Great Britain. Studying the windlass that was used to hoist cattle in the slaughter-house, George worked long into the night designing an apparatus for the 'humane accommodation of the law-breaking community'.

With the assistance of Joseph B. Atkinson, George produced a 'perfected gibbet' that came to be termed the New York pattern, and the inventors brought forth a species of machinery which, in George's language, 'was unsurpassed in simplicity and perfection of construction by any machine in the market'.

It worked so well that George, who became known as Monsieur New York, and his scaffold, were in demand for official executions all over America. He perfected another machine that could handle mass executions and, in 1866, was so keen to demonstrate it on thirty Indians sentenced to be hanged that he offered to pay his expenses to and from Nebraska solely to be able to show how all thirty persons, using his own terms, could be 'worked off at once'.

To the chagrin of George, President Johnson spoiled everything for him by granting pardons to most of the Indians. Yet the disappointed George went on to great things in the execution business. Jack Ketch would have been proud of him. There is no record of whether George died with his boots on, but it is assumed that he met a more dignified end than the Englishman who was his hero.

Things started to go wrong for Jack Ketch in the year 1686, when he was sent to Bridewell for 'affronting' a sheriff. At this time, Pascha Rose, the butcher who had been taught the hangman's trade by Ketch during the time of the 'Bloody Assizes', came back on the scene. It must have galled Jack Ketch to see his erstwhile understudy appointed hangman in his place. But Rose was only in the job for a few months before running into trouble, and Ketch got his vengeance by hanging his former pupil at Tyburn.

But Ketch hadn't returned to the job for very long before he found himself back in Marshalsea Prison for debt. He and another prisoner escaped, and Ketch went on a drinking spree before looking for a woman. He found Elizabeth White, the wife of a watchman, selling gingerbread in Moorfields. The poor woman resisted his crude advances, enraging Ketch so that he beat her almost to death.

It must have been a shock for the hangman to find himself in the dock, where he pleaded with the jury to acquit him, blaming drink for the attack on the unfortunate woman, saying: 'Everything came over black and when I came to, I found a hammer in my hand.'

His plea was rejected and Ketch was hanged in Bunhill-Fields, close to the scene of his vicious crime.

A predecessor of Jack Ketch was a man named Derrick, who was as black a character as the hangman who was to follow him, and had a violent but intriguing background. Derrick gets a mention in Dekker's *Bellman of London* (1608), and his method of hoisting his victims on the scaffold is credited as having given his name to a type of crane. Enduring though this may be, if true, it fails to match the story of his career.

When Robert Devereux, second Earl of Essex, a favourite of Elizabeth I, captured Cadiz, Derrick had been part of the apparently unruly expedition on which he was sentenced to hang for an outrage upon a woman. Derrick was in good, or, rather, bad company, for twenty-three of his companions on that voyage were also sentenced to be hanged after being convicted of various offences.

Unable to find a hangman, the Earl of Essex granted Derrick a pardon and appointed him executioner. It was a bad move by the Earl, who fell from grace, was imprisoned, sentenced to death, and later beheaded by Derrick, an irony that was taken up in a contemporary ballad entitled *Essex's Good Night*, the words of which were:

> Derrick thou know'st at Cales I saved
> Thy life – lost for a rape there done;
> As thou thyself can testify
> Thine own hand three-and-twenty hung.

But now thou see'st myself is come
By chance into thy hands I light.
Strike out thy blow, that I may know
Thou Essex loved at his goodnight.

Possibly the most famous execution of all was the one that never took place – hangman James Berry's unsuccessful attempt to put to death John Lee, 'The Man They Couldn't Hang'. That story comes later, but first is the sad tale of Tom Savage, who achieved fame the hard way by becoming the man they hanged twice.

Tom was just seventeen years old when he was taken to Tyburn. From the age of fifteen, and quite possibly long before, he had lived a fast and loose sexually active life. The Newgate *Calendar*, a kind of catalogue of crimes, records Tom Savage's offences as: 'Breaking the Sabbath, he never having once heard a whole service during that time, was the first inlet to his vices, especially whoredom, drunkenness and theft, for he used commonly to pass away the Sabbaths at a bawdy-house in Ratcliff Highway, with one Hannah Blay, a vile common strumpet, who was the cause of his ruin, and brought him to his shameful end.'

The thrill of having a toy-boy was not enough for the mercenary Hannah, who told Tom that he, just like the other punters, would have to pay for her services. She suggested that Tom steal from his master, and when Tom said that was impossible because a maid was always present, the hard-hearted Hannah advised, 'Knock her brains out.'

The gullible Tom did as he was told. Battering the maid's head in, he snatched a bag of money and ran to Hannah. Seeing the boy as trouble, she tried to keep the money but get rid of him. Giving her half a crown, a disappointed Tom ran off. When captured he was full of remorse and made a full confession in the dock of the Old Bailey.

At Tyburn, Tom went through the prolonged and agonising form of dying that was considered normal in those days. He writhed, heaved and struggled so much that a friend mercifully beat him heavily on the chest to hasten the end.

After some time, the boy's body was cut down and handed over to his friends, who carried it to a nearby house to prepare it for burial. There was considerable shock among them when Tom showed signs of revival. He was quickly taken to a bedroom. Put to bed, under warm blankets, he showed much stronger signs of recovery, to the delight of his pals. To escape the hangman was nothing short of a miracle.

But the startling news of the resurrection of Tom Savage reached the ears of the sheriff's officer, who hurried to the house. Tom was returned to the same gallows, and this time the hangman made no mistake.

Then, and in the years to follow, there was no law against hanging a person for the second time if the occasion should arise. Berry the hangman placed John Lee on the trap thrice before giving up.

An important place in the history of Newgate and the Old Bailey is held by executioner William Calcraft, who, on 26 May 1868, officiated at Britain's last public execution.

The victim who shares this legal milestone with his executioner was Michael Barrett, who is featured in a later chapter entitled 'The Fenians'.

It is difficult for normal-thinking people to imagine what kind of man would volunteer for the job of State Executioner. One ill-fated family of hangmen was the Billingtons – father James and sons Thomas, William and the much younger John. They carried out judicial hangings between 1902 and 1905. James Billlington died after a short illness in the winter of 1901, at the age of fifty-four. A month later his eldest son, Thomas, succumbed to pneumonia at the age of twenty-nine. William, who was a heavy drinker and had a liking for women, continued the family trade. William, or 'Billy' as he was known, retired in 1904 to live a chaotic kind of life that included divorce, imprisonment and stormy remarriage. William's younger brother John, or 'Jack', then aged just twenty-two, took over as hangman. A God-fearing, church-organ-playing young man, John fell through the trap doors while preparing an execution. He recovered enough to hang the prisoner the following morning, but then took to his bed and died at the age of twenty-five.

Another man who seemed to be badly affected by work as a hangman, John Ellis, learned his trade at Newgate Gaol. First working at a mill in Rochdale, he applied to the Home Office for the post of hangman, and while waiting he set up in business as a hairdresser. A man who liked publicity, he upset the Home Office, and was rapped over the knuckles, when his supposedly secret appointment of 'assistant executioner and executioner' was announced in his local newspaper. Ellis didn't learn his lesson, and when a similar announcement appeared in the *Daily Mail* he was cautioned and suspended before he had even started the job.

As a result, the more low-key Henry Pierrepoint (uncle of the more famous Albert) got the top jobs, while John Ellis, a man who displayed an unusual nervousness when doing his job, remained in the main an assistant.

It was at Leeds prison on 29 December 1903 that the real problems of John Ellis began with his first execution of a woman. Emily Swann and her lodger lover, John Gallagher, had been convicted together at York Assizes of the murder of her husband, William. Ellis, who never did adjust to hanging a woman, found Emily Swann moaning pitifully on the floor of her cell. He gave her a glass of brandy and she regained control of herself. She and her lover were to hang side by side, and it must have been a chilling scene when Emily met Gallagher below the two nooses with the cool and conversational greeting: 'Good morning, John.'

'Good morning, love,' Gallagher replied, although he had to clear his throat a few times before being able to speak.

As the trap dropped, Emily cried out: 'Goodbye. God bless you!'

It was another landlady/lodger/lover execution, this time at Pentonville Prison in 1923, that was the undoing of John Ellis. Edith and Percy Thompson lived in Ilford. They were a happily married couple, in spite of the fact that Edith was a lively, handsome, fun-loving twenty-eight-year-old, while her husband was a much duller, reserved person. Edith, a cashier, advertised for a lodger, and Frederick Bywaters, a good-looking young man aged twenty, replied to the advertisement. His job meant that he was away at sea a lot, but when he was at home he stayed with the Thompsons.

Edith and Bywaters soon became lovers, but, probably due to his youthfulness, Bywaters wasn't prepared both to have his cake and eat it, so to speak. Jealous of the husband, he wanted to get rid of Percy Thompson. Hopelessly and foolishly in love, Edith wrote Bywaters letters in which she said that she was doing her best to finish off her husband – one method she was using was putting ground glass in his food. This was untrue, plainly written to please her young lover.

Bywaters accompanied the Thompsons on a trip to Shanklin on the Isle of Wight, quarrelling with Percy Thompson on the return to Ilford, who banned Bywaters from his house. On the evening of 3 October 1922, Percy and Edith were walking along the almost deserted Belgrave Road, Ilford, on their way home from a visit to the theatre, when Bywaters, reeking of alcohol and wielding a ship's knife, jumped out of the shadows to stab Percy Thompson several times, killing him.

Taken completely by surprise, Edith Thompson screamed: 'For God's sake, don't do it!'

She had neither planned nor wanted the death of her husband, but Mrs Thompson's stupidity in writing those letters to Bywaters had her convicted of murder at the Old Bailey in December 1922 and sentenced to death.

In his memoirs, Major Blake, who was Governor of Pentonville at the time, but resigned (or was pushed) because of his humane outlook, writes of how he liked Bywaters and was so upset that he had the boy brought to his office on the eve of his execution. They talked of many things, including Bywaters' voyages around the world, but the boy's thoughts were for the woman he loved, and he asked Blake: 'Do you think they will hurt her? I am always thinking of it, sir. I wish to God I had never done what I did. I must have been mad; but I loved her so much. Please see they do not hurt her. It was my fault; she is innocent. Everyone should have been able to see that. She never did anything – it was me.'

Bywaters went courageously to the Pentonville execution chamber, where he was despatched by hangman William Willis and his assistant, Seth Mills, on 9 January, while on the same date, Edith

Thompson was executed, under terrible circumstances, at Holloway Prison by John Ellis and his assistants Robert Baxter and Thomas Phillips.

Major Blake wrote:

> I had been suffering with neuritis in the night [the night before the execution of Bywaters and Thompson], and was rather late visiting him in the morning, but he looked at me with gratitude in his eyes and thanked me. The question that was on his tongue, about Mrs Thompson, he did not ask. But his thoughts were of the woman he loved, and his heart went out to her.
>
> They hanged Mrs Thompson. Her end was terrible. She had been moaning for days, and often the words, 'Why did he do it? Why did he do it?' came from her lips. In the last few days of her life, her hair was going grey, and her sufferings had been so great that she had had a complete collapse. They carried her to the scaffold, and had to hold her while they fixed the cap round her head; she was moaning all the time. They hanged a practically unconscious woman.

At the jolt at the end of the drop, some inner part of Mrs Thompson passed from her to saturate her underclothes with blood. It was tentatively assumed that she had been pregnant without being aware of the fact, and had miscarried as she died. Whether or not this was true, it was an upsetting experience for all who were involved, and from then onwards all women hanged in British prisons wore special canvas knickers at their executions.

Worst hit of the many affected by Edith Thompson's gruesome death was hangman John Ellis. His grim profession was not in his genes, for, unlike other executioners, hanging was not a family business for Ellis. In fact, when he first applied for the job, his father was so repelled that the two of them didn't speak for some time. Ellis had, without apparent ill effect, sent something like two hundred persons, including Irish rebels and killers such as

Crippen, George Smith (the 'Brides in the Bath' murderer), Sir Roger Casement, Seddon and Major Armstrong to their deaths, but it was the ghost of Edith Thompson which came to haunt him.

By that time he had four children and, after having run a public house for a time, was working as a barber. He would sit for hours, still and alone, staring straight ahead. Often he was heard to whisper: 'I wish I hadn't done it, I wish I hadn't done it.' When asked what he was referring to, Ellis would reply, 'I hanged an innocent woman', sometimes adding, 'It's a wicked thing to hang people, but it's the State, they are the murderers, they make us do it.'

On 10 October 1923, John Ellis, still suffering and close to breaking down, was at Duke Street Prison, Glasgow, to carry out the first execution of a woman in Scotland for more than half a century. The condemned was Susan Newell, a spiteful, violent woman aged thirty. She had once attacked her husband so viciously that he had reported her to the police. One evening in June she had called a thirteen-year-old paperboy into her home in Coatbridge and attempted to get a free newspaper from him. When the boy refused, Susan Newell flew into a rage and strangled him. Keeping the body on a settee, she had her daughter Janet, aged eight, help her wrap it in an old rug the next morning and put it in a handcart. She was arrested while pushing the body into Glasgow, with Janet sitting on top of the rug that covered it. She blamed the killing on her husband, claiming that she was protecting him by trying to dispose of the body.

Police inquiries proved that the husband had taken no part in the crime, and he was released. The defence entered a plea of insanity, which was rejected, and Newell was sentenced to death.

Dreading the execution, Ellis contacted the sheriff to stress that there were special problems in hanging a woman, asking for the special knickers produced after the hanging of Edith Thompson. Nerves got the better of him, and he left himself open to another terrible ordeal by not properly securing the woman's arms. Able to wrestle free, Susan Newell pulled the white hood – worn after public executions had been abandoned – from her head. A harrowing scene then ensued in which she fought like a wildcat before she could be subdued and her arms strapped before the hood was replaced.

Susan Newell is said to have then died bravely, but her death was the last straw for hangman John Ellis, who resigned.

Like other executioners before him and since, Ellis settled down to writing his memoirs. They were published in the spring of 1924, and he celebrated the occasion by trying to hang himself, the first of many suicide attempts. In 1927 he tried to escape his terrors by going into the twilight world of acting, playing the part of Marwood in Congreve's *The Way of the World* on the stage. This would seem to have increased his instability, and on 20 September 1932 he chased his terrified wife, threatening to kill her, before slashing his own throat with a razor. By choice John Ellis, at the age of fifty-eight, had joined those whose deaths he had been unable to live with.

Being an executioner never got the better of James Berry, but the operation of the gallows at Exeter Gaol defeated him on the morning of Monday, 23 February 1885. Berry was there to execute John Lee, a footman who had battered in the head of Miss Emma Keyse, his elderly mistress, and set her room ablaze in her beautiful home overlooking Babbacombe Bay in Devon.

After a thorough trial before Mr Justice Manisty, Lee was found guilty, and when asked if he had anything to say, quietly replied: 'The reason I am so calm and collected, my lord, is because I trust in the Lord. I am innocent.'

The night before his execution, John Lee had a dream in which he had stood on the gallows but the trap door had refused to drop. He told several people, including the chaplain, about the dream, but it meant nothing to James Berry when he came into the cell to pinion Lee.

The hangman had overnight satisfied himself that the scaffold was working perfectly, and he had no doubts as, with the chaplain murmuring the usual prayers, he knelt to strap Lee's ankles, as Lee was unflinchingly toeing the chalk marks on the trap door. Standing back upright, Berry pulled the lever. Nothing happened. Lee still stood calmly on a trap door that hadn't moved a fraction of an inch. The governor of the prison, as shocked as all others present, apart from Lee, signalled to the warders to take Lee back to his cell.

Berry made some adjustments and again pulled the lever. The sides of the drop fell swiftly and smoothly open.

Lee was hurriedly brought back and placed on the trap door with his toes once more against the chalk marks. Berry pulled the lever, but again nothing happened. Once more Lee was returned to his cell. Wood was trimmed from the sides of the trap door and the apparatus tested again and again, never failing each time.

The calmest of all present, Lee was brought back to the scaffold for the third time. Yet again the trap door wouldn't drop. The chaplain cracked up, wanting nothing further to do with the bizarre proceedings, while the frantic prison governor telegraphed a message to the Home Secretary, who wired back to order that, in the circumstances, the sentence be commuted to one of penal servitude for life.

John Lee served twenty-three years in prison, and on coming out wrote a book, fittingly entitled *The Man They Couldn't Hang*, got married, toured the music halls, ran a public house, then went to the United States, where he died in 1933.

Hangman James Billington hung his noose on a peg of history when he executed twenty-four-year-old Ada Chard Williams, the last woman to be hanged at Newgate Gaol. Ada's husband William was forty-two. A talented artist, for some reason he worked as a clerk, a position with such a poor salary that the couple had money problems. It was their financial distress that had them rent 3 Grove Villas, Barnes, under the name of Goodwin.

In August 1989, Ada Chard Williams used a false name and an accommodation address in Hammersmith to place in a Woolwich newspaper an advertisement that read:

> A young married couple would adopt healthy child, every care and comfort, good reference given, very small premium. Write first to Mrs M. Hewetson, 4 Bradmore Lane, Hammersmith.

Reading this advertisement gave hope to a young unmarried mother who was in dire straits. Florence Jones dearly loved her twenty-one-month-old daughter Selina, but simply couldn't afford to keep her. Replying to the advertisement, Florence arranged to pay Mrs Hewetson (Ada Chard Williams) three pounds when passing over the child, complete with a new outfit, with a further two pounds to be paid at a later date. Florence was willing to pay out in the short term an amount of money that was small compared to what it would cost her to raise the child.

The handover of the baby took place at Charing Cross on 31 August. There the bogus Mrs Hewetson told Florence Jones that she and her husband were moving to a new address, and offered to allow the mother to see the baby there every other week. On paying her first visit, Florence Jones discovered that Mrs Hewetson didn't live at that address. Alarmed by this turn of events, she went to the police.

Soon afterwards the body of a baby was found floating in the Thames at Battersea. Neighbours, who were aware that the Chard Williams' had had a child in their house and that it was now missing, started to gossip. As rumours spread, Ada Chard Williams boldly wrote to Scotland Yard on the subject, saying:

> Dear Sir, I must apologise for taking this liberty, but I see that I and my husband are suspected of murdering a little female child found in the river at Battersea. The accusation is positively a false one.
>
> The facts are these: I, much against my husband's wish, advertised for a child to make a little money, and as a result we adopted this little child. My next act was to advertise for a home for the little girl. I used the address of some shop in Warwick Road, Kensington, and I received several answers.
>
> I chose one in Grange Street or Road, Croydon, from a lady of the name of Smith. She agreed to take the child for one pound, together with the clothes for the child. I met her at Clapham Junction – the Falcon Hotel – about the middle of September, and I handed the child and the clothes over to her.

It was then quite well. That was the last I saw of the child. I have, it is true, carried on a sort of baby-farming – that is, I advertised for children and then got people to readopt them for less money. I have had five in this way. Two died while in my care, but I can prove that every kindness was shown them, and the others I have readopted.

I have been accused of carrying on this kind of thing for six years, but that is wrong as I only started it in 1897. You will say that if I am innocent why don't I come forward? But there have been innocent people hanged, and I must say the case is rather black. Things look very much against me and it is not fair to go entirely on circumstantial evidence.

I am trying to find the woman to whom I gave the child. If I come forward I must clear myself unless I give a clue to the woman. My husband is not to blame, as he has always looked on the whole thing with abhorrence. We left Barnes because we couldn't pay the rent.

The bravado or stupidity that had Ada Chard Williams contact the police direct was her undoing. There was evidence to link her with other infants found dead in the Thames. With her husband, Ada Chard Williams stood before Mr Justice Ridley at the Old Bailey on 17 February 1900. As was to be suspected from her behaviour in the magistrates' court, where she had been smiling at people in the court, and had snapped at a police inspector, 'Mind your own business', when requested to face the front, her attitude was overly self-confident and callous.

The jury found her guilty of murder, and her husband of being an accessory after the fact. Judge Ridley ruled that William Chard Williams had not been indicted on that charge, however, and he was discharged.

Donning the black cap to sentence Ada to death, the judge advised her to seek repentance, and she replied, 'Thank you, my Lord', and when asked if she wished to make representation for a stay of execution, she replied firmly and clearly, 'I have nothing to say, gentlemen.'

Her mother, brother and husband visited Ada in the condemned cell, and her final farewell to the latter distressed him greatly. Although her demeanour had mellowed since her time in court, she showed no trace of fear when she met hangman James Billington in her cell at three minutes to nine on the morning of 8 March 1900. Quietly allowing him to pinion her arms, she walked without assistance to the scaffold, where she died without a murmur.

It was William Billington, the second son of hangman James Billington, who carried out the last execution of a man at Newgate Gaol. The condemned man was twenty-one-year-old George Woolfe, a particularly nasty bit of work from Hoxton. After seducing factory girl Charlotte Cheeseman, who was madly in love with him, Woolfe caused her all kinds of trouble after tiring of her, and eventually, on the night of Saturday, 25 January 1902, he decided to rid himself of the girl once and for all.

The next morning a lad playing football on Tottenham Marshes found Charlotte's terribly battered body in a ditch. She had been savagely and repeatedly kicked, and seventeen stab wounds had been inflicted. Despite being covered in blood, her nose broken and her skull smashed in, a post mortem established that the girl, whose body still had some warmth when discovered on a bitterly cold morning, had taken a long time to die and must have suffered severely.

On the run, Woolfe had enlisted in the Surrey Regiment under the name of Slater, and the police didn't catch up with him until 6 February. Tried and convicted at the Old Bailey, the despicable Woolfe was both the last man to die in Newgate, and the first murderer whose hanging was delayed by the new regulation requiring three clear Sundays to pass to enable the condemned to make his peace with God. (Although this had been common practice since the earliest times, it was made law in 1902.)

For most of us alive at the time of the abolition of hanging in this country, there would seem to have only ever been one hangman – Albert Pierrepoint. Sadly, his autobiography is diluted by inaccuracies and Home Office restrictions, and he perhaps clicks into the memory most easily in association with the well-remembered execution of Ruth Ellis, the fifteenth woman, and the last, to be hanged in the twentieth century.

Mrs Ellis, a hostess in a Soho drinking club, shot and killed David Blakely, the racing driver with whom she'd had a stormy affair. Her conviction in court was made certain by her own statement on the shooting to the prosecutor, when she said: 'It is obvious that when I shot him I intended to kill him.'

This frank admission left two defending barristers, paid for by a newspaper, high and dry. Even so, the press kept a campaign going for Ruth Ellis to be reprieved. No one could argue that she was not a murderer, and most of the clamour for her to be spared seemed to rest on the fact that she was a glamorous woman.

Wearing the regulation canvas knickers that were a legacy from Edith Thompson, she went silently and with dignity to meet her death at the hands of Albert Pierrepoint on 13 July 1955. As was the custom for the executed, Ruth Ellis was buried within the precincts of the prison. Because it lay in the path of a proposed access road, in 1971 her body was moved and reburied at Amersham, Buckinghamshire. Denied a reprieve by law, Ruth Ellis was given a respectable grave by progress.

Hangmen came and went in the lengthy history of Newgate Gaol and the Old Bailey, and now they have gone, most probably forever. Many, including Albert Pierrepoint, expressed regret, but that doesn't explain how they were able to carry out their trade. The hangman killed poor creatures for money, irrespective of their sex, calling or the motive behind their awful crimes. Should the passing of the State Executioner be mourned?

5. THE FENIANS

The aim of the Fenian movement was the severance of Ireland from England, and the conversion of Ireland into a republic. In pursuit of this aim there were active units in England during the second half of the nineteenth century. They operated in a spasmodic manner, but often with devastating effect. What was, in terms of loss of life and damage to property, the climax of the campaign, occurred in 1867, following the arrest of two Fenians named Burke and Casey, who were held for trial at the Old Bailey on a charge of treason-felony. They were detained in Clerkenwell Prison, which was built in 1845 and known as the House of Detention. It was constructed on the site of the Bridewell in Clerkenwell Green, which had been known as the New Prison, a misnomer because it had been very old and decaying when demolished. The boundary wall of the previous structure was retained, and the House of Detention was one of the first 'cellular' prisons to be built. It was a modification of the separation-of-prisoners system that was then in use at the 'model' prison of Pentonville. Until this time prisoners had been herded together. There were individual cells at Clerkenwell for 286 prisoners. It was the last of several prisons that had from time to time been located at Clerkenwell, and was situated in a slum neighbourhood close to Corporation Row.

Holding Burke and Casey made the authorities nervous. The two men and their cause had many sympathisers, not all of whom were Irish, and the Fenians were known to take care of their own. An attempt to free the men was expected, and that it would involve force was fully accepted. Burke and Casey were included in the custom of exercising the prisoners daily in the prison yard, the boundary wall of which faced the buildings in Corporation Row.

The prison authorities were suspicious and sure that some plan was being hatched. Consequently, a vigilant watch was kept on the two Irishmen. During one exercise period a small india-rubber ball came in over the wall. A prisoner officer caught it when the ball had bounced only once. When opened up the ball was found to contain materials for writing letters in invisible ink. The prison authorities gave themselves a pat on the back for depriving the Irish prisoners of these items, but they were to learn later that Burke had obtained similar materials prior to this, and had smuggled out a note to his comrades, which read:

> Dear Friend. – You know my position here. You know how
> I am situated here. There is a house here called the 'Noted
> Stout House', and at that house there is a sewer and a weak
> part of the wall. If you get a barrel of gunpowder and place
> it there, you will be able to blow the wall to hell. Get the
> men to buy it in small quantities. The job must be done at
> 3.30 or 4 o'clock. If you do not do this you ought to be shot.

The house referred to was a public house close to the prison. Had the authorities been astute enough to intercept this communication, a disaster would have been averted.

A warder was watching Burke one day, and saw him stand in a position that guaranteed him being seen by anyone who might be looking out of an upper window in a house in Corporation Row. Burke stooped to remove one boot, then took off the sock and wiped his foot with it. Replacing the sock and boot, Burke wiped his hand across his forehead. It was obvious that he was signalling to someone in the houses opposite.

Burke's comrades did as he asked. Obtaining the powder in small quantities, they accumulated a full barrel. That done, they, at the hour specified by Burke, on 13 December 1867, wheeled the heavy barrel to the section of wall Burke had indicated in his instructions. They laid a trail of gunpowder as a fuse, and touched it off.

The explosion that ensued was terrific. Several houses were completely wrecked, four people died instantly, and the blast seriously injured about forty more, some of whom subsequently died from their injuries.

A massive hole was blown in the wall, but the object of the Fenian attack was defeated by the authorities having been suspicious enough to move Burke and Casey further into the prison.

A considerable reward was offered for information regarding the perpetrators of the frustrated attempt at breaking out the two prisoners, and the informer, the ever-present blight of Ireland's patriots, turned up once more. This time there were two of them, named Mullany and Vaughan.

Their information, which came at a high price, led to the arrest of five men and a woman. The men were William Desmond, Timothy Desmond, John O'Keefe, Nicholas English and Michael Barrett. The woman, ironically for someone destined to stand in the dock at the Old Bailey, was named Ann Justice. The six were jointly charged with the murder of Sarah Ann Hodgkinson, one of the victims of the explosion, and appeared at the Old Bailey in April 1868.

The case was heard before Lord Chief Justice Cockburn, a ludicrously peculiar-looking little man with an eccentric liking for old-fashioned clothes. The collar he wore tied at the back of his neck, with points which came up over his cheeks on both sides, imparting the harmless appearance of a clown. Anyone in court, whether an accused or counsel, who was led to regard Cockburn as a buffoon, and acted accordingly, soon regretted doing so. Lord Chief Justice Cockburn was a stern judge and a stickler for legal etiquette. Yet if womanising had been a crime, Cockburn would have been a very guilty man. His bedroom activities probably contributed to the heart attack that was later to cause his death.

With Cockburn at the trial of the Fenians was Baron Bramwell, and the big guns of counsel were brought in for the prosecution – the Attorney-General, the Solicitor-General, Mr Hardinge Giffard QC (who became Lord Halsbury), Mr Poland (who afterwards became Sir Harry Poland, and lived long enough to come close to celebrating his hundredth birthday) and Mr Archibald.

It was plain that the funds of the Fenian Brotherhood were limited, for facing these prominent members of the Bar were juniors acting for the defence.

The defendants, probably due to a protracted period on remand in prison, were woebegone, dejected and ill-looking, apart from Michael Barrett, the man whose intelligence, appearance and general demeanour had him regarded as the leader. There were many women present in a court that was crowded to suffocation, and in spite of the tragic deaths caused by the explosion, there was much sympathy for, and admiration of, Michael Barrett. He was a broad-shouldered man standing about five foot seven or eight inches tall, with a handsome, good-natured face that made it difficult for anyone to associate him with the crime that he was accused of. He was calm and self-possessed throughout the hearing, a fine specimen of manhood compared to the two men who had informed on him and the others. When they were in the witness box, Barrett stared at them with disgust and loathing. His steady gaze had them writhing and faltering in their evidence.

It was all a very open-and-shut case, with the prosecution giving details of the plotting and planning so that there could be no doubt of the guilt of the Fenians. Convincing evidence of the secret communications between Burke and Casey and Fenians on the outside came from prison warders. These officers also testified that Ann Justice had visited Casey in Clerkenwell on the day of the explosion, passing herself off as his sister while a woman with her, who gave her name as Mrs Barry, claimed to be Casey's aunt. Further evidence against Ann Justice was that she had been seen with Timothy Desmond close to the prison wall on the afternoon of the attempted jail-break, as well as being seen running away with Desmond after the explosion.

Michael Barrett was seen to be the prime mover in the conspiracy, with evidence given that he had been witnessed setting fire to the trail of gunpowder. There was barely any defence other than pointless contradictions of the evidence for the prosecution and the putting forward of weak alibis.

Yet the trial went on late into each day, with even the corridors and approaches to the court densely packed, while the crowd gathered outside was so large that the buzz of general conversation from it could be heard inside the court.

It displeased no one when the prosecution withdrew the case against Ann Justice due to insufficient evidence. Before the trial she had tried to hang herself in her cell, but was cut down in time. She was then allowed to leave the dock, but before going to the stairs leading down to the prison, where she would be formally discharged, Ann Justice, with tears streaming down her face, walked to Michael Barrett. The courtroom was hushed as she took his hand and reverently kissed it. Then she left, and so ended one of the most memorable little dramas ever witnessed at the Old Bailey.

When the final day came, the power in the closing speeches lay, as expected, with the prosecution. There was not much the defence counsel could say on behalf of those they represented. However, Mr Baker Greene, who defended Barrett, remembered something worth saying at the time the judge was summing up. It was so important, at least to Greene, that he jumped to his feet and broke in upon his Lordship's observations for the jury to consider. The funny little judge turned into an angrily snarling creature who stopped the lawyer before the poor man had got many words out. Eyes flaming, voice cutting, Mr Justice Cockburn shouted: 'Sit down, sir, sit down! How dare you interrupt me!'

Mr Baker Greene's moment of recklessness was over. Psychologically dismantled by the irate judge, he collapsed into his seat and remained silent.

The jury went out, leaving everyone agog and eager to learn the verdicts. They weren't kept waiting long, for an agitated jury returned quickly, its foreman's face ashen, to deliver a series of verdicts that took all of the people by surprise, and brought cries of disgust from several of them. One after the other, all of the prisoners were acquitted until it came to Michael Barrett. There was a pregnant pause, and the foreman seemed reluctant to announce the verdict on Barrett. At last he uttered it, but in an undertone: 'Guilty.'

It was difficult to believe that the jury had unloaded the total guilt onto the shoulders of just one of the accused. The failure lay in the preparation and presentation of the case by the prosecution. The best legal heads in town had produced a cock-up that made it impossible for the jury to convict on the evidence placed before them.

After the verdict of guilty, Michael Barrett was boredly asked the usual question of whether he knew of any reason why sentence should not be passed. The usual replies ranged from total silence to a vehement, but not usually articulate, protestation of innocence. With Michael Barrett it was very different. In his *The Old Bailey and its Trials*, Bernard O'Donnell wrote:

> A less murderous face than Barrett's was never seen in the dock at the Old Bailey. It expressed good humour, frankness and intelligence. After the verdict he was asked if he had anything to say, and in one of the most amazing extempore speeches ever heard in court, he courteously, and without bravado, addressed the judges. With infinite skill he analysed the evidence against him, denying that his was the hand that fired the barrel.
>
> He wound up with a peroration during which men and women openly wept, the sobs of women punctuating his speech. Two or three fainted and had to be carried out, so great was the emotional stress caused by his eloquence.

Portions of what Michael Barrett said in his address to the court are quoted here. He began with:

> In answer to the question that has been put to me, I have a great deal to say why sentence should not be passed upon me. Nevertheless, I do not intend occupying your Lordship's time with anything I may have to say now, being fully conscious that no words of mine would in any way alter your Lordship's mind on this matter. But I cannot allow this opportunity to pass without making a few remarks, as it is likely to be the only one I shall have this side of the grave, to endeavour to at least place myself as I should like to stand before my fellow

men. In doing so, however, I shall be compelled to expose the means that have been resorted to in order to secure my conviction. I am not going to whine for mercy, yet, as a humble individual, will I address your Lordship, and as one whose character has been ruthlessly and mercilessly assailed, and whose determination is to defend it against all odds so long as I have sufficient life left to enable me to do so.

Conscious I am of never having wilfully, maliciously and intentionally, as I am charged, injured a human being, that I am aware of – no, not even in character. True, I stand charged with the most repulsive of crimes – that of murder; yet, when we come to examine the nature of the evidence on which I stand convicted, it will be found that there are no two witnesses who have not more or less – nay, directly – contradicted each other. If we place any reliance on those who profess to be eye-witnesses of the deed, they all agree in describing the man who fired the barrel as a tall man, evidently five foot ten inches, or more, in height. Consider the impossibility of mistaking a person of my humble appearance – five foot six inches, or so, high; and, taking these things into consideration, apart from the testimony – the incontestable testimony – which has been advanced in this court, that I was not present at the time, I express it as my most firm conviction that there is not an unprejudiced man here – if it is possible that such a man can be found here – who can honestly believe me guilty.

It is my conscientious conviction that the jury, who have so far descended to meet the requirement of the prosecution, do not, in their hearts, believe me a murderer.

At that point Barrett most skilfully proceeded to analyse the evidence of the prosecution, and lay great stress and bitterness on the testimony of the informers.

He went on:

With reference to that fiend of iniquity, Mullany, I will pass him over with as few words as possible, for to mention his very name is to inhale the most deadly poison. I will allow him to remain in his misery and wretchedness without further reference. And now, my Lord, in reference to the Clerkenwell explosion, I will just say a few words. It is, I know, useless for me, nor do I intend to enter upon any protestations of innocence, being conscious that no declarations of mine will have the slightest tendency to prevent your lordship from taking the course you have already determined to pursue; but this I will, and can, most solemnly declare, that there is no one who more deeply commiserates the sufferers from that explosion, and no one who more earnestly deplores the fatal consequences of that occurrence, than I do. No, I am not one who can rejoice over the miseries and sufferings of my fellow creatures, the statements of Mullany notwithstanding. Him, even him, I can forgive, and pray that his sufferings may not be so great as he deserves. I also wish to correct a statement which has been made here – an inference, at least, which has been made, and which I think has been more or less believed – that I am the author of the explosion. I can honestly declare that never has a greater mistake been made; indeed there is no one, unless their reason is completely clouded by their prejudices, who could for a moment entertain such an idea. To give me credit for such an undertaking is absolutely absurd; being, as I am, a total stranger to acts of daring, and without any experience which would in any way fit me for engaging in such an enterprise . . .

Michael Barrett ended this oration, which had even the court-hardened Lord Chief Justice Cockburn betray great emotion, with:

If it is murder to love Ireland more deeply than life, then indeed I am a murderer. If I could in any way remove the miseries or redress the grievances of that land by the sacrifice of my own life, I would willingly, nay, gladly, do so. If it should please the God of Justice to turn to some account, for the benefit of my suffering country, the sacrifice of my poor, worthless life, I could, by the grace of God, ascend the scaffold with firmness, strengthened by the consoling reflection that the stain of murder did not rest upon me, and mingling my prayers for the salvation of my immortal soul for the regeneration of my native land.

Time distances us from the full impact of this speech, but in *Old Days at the Old Bailey* Hargrave Lee Adam helps us with a paragraph reading:

These are but the words of the speech, and they necessarily lack the facial display, the eloquent gestures, the emotional voice of this remarkable deliverance of a remarkable man. The scene in the court at the time was one of but few such scenes which were witnessed from time to time in the gloomy precincts of the Old Court. There was scarcely a dry eye in the court, women, particularly, being affected, several of whom fainted from stress of emotion. Also the idea was definitely prevalent that, after all, this man might not have been guilty of the acts attributed to him. But that he was a member of the group of conspirators who planned the outrage seemed beyond dispute. The act of Ann Justice before leaving the dock suggested that much. She was bidding a tearful farewell to a comrade. It was a foolish thing for her to have done, under the circumstances, but it was just the slip that one might expect from a woman carried away by her emotion. Barrett must have realised this, but was too manly to resent it. In fact, he did not seem to take much notice of it.

Is it possible then that Michael Barrett was an unfortunate forerunner of the 'Birmingham Six' or the 'Guildford Four', with the awesome handicap of requiring a resurrection rather than a review of his case? He had the misfortune, too, of living at a time when no campaign would be mounted on his behalf. The contemporary newspapers were dissatisfied with the case, not because Michael

Barrett was convicted, but because the others weren't. The leading article in one respected morning paper read:

> Interesting in one respect, the issue of the trial is strangely unsatisfactory. While the police charged six persons with the crime, they have afforded proof sufficient to convict only one. The case against O'Keefe and Ann Justice utterly broke down, and when sifted, that against the Desmonds and English are seen to be far from complete. The police have manifestly failed in some way. Barrett must have had accomplices, either in the persons arraigned along with himself, or in others who are still at liberty. We do not wish to bear hardly on the police, who have had to perform an intensely perplexing task, and, in many respects, have performed it well. But it is difficult to avoid the conclusion that they have fallen into their old blunder of sticking too closely to one line of search; that they have been content to follow the clue which they first obtained, and they have allowed the real culprits to escape. The Cannon Street murderer is still at liberty. So is the person who shot the bandsman, M'Donnell, and now we have a nest of murderers defying our search. It is impossible for the public to regard such repeated failures of justice with anything but grave disquiet.

The Cannon Street murder referred to occurred on the night of 11 April 1866, when Sarah Milson, a housekeeper living above the premises of her employers, a furriers and leather dressers named Bevington, answered the door and was battered to death. The attack was a violent one, and there was much blood splashed about. The first curious thing about this case – which was forever to remain a mystery – was that the crowbar that had been used as a weapon and was found nearby had no bloodstains upon it. After a lengthy police investigation, a man named William Smith, of 6 Eton Square, London, was arrested and tried at the Old Bailey for the murder of Mrs Milson, on 13 and 14 June. The prosecution failed, the jury returned a verdict of not guilty, William Smith was released and the murder of Sarah Milson was added to the mountain of unsolved cases.

As for the unfortunate bandsman M'Donnell mentioned by the newspaper, no other reference to his killing seems to exist anywhere.

As these protests and arguments went on about the Fenian case, Burke and Casey, together with a man named Shaw, were placed on trial at the Old Bailey the day following the condemnation of Michael Barrett. The charge was that they did, 'with divers other persons unknown, feloniously compass, devise, and intend to depose our Lady Queen from the style, honour, and royal name of the Imperial Crown of the United Kingdom'.

The charge was cumbersomely worded, but the overt acts they were said to have committed were set out in the indictment. Ironically, the attempt to rescue Casey by blowing down the prison wall was unnecessary, as he was acquitted. Burke fared the worst, being sentenced to fifteen years' penal servitude, while Shaw was sent to prison for seven years.

As for Michael Barrett, he went to his death white-faced but brave, with the indifference he had shown since taking on a fatalistic attitude in the wake of his impassioned oration at the Old Bailey. At eight o'clock in the morning of 26 May 1868 he was led out of Newgate, watched by a crowd that was unsure whether to jeer or cheer, so did both. He walked with a placid calmness to the scaffold where he prayed fervently with the Roman Catholic priest who accompanied him. Hangman Calcraft then put the noose around Barrett's neck in a way that must have caused him some discomfort, for he turned and, speaking through the hood, asked for the rope to be adjusted. Calcraft obliged, then Barrett plunged to his death. His body was cut down one hour afterwards. Three days later a new law received the royal assent. It required all future executions to be held privately inside official prisons. So it was that Michael Barrett was posthumously credited as being the last person executed in public.

Although perhaps the most remarkable, Michael Barrett was not by any means the only Fenian to stand in the Old Bailey dock. One of note was the one-armed Michael Davitt, whose background was the stuff that rebels are made of. The son of peasant parents, he was born in the village of Straide, Foxford, County Mayo, on 25 March 1846, to grow up in the disastrous years of the Irish famine. When Davitt was aged six his parents were evicted from their homestead and had no choice but to take the emigrant ship to England. They settled at Haslington, Lancashire, where Michael was employed as a child labourer in a local cotton mill. At the age of eleven he was put in charge of a machine normally operated by a youth aged eighteen. On the first day his right hand was mangled by the machine and had to be amputated. It was an accident that, though unfortunate, meant that Michael Davitt could use his clever brain rather than his now crippled body. At the age of nineteen he joined the Fenian Brotherhood, touring England in the guise of a commercial traveller to raise arms for the Fenians in Ireland. Despite his physical handicap he took part in the 1867 attack on Chester Castle.

On 14 May 1870 he was arrested at Paddington Station in London. He appeared at the Old Bailey charged with (1) Feloniously intending to deprive the Queen of her style and title as Queen of the United Kingdom of Great Britain and Ireland; (2) Feloniously conspiring to levy war against the Queen in Ireland in order by force to compel her to change her measures and counsels.

The chief piece of evidence brought against him was a letter he had penned to a young Fenian in which he had dissuaded his comrade from assassinating a supposed spy. Ironically, this saving of another man's life cost Davitt fifteen years of his, the term for which he was sentenced to penal servitude. During his imprisonment at Millbank, Portsmouth and Dartmoor, he was poorly fed and badly treated. He did his suffering quietly, his deepest regret as an intelligent person being the fact that he was deprived of suitable reading material.

Released on 9 December 1877, on a ticket-of-leave, Davitt went to America where he laid the foundations for his Land League to help tenants against absentee landlords, which came into being in 1879.

On 3 February 1881 Davitt was again arrested and once more found himself in the dock at the Old Bailey. He was sentenced to penal servitude, and while in Portland Prison in Dorset he was elected as Member of Parliament for County Meath, but was automatically disqualified by being a convict. Released from Portland on 8 May 1882, he was re-arrested in January the following year, and spent four months in the Richmond Bridewell in Dublin.

After this he travelled the world as an activist, marrying Mary Yore of Michigan. The people of Ireland presented the happy couple with a delightful residence at Ballybrack, Co. Dublin, which soon became known as 'Land League Cottage'. In a literary sense, Michael Davitt was the most successful graduate from the Old Bailey, for as well as being a distinguished journalist he wrote several books, his best-known titles being *Leaves from a Prison Diary*, *The Defence of the Land League*, *Life and Progress in Australasia*, *The Boer Fight for Freedom*, *The Fall of Feudalism in Ireland* and *Within the Pale*.

Davitt had twice visited the dock at the Old Bailey, yet on neither occasion had the threat of the noose hung over him as it had fellow-Fenian Michael Barrett. Yet Davitt's end did come suddenly. Catching cold after a dental operation, blood poisoning set in and he died just after midnight on 31 May 1906.

It was not a Fenian but a murderer who opened up a new era of executions at the Old Bailey after Michael Barrett had brought the old bad times of public executions to a close. Mentioned briefly at the end of Chapter 2, it was Alexander Mackay, convicted of battering his mistress to death, who was the first to go to the execution shed in Newgate Prison.

Strangely, the officials involved, accustomed to the raucous, drunken masses milling around them during a public execution, were unnerved by the awful silence of the first private ceremony. For no reason, they spoke in whispers as they prepared the scaffold, and many of them were physically sick. The atmosphere got to the condemned man, with Mackay a quivering, whimpering wreck having to be dragged to the gallows.

But the human being is said to be able to get used to anything, and familiarity with the newfangled private hangings soon had prison officers carrying out their duties without any great distress.

6. THE HIGHWAYMEN

Unlike other criminals, highwaymen evoke a romantic image. Although the robberies they committed were as brutal as any others, more so than some, their adventures are seen as picturesque. Possibly this view owes much to the 1940s Margaret Lockwood film *The Wicked Lady*, in which the tall, dark and handsome James Mason starred. Fiction collides with reality when one of the better-known highwaymen, Jack Sheppard, is compared physically to Mason. The baby-faced Sheppard stood only five foot four inches tall. He was of slender build but of disproportionate, prodigious strength, despite spending most of his time drinking and whoring.

As the son of a hard-working, respectable Spitalfields carpenter, Jack Sheppard had all the advantages that make a life of crime unnecessary. In fact, until the age of nineteen he lived a good, clean life as an apprentice joiner. But then he fell into bad company and discovered that a dissolute way of life appealed to him. The whores with whom he drank and slept taught him how to pick pockets. But the profits from 'dipping' were not sufficient to support his new lifestyle, so Jack went in for burglary.

His daring and strength caught the attention of Joseph Blake, a highwayman known as 'Blueskin', and they became partners who were much feared on the roads. As a successful robber, Sheppard spent his money freely, enjoying himself immensely. But this 1724 version of *la dolce vita* ran into trouble when Jack reached the age of twenty-one.

Betrayed by his brother, he was captured and placed in St Sepulchre's watch-house. Known as the Round House, this was a grim place consisting of three rooms, a basement, a ground floor and a first floor. The basement was a foul-smelling, cramped 'black hole' in which male prisoners were confined. It was so overcrowded on one occasion that several of the prisoners died from suffocation during the night. The first floor was used as the office of the watch.

It was a bad place to be, but Jack Sheppard didn't stay there long. Blueskin smuggled a file to him, and the resourceful young highwayman was soon free and back on the road. Caught again and taken to New Prison at Clerkenwell Green, he was shackled but freed himself from them by using a bent nail to chip away at the concrete into which the irons were fastened. His subsequent escape, in which he cut through a double grille of iron and oak bars, as well as scaling high walls, was a fantastic achievement.

But his liking for strong wine and loose women was his undoing. Recaptured and sentenced to death, Sheppard was put into the secure condemned cell at Newgate Prison. But the great escaper did it again. This time it was with the assistance of a dead man. With the grand-sounding name of Lumley Davis, this man had also been in a Newgate condemned cell. He had collected escape gear but had failed to use it. When visited by some whores, Davis passed them the gear, and they took it to Jack Sheppard.

On 28 August 1724 Lumley Davis was hanged at Tyburn Tree for a crime that has escaped the records. A small-time criminal, he is remembered only for having passed escape equipment to Sheppard.

Three days later, on 31 August, just four days before he was due to be executed, Jack Sheppard cut through his leg-irons and loosened the fastening of the hatch to his cell. The two whores who had brought him Davis's gear paid another visit, pulling him out through the hatch. With his broken leg-irons tucked up under his trouser-legs, he walked out of Newgate Prison in the company of the two women.

About a week later he was caught robbing a watchmaker's premises in Fleet Street, and this time the prison authorities were taking no chances. Sheppard was placed in the Castle, the most secure condemned hold in Newgate Prison. Handcuffed, he had the heaviest fetters tight round his ankles, the centre link of which was firmly attached to a ring set in the concrete floor. Content that every precaution against escape had been taken, the turnkeys left him unattended.

Somehow, and it seems impossible, Sheppard slipped out of his handcuffs, broke the chain holding him to the floor, and stood up. Taking off his stockings, he lashed the chains of his fetters to his legs, and began a climb up a chimney to the room above. In the unlikely event of something like this happening, the prison authorities had fixed an iron bar across the chimney, the ends of which were set in the stonework. Sheppard took the bar with him, and using that and a nail from when he was up in the other room, broke through six firmly bolted doors, one of which was said not to have been opened for seven years. Out on the roof of the prison, he dropped onto the roof of a private house, climbed in through an attic window, and went out of the front door unseen and unheard.

Yet when free Sheppard seemed to exchange the ingenuity involved in his prison escapes for a crass stupidity. Within two weeks he was easily arrested while lying hopelessly drunk in a tavern.

Heavily chained once more, Sheppard was now the subject of a twenty-four-hour watch by two guards. The Duke of Newcastle, who was Secretary of State at the time, was keenly aware that the young highwayman couldn't be allowed to make the prison system look inept again. On 10 November he was brought to trial. The following day, his partner in crime, Joseph Blake, or Blueskin, was hanged at Tyburn Tree for house-breaking. Another in Jack Sheppard's position may well have viewed this as a bad omen, but he, undaunted, was already forming a plan for yet another escape.

He had somehow obtained a pocket-knife and concealed this in his clothing. Aware that there would be a large crowd assembled to see him taken in the cart to Tyburn, he intended to cut his rope bonds, leap off the cart into the crowd, and run off down a narrow alleyway close to Little Turnstile. But his luck had completely run out, and a warder discovered the hidden knife as he was ready to be taken from the prison.

A sensation in life, Jack Sheppard caused a riot in death. An already excited mob, siding with the underdog, became enraged by a rumour that his body was being taken away for dissection by surgeons. Things got out of hand, the police couldn't gain control, and the military had to be called in to quell what was by then a very serious riot.

Few visitors to the National Gallery near Trafalgar Square know that they tread where twenty-two-year-old Jack Sheppard was once buried. Workmen found his coffin when digging at the site in 1866

Although the strength, determination and escape skills of young Jack Sheppard are admirable, he lived a base life of heavy drinking. It was Claude Duval, a Frenchman called Du Vall in official records, who brought class and dignity to the profession of highwayman.

Born in 1643 in Normandy of poor parents who planned for him to go into domestic service, Claude didn't fancy so dull a life. At the age of thirteen he set off to see something of the world, Paris being his chosen destination. But at Rouen he met the Duke of Richmond, who was in the company of a group of Royalist exiles from the English Civil War. Richmond liked the young fellow, and when the English monarchy was restored he took Claude to England with him as a footman.

There was much unbridled celebration at the return of Charles II. The merrymaking turned it into an era of debauchery, which interested Duval, but was beyond his reach on the low wages of a footman. So he crossed the great financial divide in the only way open to him, by the hold-up of carriages on the highway in his spare time.

Finding his new activity more exciting, and definitely more lucrative than being a servant, Duval became a full-time highwayman and soon a proclamation was issued for his arrest and 'wanted' posters bearing his name were going up all over the countryside.

The famous story of his hold-up on Hampstead Heath has been romanticised through the years, if there is any truth in it at all. Nevertheless, it typifies Claude Duval, as well as showing how the highwayman became a loveable rogue as far as the general public was concerned.

According to this tale, a suitably young and beautiful woman, with a conveniently aged and wealthy husband who reportedly was a knight, had their carriage stopped by Duval as they crossed Hampstead Heath. When he made his customary demand of 'Stand and deliver', the young woman, perhaps out of bravado, began to play upon a flageolet (a flute-type instrument). Handsome in spite of being masked, Duval appeared at the carriage window gallantly and challengingly to wager that so lovely a woman could dance as well as she played.

Accepting his invitation to step out of the carriage onto the roadway, the fair lady, there in the moonlight, joined an expert partner in a *coranto*, a fast, sensuous dance. When it was over and Duval was assisting the now breathless young lady back into her carriage, the husband irritably ordered the coachman to drive off. A remarkably informed Duval politely reminded the old man that he had not paid for his entertainment. Doubtless in fear of his life, the aged knight took a bag containing one hundred pounds from under his seat, passing it to Duval.

With a flamboyant sweep of his feathered hat, Duval told the old man that a voluntary gift was worth ten times more than one produced by force, and that therefore he wouldn't take the other three hundred pounds that he was aware his victim was carrying.

The style of Claude Duval, who lived wildly and lavishly, permitted him to take his pick of the girls, wives and widows, from among all classes, of his day. He bedded the poor and rich, the refined and vulgar alike.

Not only the English were to be robbed by, or succumb to, Claude Duval. When he was pursued too hotly and too closely for comfort, he returned to his native France for a time, where he carried out hold-ups that were greatly rewarding.

On his return to London, Duval let having a good time suspend his normal alertness. During the drunken festivities going on one night early in 1670 in the Hole in the Wall Inn in Chandos Street, located uncomfortably close to the Tyburn Tree, he was arrested. On the occasion of his appearance at the Old Bailey, there was a gathering there of noblemen with their ladies, many of whom had enjoyed the favours of Duval. When sentenced to death he maintained the brave, calm demeanour expected of him. He prepared for death by holding court to a number of society beauties in his cell.

When he was hanged at Tyburn Tree on 21 January 1670 by Jack Ketch, Duval had the sympathy of a watching public accustomed to jeering prisoners executed for other crimes.

A contemporary writer recorded that after Duval had 'hanged a convenient time he was cut down, and, by persons well dressed, carried into a mourning coach, and so conveyed to the Tangier Tavern in St Giles, where he lay all night, the room hung with black cloth, the hearse covered with escutcheons, eight wax tapers burning, and as many tall gentlemen with long black cloakes attending'.

It seemed fitting that Claude Duval should 'lie in state' in a tavern, the kind of place in which he had spent considerable periods of his life. The tall gentlemen with 'long black cloakes' were either fellow highway robbers or professional mourners. But the establishment resented such recognition being afforded a common criminal, as the narrator of the day revealed when he continued with: 'Mum was the word, great silence was expected from all that visited for fear of disturbing this lion. And this ceremony had lasted much longer had not one of the judges (whose name I must not mention here, lest he should incur the displeasure of the ladies) sent to disturb this pageantry.'

In some memoirs with the top-heavy title of *Intended as a Severe Reflexion on the too great Fondness of English ladies towards French Footmen: which, at That Time of Day was too common a Complaint* that were ascribed to William Pope, and had that writer's satirical style, it is stated that on the tomb of Duval in St Paul's Church, Covent Garden, the following epitaph appears under the family arms:

> Here lies Duval; reader if male thou art,
> Look to thy purse, if female, to thy heart.
> Much havoc hath he made of both, for all
> Men he made stand, and women he made fall.
> The Second Conqueror of the Norman race,

> Knights to his arms did yield, and ladies to his face.
> Old Tyburn's glory, England's bravest thief,
> Duval: the ladies joy: Duval, the ladies grief.

Other highwaymen, perhaps less chivalrous than Claude Duval, maybe lesser men than he, were characters in their own right, but made a much lighter impression on history than did the French 'knight of the road'.

None was a harder man than Dorsetshire's Tom Cox, the younger son of a Blandford titled family. Though fairly well-off financially, Tom, being the last-born, didn't get much of a share of the family fortune on reaching maturity. Moving to London, where his handsome features ensured him a female following, Tom Cox became a highwayman. It was an active but short career, which ended with Tom being arrested. At the Old Bailey he was convicted and condemned. His last days were spent well in Newgate Prison, where he partied, enjoying succulent food, good wine and bad women.

When the prison chaplains beseeched him to repent, Cox scorned them, and his spirits never flagged when he took the cart for Tyburn Tree on 3 June 1691. Aged just twenty-six, he was tough and untamed. The chaplain officiating at the gallows asked him to join in final prayers with another prisoner who was to die beside him. Tom didn't just refuse – he kicked the clergyman off the gallows. Springing forward in an attempt at saving the chaplain, the hangman was also kicked off by Tom Cox.

One of the worst highwaymen, a disgrace to that criminal profession, was the well-educated but brutally coarse William Cady, the son of a Norfolk surgeon. Following in his father's footsteps, Cady went to Cambridge University, where he took his BA, after which he practised medicine for a short while. But then he tried his first crime, drawing his pistols to rob Lord Viscount Dundee, after sending the Viscount's footmen off on a wild goose chase after an imaginary footpad.

Cady took to the road then, with such effect that a reward of one hundred pounds was offered in the *London Gazette* for his capture. Fleeing to France when the law was closing in on him, Cady hid in a seminary, amusing himself by hearing the confessions of penitents. Two wealthy young women were among those who revealed their innermost thoughts and outward actions to him in the confessional. When he tired of hearing their intimate secrets, he decided that these two women would fund his return to England.

When the unfortunate pair visited his room one day, he threatened them with his pistols, robbed them of their money, took their rings and other jewellery, raped them, then tied them up and made off. There was none of the Claude Duval-style chivalry here.

There was worse to come back in England. Back on the highway, William Cady held up a rich merchant named Sandal and his wife. Sandal, who dealt in hops, was no pushover. He made a fight of it, but Cady shot his horse from under him, jumped on him before he could recover, and tied him up so securely that Sandal was helpless. When he demanded the wife's wedding ring, she cried, begging him to let her keep it because the ring was of great sentimental value.

'You whining bitch,' Cady shouted, threatening to cut off the woman's finger unless she surrendered the ring. Drawing it off as if she was going to hand it to him, the woman quickly popped the ring into her mouth and swallowed it.

The thwarted Cady flew into a rage, shot the woman in the head then, watched by her horrified, helpless husband, sliced her open with a knife. Aided by his medical training, Cady probed the mutilated body with his fingers and retrieved the ring.

William Cady committed two further murders before he was arrested after a shoot-out. He was sentenced to death when brought to the Old Bailey. His wait in the condemned cell was not a joyous pre-death party as it was with others of his profession. Cady sang and swore, ranting and raving at the top of his voice.

On the way to Tyburn he continued to display an ugly arrogance, and as he stepped onto the gallows there was not one person to mourn the passing of this particular highwayman.

Two other highwaymen, brothers George and Joseph Weston, had gained fame for the Royal Mail Robbery of 1781. Acquitted for lack of evidence, they were hanged at Tyburn a year later, not for highway robbery but for attempted murder.

There is no way of knowing just how many highwaymen existed, so the percentage that were caught and hanged cannot be determined. The successful seemed doomed to a short career, and among these was Jack Rann, who became something of a folk hero by regularly appearing in magistrates' courts but walking away each time due to the lack of sufficient evidence to convict him.

A native of Bath, Rann had first travelled the roads as a pedlar, before working as a stable lad and then graduating to a coachman. His habit of wearing eye-catching clothes led to him being nicknamed 'sixteen-string Jack' when he was noted for the eight strings of brightly coloured beads he wore dangling from each knee.

Those who were robbed by Jack Rann were faced by a highwayman dressed in the height of fashion, and he appeared in court at one time with his leg-irons brightly decorated with ribbons. Perhaps it was his stylish dress making him so distinctive that ensured his career was a brief one. Captured in September 1774, he was charged with robbing the King's chaplain, Dr William Bell, on the Uxbridge Road.

Jack arrived in court splendidly dressed, complete with his sixteen-string trademark swinging from his knees. Being found guilty and sentenced to death didn't put the slightest dent in his extroverted personality. It would appear that he made himself a silent vow to spend what little time he had left in the same riotous way he had lived as a free man.

In the condemned cell he wined, dined and otherwise entertained a party of seven girls, possibly putting more living into that one night than most men manage in a lifetime.

Most probably those seven girls were among the crowd that enthusiastically cheered him as hangman Edward Dennis put him to death at Tyburn Tree.

Many highwaymen followed peculiar routes to their profession, and how James Maclane came to the roads is a strange tale. From a family of clergymen, Maclane inherited a fortune but quickly blew the lot on high living. Taking unto himself a wife, he used her dowry to set himself up as a grocer. When his wife died he sold up, but was all too aware that the money he got for the business would soon run out because of the way he lived. So he started a career as a highwayman in grand style, one of his early victims being Horace Walpole.

Forming an ambitious partnership with a highwayman named Plunket, Maclane robbed the Earl of Eglington on 26 June 1750, with Plunket and himself riding far and fast the same day to hit the Salisbury Stage. Although neither of them was caught at the scene of these robberies, Maclane was arrested when trying to sell the spoils from the Salisbury Stage hold-up.

It is unclear why, but Maclane gained a large following from among the public, and was dubbed the 'Gentleman Highwayman', while it had always been evident that a gentleman was something that he had never been. He was tried and found guilty at the Old Bailey, and on the following Sunday, as reported by Walpole, there were three thousand people crowding Newgate Prison, all trying to gain an 'audience' with the condemned highwayman.

There was a vast crowd at the gallows, too, on 3 October 1750, when James Maclane, then aged twenty-six, met his executioner, John Thrift. As the noose tightened on his neck, most of his unexpected and unexplained popularity died with him. The film *Plunkett and Macleane* (1999) was based on some of their exploits.

A highwayman who survived at the game long enough to become possibly its only veteran was William Hawke. It is likely that he had more brains than all the others put together. Claude Duval may well have been comparable in intellect, but he gave more thought to taking his next woman than he did to planning his robberies. William Hawke was very different. He moved fast, using three speedy horses for getting away. One was a grey, the second a sorrel, the third a black horse with a distinctive bald face that he covered up with the skin of a black cat. Each of the three horses was a jumper, too, and could lift him with ease over the turnpike on any road.

Though he wasn't the only one plying his trade to be called the 'Flying Highwayman', he most deserved the title, and it stayed with him. Ironically, he was never apprehended for the crime of highway robbery; Hawke was arrested, tried at the Old Bailey, and sentenced to death for the theft of a modest amount of linen.

To most people it seemed cruel that a man such as William Hawke should die for so ignominious a crime. On his last days in Newgate he had a long queue of noted people and gentry visiting him. A Colonel Hanger gave him fifty pounds with which to bribe warders to permit him to escape. When he was unable to find a turnkey prepared to take the risk, honest William Hawke returned the money to the Colonel.

On his last night in the condemned cell there was no carousing for William Hawke. Instead, he prayed with other prisoners and sang hymns. When he went to Tyburn it was bravely and with his head held high. It must have been an unimaginably traumatic experience for him, as there for him to see was his own black coffin with a plate attached engraved with his name and the date of his death, 'July 1st, 1774'. His funeral at Uxbridge was a moving, well-attended one, with Edward Dennis, the man who had hanged him, among the mourners.

In contrast to the dignified death of William Hawke, the hanging of John Ashton, another highwayman, outside the Old Bailey in February 1814, would have been a thoroughly disgusting affair could it not have been excused by the insanity of the condemned man. He is numbered among the few criminals in history to be hanged twice.

There were five in all to be hanged that day, but Ashton took centre stage. Running up the ladder, he leapt up and down, shouting: 'I'm Lord Wellington! Look at me, I'm Lord Wellington!'

It must have been an odd, even frightening sight when the trap fell and John Ashton bounced back up onto the platform, the noose around his neck, unhurt. Once more he started up a crazy dance, calling out to the crowd: 'What do you think of me now? Am I not Lord Wellington now?'

When the executioner and his assistants grabbed him, Ashton put up a tremendous struggle but was overpowered. He was put on the trap once more, and this time, to the relief of everyone, possibly even John Ashton himself, he died.

Many more highwaymen were sent from the Old Bailey to the gallows, leaving nothing of themselves for posterity but their names. They were Joseph Redguard, William Kelly, William Davis, John Robinson, Andrew Barton, William Burke, William Rea, John Germaine, John Everett, John Lewis, Thomas Crowther, George Gates, William Wyell, Thomas Clark, William Thompson, John Kennedy and Henry Powell.

For all its romantic image, the black mask around seductively dark eyes, the fine horse standing high on a hill with a background of pale moonlight, highway robbery must have produced more losers than any other branch of criminality.

7. THE TRAITORS

Treason is an emotive issue. Fundamentally it is no more than a decision to follow a foreign flag, but the traitor is feared greatly as a threat to his country's status quo. Consequently, the offence of treason has both attracted the severest of punishments and been the subject of hideous injustices.

When in 1660 the monarchy was restored with King Charles II on the throne, the signing of an Act of Pardon for Past Offences didn't extend to the regicides. These were the sixty-seven judges and parliamentarians who, with Oliver Cromwell at their head, tried and sentenced to death Charles I, who was beheaded outside the Banqueting Hall in Whitehall on 30 January 1649.

Twenty-nine regicides stood trial for treason at the Old Bailey. They were put at a distinct disadvantage by being outnumbered by judges and having a packed jury. All were sentenced to be hanged, drawn and quartered. The sentences were carried out at Charing Cross on 13 October 1660. One of the condemned men, fifty-four-year-old Major-General Thomas Harrison, watched by thousands of people, with Charles II and many nobles and ladies of the court in an excellent viewing position, was able to strike a blow for all those who have suffered the wickedness of judicial monsters. After being hanged and remaining conscious to witness his own bowels being cut out and thrown into the fire, Harrison incredibly found enough strength to catch the executioner, Edward Dun, a stunning punch to the head.

This was at a time when most prisoners coming to court were

morally superior to the judges and officials, which meant that justice was unattainable. When, in 1679, five Jesuit priests stood accused of high treason at the Old Bailey, they had even less chance of a fair trial than had the regicides. The Recorder was a young lawyer named George Jeffreys, who would later be the notorious 'Bloody Assizes' Judge Jeffreys. A principal witness was the unscrupulous Titus Oates, who was backed by a line-up of professional witnesses.

Early in what became known as the Popish Plot, an alleged comprehensive Catholic scheme to overthrow the Crown, Titus Oates, a convicted perjurer, swore allegations before a prominent magistrate, Sir Edmund Berry Godfrey. An outline of Oates's story was that the Catholics would fire London, put to death every Protestant who refused to recant and, with the aid of French and Irish arms, forcibly convert the country to the Roman faith, murder the King and place the Duke of York, a Catholic, on the throne. Oates claimed to have been present at a Jesuit meeting in the White Horse Tavern in the Strand earlier that year, 1678, when the plan had been formulated.

Not believing Oates, Sir Edmund, a Protestant with Catholic friends, warned these friends of the scheme the informer was hatching. He paid for this with his life, disappearing when taking a walk from his house in Hartshorn Lane on the morning of 12 October. Within hours, too soon for it not to be a deliberately engineered rumour, there was talk that Sir Edmund Berry Godfrey had been murdered by the Papists. When, five days later, the body of Sir Edmund was discovered in a ditch at the foot of Primrose Hill, public anger was inflamed against the Catholics.

The death of the magistrate was only a slight hitch in the scheming of Titus Oates, who had gone before the King and Privy Council to repeat his allegations. Parliament ordered all Papists to be held, and there were rushed preparations for a spectacular series of State trials with the intention of convicting the high number of Catholics already in custody.

At the trial of the five priests before the Lord Chief Justice, Sir William Scroggs, and twelve other judges, the testimony of the paid

witnesses, and that of Titus Oates, was totally disproved by witnesses called by the prisoners. Some twenty witnesses were proved
in court to be lying, but the Lord Chief Justice held them up to the
jury as witnesses of truth and integrity.

Despite being constantly interrupted and ordered to stay quiet,
the five Jesuits were successful in establishing alibis that couldn't be
faulted. Yet the five priests, and a middle-aged Roman Catholic
barrister named Richard Langhorne, who had been tried with them,
were found guilty and sentenced by Recorder George Jeffreys to be
hanged, drawn and quartered.

At that time a further eight priests were put to death under the
newly revived penal laws which made it a capital offence for a
Roman Catholic priest to be in England.

In more recent times it has been wars and not religion that have
produced the curious creature, the traitor. A side issue that has
confused the law, and possibly fractured it once, in these cases has
been the nationality of the accused.

Out of the Boer War, a conflict that stained British history, came
Arthur Lynch, an Australian of Irish descent. Born near Ballarat,
Lynch obtained a degree at the University of Melbourne and
became a qualified engineer. Of a restless nature, he travelled
extensively in Europe before settling in Paris for some time.

Working in the French capital as a journalist, he became corres-
pondent for the *Daily Mail* until the Boer War began and he
changed to the Paris newspaper *Le Journal*, a post which gave him
the opportunity to go to South Africa. He went aboard the German
steamer *Herzog* which was captured and detained by a British
warship off Durban.

Eventually going ashore at Delogoa Bay, Lynch went in search of
news to send back to Paris, and approached General Louis Botha. A
disappointed Lynch was told that he couldn't send news or pictures
to France in case they fell into British hands, but he was sympathetic
when learning that the Boers' resources were extremely limited, a
fact Botha was desperate to keep concealed from the enemy.

Due perhaps to an innate dislike of the British, Arthur Lynch was
easily persuaded to become part of an international army being

raised in Johannesburg. There already was an Irish Brigade, led by a Colonel Blake, but Lynch was made a colonel in the new organ- isation which, made up of Irishmen, Germans and Cape Colonists, was later called the 2nd Irish Brigade. Becoming a naturalised Boer, Lynch made such a good impression that President Kruger put him in charge of the new army.

Lynch led his brigade well in many a fight up to close to the end of the war. Then, with it evident that the Boers had suffered so much that there was little fight left in them, and on the news that President Kruger had fled, the brigade fell apart.

But Botha still had a cause and faith in Arthur Lynch. The General asked Lynch to go to the United States to promote the Boer Republic. This he did with some dash, and when in 1901 he was living back in Paris, his fame was such that a deputation of Irish Nationalists from Galway arrived to persuade him to stand for Parliament in the coming election.

That he would win wasn't a foregone conclusion. Lynch's experiences in the South African war had left him opposed to any policy of physical force, whereas Ireland's intention of freeing itself from Britain was coming violently to a head. The Galway Nation- alist Parliamentary Party was keen to adopt him as a candidate, but there was considerable opposition to him from the Irish Parliamentary Party. The latter organisation's policy was to show a dove-like approach to politics, while surreptitiously using extreme measures to achieve its ends when necessary. The members doubted that Arthur Lynch could walk their particular tightrope in the House of Commons.

There was much support from other quarters, with the chairman of Ireland's Nationalist Party, John Redmond, sending a telegram from America in support of Lynch's candidature, describing him as 'this soldier of freedom'.

Ireland, however, wasn't the only country to take an interest in this particular soldier of freedom. When Arthur Lynch was elected by a comparatively large majority to the Parliament in London as an Irish Nationalist, the British government immediately reacted by issuing a warrant for his arrest. By fighting on the side of the Boers he had brought himself to the notice of the law. To attempt to take his seat in Parliament would have him arrested for high treason. He couldn't stay in Ireland, the country which had chosen him to be its representative in Parliament. The only other options would be to return to Paris and live in security, or go to the United States where he would be warmly welcomed.

Being a man of principle, Lynch couldn't let down those who had elected him as their Member of Parliament. He reasoned that since the Boers had signed an instrument that made them British subjects, the position that he was in could be resolved by a tribunal rather than a court.

So Lynch wrote a letter to the Speaker of the House of Commons 'to inform you of my intention to return to England at an early date in order to present myself at the House of Commons and to undertake the duties which have been imposed on me by my election for Galway'.

The British didn't quite see it in the same way that Lynch did. A detective met him on his arrival in England. Lynch was arrested and when he appeared in the police court he said that his sole reason for going to South Africa was to work as a journalist. It was to have unrestricted movement to carry out this purpose that he had taken the oath to become a naturalised burgher. It had never been his intention to join in the fighting until he had met General Botha and had agreed to help in raising the 2nd Irish Brigade. Fighting as a burgher, he had been assured, and still believed, that his naturalisation was in due form and complete. Lynch expressed his opinion to the court that he could not be held guilty of any treasonable act for the clear and simple reason that he was a bona fide subject of the State with whose army he was serving.

The magistrates were not convinced, and on 21 January 1903 he appeared at the Old Bailey for the first high treason trial to have taken place in England for sixty-two years. Here the defence would rely heavily on the usual traitor case questions as to whom, if anyone, the accused owed allegiance. The whole of the second day was taken up by defence counsel, Mr Shee KC, using an argument based on section 6 of the Naturalisation Act of 1870.

There was so much interest in the trial that crowds blocked the streets. In his *Life of Lord Carson*, Edward Marjoribanks writes of how the Solicitor-General, Sir Edward Carson, who together with the Attorney-General was for the prosecution, was unable to get through to the court and asked a police constable to assist him. 'I am the Solicitor-General,' Carson said.

'That's what they're all saying,' the policeman replied.

In court the grounds of the indictment were that Lynch had adhered to and aided and comforted the governments of the South African Republic and the Orange Free State, enemies of the late Queen, and several covert acts were alleged: taking the oath as Colonel of the Irish Corps, departing from Pretoria with intent to join the enemy in Natal, commanding the 2nd Irish Brigade, and fighting against British troops at Sunday's River.

After reading the indictment, the King's Coroner spoke the words: 'How say you, Arthur Lynch? Are you guilty or not guilty, in respect of the High Treason in respect of which you have been indicted?'

As the Lord Chief Justice, two High Court judges and a jury waited for a response, Mr Horace Avory KC, one of Lynch's counsel, stood to move that the indictment be quashed on technical grounds. But in the wake of a legal argument between Avory and the Attorney-General, Sir R. Finlay KC, the court decided that at that stage of the trial the motion couldn't be entertained.

From the outset of the trial the difficulties facing Lynch's legal representatives were plain. He had made a declaration that he was willing to take up arms for, and had sworn an oath of allegiance to, the South African Republic. Lynch had sworn further oaths, one in his capacity as 'Colonel of the Irish Corps' and the second as 'Special Justice of the Peace for the Irish Corps'.

In addition he had drawn up an invitation to Irishmen or those of Irish descent to join in the war. This, which pleaded the Irish cause as much as that of the Boers, was printed and posted up in camp, and was also published in the *Standard and Digger's News*, a Johannesburg newspaper. Containing a historical allusion to the Battle of Fontenoy of 11 May 1745, when the British Army was holding against the attacks of French infantry under Marshal Saxe, but succumbed to the final charge of the Irish Brigade, which was on the French side, it read:

To Irishmen

The events of the war are daily becoming critical and important . . . Irishmen and men of Irish descent have never been backward when battle has sounded its clarion call . . . rally to the Green Flag! Never since Fontenoy have Irishmen been so blessed with fortune.

Remember how that name has resounded in Irish history . . . All Ireland and Irish America are looking at your actions and your valour has already sent the electric thrill of enthusiasm throughout the ranks of the 'sea-divided Gael' and raised the prestige of the Irish name.

Indisputable evidence in court included that Lynch had been leading the 2nd Irish Brigade on the occasion of a Boer Commando engagement of British forces at Sunday's River Bridge, near Elandslaagte in Northern Natal, in April 1900. After suffering heavy losses, an advance British brigade had to fall back on Ladysmith. An American named Gregg and an Englishman by the name of Holder, both civilians, testified that they had been arrested by the Boers, who suspected them of being spies, and were questioned by Colonel Arthur Lynch.

All that was left to the defence was to attempt to prove that Lynch had not at the time been 'a subject of our late Lady Queen Victoria'. This was made difficult by the Naturalisation Act, before the passing of which it was possible, albeit confusingly so, to have double or treble nationality. Mr Shee's contention was that the legislature responsible for the Act of 1870 was concerned with naturalisation in time of war, not of peace.

It was a sound argument, for less than a century earlier, at the start of the war between England and America in 1812, there had been up to twenty thousand English-born subjects serving in the

American Marine, and some twenty million citizens of the United States could also claim British nationality at that time.

When Mr Shee had ended his effort to prove that Lynch had been a naturalised Boer during the fighting in South Africa, Horace Avory, also for the defence, opened up a second front. His contention was that the prosecution had been brought under the Statute of Edward III, the important wording being, 'adherent to the King's enemies in his realm'. This, Avory contended, could mean one of two things. For Lynch to be guilty he would have needed to have been adherent to the King's enemies while he was in the King's realm, no matter where they had been at the time, or it must be that he had aided the King's enemies when they had been in the King's realm.

Logical though this was, it was contemptuously dismissed by Mr Justice Wills. Much bad feeling towards Arthur Lynch, as there would be towards William Joyce (Lord Haw-Haw) in a war yet to happen, stemmed from him helping the enemy at a time when the war was going extremely badly for Britain.

At the closing stages of the trial, Mr Shee, without having anything worthy of an oration, made a long and eloquent speech. This was probably an error. Lynch later stated that it had been. His idea of a defence, and he complained that he hadn't been consulted, was to invoke the Peace of Vereeniging, a treaty that said anyone prosecuted after fighting on the Boer side had the right to be tried in his own country. General Botha had objected to this clause until he had been assured by Lord Roberts and Kitchener that no British subject who had fought on the side of the Boers would be prosecuted for high treason. Possibly due to the problem of proving this undertaking, it was not honoured at the Old Bailey trial of Arthur Lynch.

It took no more than twenty-six minutes for the jury to return a verdict that Lynch was guilty upon all counts. Mr Justice Wills then pronounced a viciously protracted sentence of death that would have a modern-day court aghast and himself torn to pieces by the tabloid newspapers.

'The jury have found you guilty,' said Wills, his small body trembling with excitement, repugnance on his face, anger in his tone, 'of the crime of High Treason . . . and the misdeeds you have done in this case . . . must surely convince the most sceptical and the most apathetic of the gravity as well as the reality of the crime . . . in the darkest hours of your country's fortunes, when she was engaged in the deadly struggle from which she has at last emerged, you joined the ranks of your country's foes . . . you fought against your country, not with her . . . nor can I forget that you have shed the blood of your countrymen who fought for their country. How many wives have been made widows, how many children have been made fatherless by what you and those who acted under your command have done, Heaven alone knows and no one on earth can tell. You thought it safe at that dark hour of the country's fate, when Ladysmith, Kimberley, when Mafeking were in the jaws of dreadful peril, to lift a parricidal hand against your country. You thought, no doubt, that your country would shrink from the costly struggle . . . and that at the worst a peace would be made which should comprehend a general amnesty that should cover up such acts as yours and save you from personal peril. You misjudged your country, you failed to appreciate . . . that she is seldom so dangerous to her enemies as when an hour of national calamity has roused her dormant energies, knit together every nerve and fibre of the body politic, and strung up her sons to do all, to bear all and sacrifice all on behalf of the land which gave them birth. And against what a Sovereign and what a country did you lift your hand! . . . Against a country which has been the home of freedom and of progress, under whose beneficent sway, wherever you have chosen to abide in any part of her dominions, you have enjoyed a liberty of person and a freedom of action and speech such as you could have enjoyed in no other country in Europe and, it is not too much to say, in no other country in the world . . . He who has attempted to do to his country such irreparable harm must be prepared to submit to the sentence which it is now my duty to pronounce upon you . . . that you will be taken hence to the place from which you came and thence to a place of execution, and thereby hanged by the neck until you are dead.'

Mr Justice Wills had either forgotten to add the customary words 'and may the Lord have mercy upon your soul', or feared that they would stick in his throat if he attempted to utter them.

Arthur Lynch sat unmoved throughout this tirade by a judge who was on the verge of tears when he had finished speaking. But the government was uneasy about the whole case, doubting that it should ever have been brought to court, and the sentence of death on Lynch was immediately commuted to life imprisonment.

Early one morning a few months later, the chief warder of Brixton Prison came to Lynch's cell. Having settled into prison life, Lynch feared that the authorities had hatched some plot to punish him further, but the warder announced that he was to be released at once.

Lynch later stated that his early release came as a result of Michael Davitt, the Irish Nationalist leader, asking Sir Thomas Lipton, the tea magnate, to persuade King Edward VII to bring his influence to bear on the Cabinet.

A freed Lynch was eager to get back into politics, but couldn't do so because of his conviction as a traitor. The necessary papers were prepared for a free pardon, and submitted to the King. His Majesty signed them, and a happy Arthur Lynch was on his way back to Parliament. This time, for some unexplained reason, there was no support for him from John Redmond, the Irish Nationalist.

Despite this, when a vacancy occurred in West Clare, Lynch was elected to Parliament, and was still a member for that constituency when the war with Germany broke out in 1914.

There was a hope in Ireland that Germany would grant her Home Rule on winning the war, but Edward Shortt, Chief Secretary for Ireland, wanted to launch a recruiting campaign in that country. To this end he persuaded Arthur Lynch to join the British Army, and the Australian of Irish descent, once the sworn enemy of England, became a colonel and fought for the King against the Germans.

As Lynch, traitor turned loyalist, became a role model for the recruitment of young Irishmen, Roger Casement, a candidate for a trial of the future at the Old Bailey, was in Germany. Irishmen who had been taken prisoner by the Germans during the retreat from Mons and on the Marne and the Aisne were originally mixed with other prisoners of war throughout Germany. But in the first winter of the war they were moved to a camp of their own at which conditions were much improved. While they speculated on the reason for this, Roger Casement came along asking for volunteers to join the 'Irish Brigade' and fight on the side of the Germans.

Unlike Arthur Lynch, Roger Casement was not a man without a star to follow. He was no rootless journalist who drifted into being a traitor. Born near Dublin in 1864, Casement entered the British consular service in 1892, and served in the Boer War on special service in Cape Town. First gaining fame by exposing the oppression of natives in the Belgian Congo, and following his revelations on native Indians working on rubber plantations in Brazil and Peru, he was knighted on 20 June 1911, and was so pleased and honoured that he had written to the King to express warmly and loyally his pleasure at being honoured with a knighthood. Sir Roger Casement retired shortly afterwards for health reasons, and received a monthly pension.

This was a time when unrest in Ireland seemed likely to explode at any moment; Casement was in Washington in the early weeks of the war, and when Von Papen, the military attaché at the German Embassy in the US capital city, introduced the subject of Irish independence into the conversation, he discovered that Casement had a deep hatred of everything English. His opinion was that Ireland's autonomy would be achieved if Germany triumphed over Britain. On hearing this, Von Papen arranged for Casement to go to Berlin to discuss the possibility of Irish aid for Germany in the war. The Irish prisoners of war were brought together at Limburg Lahn Camp, where a leaflet worded as follows was distributed:

> Irishmen, here is a chance for you to fight for Ireland. You have fought for England, your country's hereditary enemy. You have fought for Belgium in England's interest though it was no more to you than the Fiji Islands. Are you willing to fight for your own country with a view to securing the national freedom of Ireland? With the moral and material assistance of the German Government an Irish Brigade is being formed. The object of the Irish Brigade shall be to fight solely for the cause of Ireland and under no

circumstances shall it be directed to any German end. It shall be formed and fight under the Irish flag alone: the men shall wear a special distinctively Irish uniform and have Irish officers. It shall be clothed, fed and officially equipped with arms and ammunition by the German Government. It shall be stationed near Berlin and be treated as a guest of the German Government.

At the end of the war the German Government undertakes to send each member of the Brigade who may so desire it to the United States of America with the necessary means to land. The Irishmen in America are collecting money for the Brigade. Those men who do not join the Brigade will be removed from Limburg and distributed among other camps. If interested, see your company commanders. Join the Irish Brigade and win Ireland's independence. Remember Bachelor's Walk! God Save Ireland!

Casement arrived at the camp shortly afterwards. He spoke to various prisoners individually, and addressed them all together at times, saying: 'Why live in hunger and misery in this camp when you can better yourselves by joining the Irish Brigade, which I am forming, and going to Berlin as the guests of the German Government?' He promised that when Germany gained control of the English Channel and the Irish Sea, the Irish Brigade would be landed in Ireland to fight against the English and win the freedom of their country. He reiterated that they could go to the United States after the war if they chose to do so, adding that they would each receive a gratuity of twenty pounds.

History tells us that only fifty out of two thousand Irish prisoners of war joined the Irish Brigade, but propaganda distorts the past just as it damages the present. Whatever the success of the renegade army, Casement didn't return to prominence until he was apparently involved in a gun-running expedition from Germany to Ireland, assisted by some of the Irishmen he had persuaded to join the Brigade.

The story begins on Good Friday 1916 with an Irish labourer, Michael Hussey of Tralee, who was returning from a visit to a friend on the night of 20 April 1916. Hussey saw a red light flash for a few seconds about half a mile out to sea. He went to the foreshore the following morning to gather seaweed, but saw a boat wedged on sandbanks above high-water mark.

Later that morning a man named McCarthy, who lived in the same village as Hussey, first saw four oars floating in the water, and then a boat aground about twenty yards out from shore. When he called a friend to help him, McCarthy could only manage to pull the boat a little way up the beach because she was filled with water.

The two men found a dagger in the boat, and a tin box containing revolver ammunition. There were three sets of footprints on the beach, and, scouting around the immediate vicinity, they found buried in the sand three Mauser pistols with two small bags filled with ammunition for them, a flash-lamp, several maps of Ireland that were foreign-made, two lifebelts and three coats. In the pocket of one of the coats they found a railway ticket from Berlin to Wilhelmshaven dated 12 April 1916.

When the police were called they searched the area and found Roger Casement hiding in an old stronghold known as McKenna's Fort. He told the police that he was an author named Richard Morton, and that he lived in Denham, Buckinghamshire. Casement said he had left Dublin on the 19th and arrived in the area on the 20th, spending the night in a nearby farmhouse.

He was arrested and taken to Ardfort Barracks. There is no record of the police searching Casement at that time. If they did do so, they were inept, because along the way to the barracks a small boy noticed the prisoner drop a document from under his coat.

This was found to be in code, and when deciphered it contained damning phrases such as: 'Await further . . . send agent at once . . . our men are at . . . send rifles and ammunition . . . send more explosives to . . . send another ship to . . . '

Casement was taken to Dublin and then across the Irish Sea to London. On a humid, thundery day in June 1916, the six-foot-four-inch knight appeared at the Old Bailey on a charge of treason in that he had conspired with the King's enemies against the King in time of war. Even in this situation he was not without the support of a number of influential Britons. One of these was William Cadbury, the nephew of George Cadbury Senior, and a friend for many years of Roger Casement. Although Cadbury did not approve of the Irishman's behaviour from the time of the outbreak of war in 1914, he was aware that Casement was without funds, and sent his solicitor two hundred pounds towards his defence. Serjeant Sullivan KC, who came from the Irish Bar and had already established a brilliant reputation in England, was briefed as defence counsel.

The British government began a character assassination by producing and circulating transcripts of Casement's private diaries to prominent people and both the British and American press. These documents revealed details of homosexual relationships that were most certainly irrelevant to the case and, as the authenticity of the diaries has never been established, might well have come under the 'dirty tricks' heading.

The opening speech made by the Attorney-General added a new and grave dimension to the prosecution's case. On that same long Good Friday at Tralee, HM Sloop *Bluebell* was on patrol and sighted a vessel flying the Norwegian flag. The British ship signalled a question, and a reply from the Norwegian ship gave her name as the *Aud* of Bergen, bound for Genoa. When the captain of the *Bluebell* ordered the Norwegian vessel to follow him into harbour, it needed a shot across her bows to have the *Aud* comply.

'On nearing the Daunt Lightship,' the Attorney-General told the court, '*Bluebell* headed for the harbour, but the *Aud* stopped her engines. *Bluebell* then went back to her and when about a cable's length away those on *Bluebell* saw a small cloud of white smoke issuing from the starboard side of the after-hold. At the same time two German ensigns were broken at her mast and two boats were lowered . . . *Bluebell* fired one shot across the *Aud*'s bows whereupon the two boats hoisted the white flag and their crews put up their hands. They were found to be German sailors, three officers and nineteen ratings, and were made prisoners and taken on board the British sloop. Almost immediately the German ship sank off the

Daunt Lightship, and later divers went below and discovered that she carried a cargo of Russian rifles.'

In an early show of avoiding the mistake made by Mr Justice Wills when sentencing Arthur Lynch to death, the Attorney-General ended his speech with the words: 'I have, I hope, outlined these facts without heat and without feeling. Neither, in my position, would be proper and fortunately neither is required. Rhetoric would be misplaced, for the proved facts are more eloquent than words. The prisoner, blinded by hatred for his country, as malignant in quality as it was sudden in origin, has played a desperate hazard. He has played it and he has lost it. Today the forfeit is to be claimed.'

Just as Lynch's counsel had, Serjeant Sullivan immediately moved to quash the indictment. The Lord Chief Justice, Viscount Reading, who sat on the bench with Mr Justice Avory and Mr Justice Horridge, told him that the proper time to make this submission was at the close of the case for the prosecution.

The defence called no witnesses, and rested solely on Serjeant Sullivan's address to the court in which he argued that Casement's allegiance was to Ireland.

'An Irishman's loyalty,' Sullivan said, 'is to Ireland, and it would be a very sorry day for the Empire when loyalty to one's own native land should be deemed to be treason in a sister country . . . No person has any constitutional right in Ireland to seek to bully or dictate to any Irishman in the name of any other section of His Majesty's United Kingdom. We are your fellow-citizens, but by no means your inferiors or your slaves.'

Under great emotional stress, Serjeant Sullivan went on speaking for more than two hours. Then he was forced to make several pauses, and was obviously close to exhaustion. Stopping the speech, he addressed the Lord Chief Justice haltingly: 'I am sorry, my Lord, I regret to say that I have completely broken down.'

When Sullivan slumped into his seat and rested his head in his hands, the crowded court, which was becoming increasingly stuffy, was adjourned until the following day.

The next morning, the final day of the trial, Serjeant Sullivan was too ill to appear, and his junior, Mr Artemus Jones, concluded the speech begun the previous day. In it he made no appeal based on sympathy for the accused.

It took less than an hour for the jury to return a verdict of guilty, and when asked by the King's Coroner if he had anything to say as to why the court should not pass sentence of death upon him, Casement asked permission to read from some papers he had in his breast pocket.

As he began the court was totally silent, which seemed to unnerve Casement for the first time. He stumbled over his words and occasionally his voice faded: 'Loyalty is a sentiment, not a law. It rests on love, not on restraint. The government of Ireland by England rests on restraint and not on law, and since it demands no love it can evoke no loyalty.'

He said that if he had done wrong in making that appeal to Irishmen to join with him in an effort to fight for Ireland, it was only by Irishmen that he could be rightfully judged.

Roger Casement ended with an impassioned plea for Ireland:

> We are told that if Irishmen go by the thousand to die, not for Ireland but for Flanders, for Belgium, for a patch of sand in the deserts of Mesopotamia, or a rocky trench on the heights of Gallipoli, they are winning self-government for Ireland. But if they dare to lay down their lives on their native soil, if they even dare to dream that freedom can be won only at home by men resolved to fight for it there, then they are traitors to their country and their dream and their deaths alike are phases of a dishonourable fantasy . . . Self-government is our right, a thing born to us at birth, a thing no more to be doled out to us or withheld from us by other people than the right to life itself, than the right to feel the sun or smell the flowers, or to love our kind.
>
> If it be treason to fight against such an unnatural fate as this, then I am proud to be a rebel, and shall cling to my 'rebellion' with the last drop of my blood . . . Where all your rights become only an accumulated wrong; where men must beg with bated breath for leave to subsist in their own

land, to think their own thoughts, to sing their own songs, to gather the fruit of their own labours and even while they beg – to see these things inexorably withdrawn from them, then surely it is a braver, a saner, and a truer thing to be a rebel in act and deed against such circumstances as these than tamely to accept it as the natural lot of man.

Casement's appeal was heard and dismissed on 17 July, but most doubted that the sentence of death would be carried out. A lesson learned was that an ephemeral moment of vengeance produced a lasting political martyr, and the British government was anxious to find a way of keeping Casement from his date with the hangman. Even the possibility of having him certified as insane was considered, but no competent medical authority was prepared to sign such a certificate.

On 3 August 1916 Casement, now plain 'Roger David' because his knighthood had been taken back, walked bravely and upright to the Pentonville Prison scaffold with executioner John Ellis. When the certificate of execution was posted outside the gaol, a large crowd cheered.

Was Roger Casement a homosexual with a craving to record erotica? It is doubtful, for when he had uncovered corruption and atrocities in Brazil and Peru, he had held back material that he wrote was 'too indecent to print'. On returning to England he brought with him a large quantity of official documents that included an indecent diary kept by an individual involved in the wrong-doing in South America. This diary was of precisely the same character as the one the British Government had made public claiming it belonged to Casement.

When preparing his *Life and Death of Roger Casement*, author Denis Gwynn wrote to the Home Secretary asking that he might be allowed to see the Casement diary. He received the following reply:

My dear Gwynn,

I have carefully considered your letter of 21 June about Casement's diaries. On inquiring I find that it was decided long ago not to make any official statement as to the existence or non-existence of these diaries. I have carefully considered whether it is still necessary to maintain this rule, and there seem to me to be very good reasons why in the public interest it is desirable not to break the official silence . . .

Yours sincerely,

J.R. Clynes.

This typically bureaucratic way of giving a convoluted non-answer to a straight question suggests that what happened to Roger Casement at the Old Bailey was something less than justice. When, in 1955, Lord Russell of Liverpool CBE, MC made a similar application to the Home Secretary, he received an almost identical reply.

There are 'traitors and traitors', defence counsel Mr Shee had said in the Lynch case, implying that some were better than others. Sir Roger Casement subscribed to this theory, for he regarded Arthur Lynch to be no more than an amateur compared to himself. Yet, if they were traitors, both these men must rank above the mixed-up Anna Wolkoff, who was tried at the Old Bailey in November 1940 for offences against the Defence Regulations.

A worshipper of the notorious Lord Haw-Haw, William Joyce, since before the outbreak of war, Anna was a naturalised British subject, the daughter of a former Czarist admiral. Like Joyce, she was a member of Captain Ramsey's Right Club, an anti-Semitic organisation. Unlike Joyce, who moved himself onto the world scene, Anna's rebellion was at first limited to flyposting at night. Carrying a bucket of paste and a brush, she would put up notices reading:

> Your New Year's resolution. We appeal to the working men and women of Great Britain to purchase the new Defence Bonds and Savings Certificates thus keeping the war going as long as possible. Your willing self-sacrifice and support will enable the War profiteers to make bigger and better

profits and at the same time save their wealth from being conscripted.

At first her activities were no more than childish, but she ran into trouble when she tried to get a coded message to Germany in the Romanian diplomatic bag. Intended for Lord Haw-Haw, the letter was addressed to Herr W.B. Joyce, Rundfunkhaus, Berlin. Intercepted by the British security service, the letter was decoded, found to contain advice for Joyce about his 'Germany Calling' broadcasts, and then sent on as if it had never been opened and examined.

Anna played a more dangerous game when she became involved with Tyler Kent, a cipher clerk at the United States Embassy in Grosvenor Square. Kent took copies of secret messages and passed them to Anna, who found herself charged under the Official Secrets Act.

Secrecy was an absolute necessity, and witnesses in the trial of Anna Wolkoff arrived in the Old Bailey courtroom in an undignified way. They were whisked into the yard in closed cars, then guided through the prisoners' corridors, hidden by glass panels that had been pasted over with thick brown paper, to give evidence.

'You,' the judge addressed Anna when sentencing her to ten years' imprisonment, 'a Russian subject who in 1935 became a naturalised British subject, at a time when this country was fighting for her very life and existence, sent a document to a traitor who broadcasts from Germany for the purpose of weakening the war effort of this country.'

Four years later, this passing reference to the man who must be the most well-known traitor of all, echoed silently in the Old Bailey when the judge who made it, Mr Justice Tucker, tried William Joyce.

A natural-born citizen of the United States, William Joyce came into the world in Brooklyn, New York, in 1906. His Irish father was a naturalised American, and his mother was from Lancashire. Around the time of the start of the Irish troubles, the family returned to live in Ireland, first in County Mayo and then in Galway City. The father, and probably William, were on the side of the

British. When the Anglo-Irish Treaty was signed the Joyces had to flee to England, getting out just before the Republicans burnt their house to the ground.

An able scholar, William Joyce did well for himself in London, and became a tutor. A gifted public speaker, he had extreme right-wing views, due, to a greater or lesser extent, to the influence of his mother's family. Discipline and uniforms attracted him greatly, and to gain entrance to London University's Officer Training Corps, Joyce wrote a letter in which he claimed British citizenship.

Initially a member of the Conservative Party, Joyce then joined the British Fascists, which became Sir Oswald Mosley's British Union of Fascists. After a falling-out with Mosley, Joyce, in 1937, founded the National Socialist League. Enjoying the support of several wealthy and influential Britons and both liked and admired by more than would later be prepared to admit it, William Joyce was on a path that would take him to his spiritual home of Germany, and to the gallows in a British prison.

When applying for a British passport in 1933 on the usual form, Joyce declared that he was a British subject by birth, having been born at Rutledge Terrace, Galway, Ireland, on 24 April 1906. He was granted a passport for the usual five years.

He subsequently twice applied for renewals of one year each. The first renewal expired on 1 July 1939, and Joyce left it until 24 August to apply for the second renewal. He did this with the intention of leaving for Germany within the next few days, where he would apply for German citizenship and make his permanent home there, never to return to England.

His mistake was in asking for a one-year passport. Had he renewed his passport, as was possible, for a two-month period, he would not have been hanged, and the only charge upon which he could have been successfully prosecuted in a British court would have been that of making a false declaration when applying for a passport. As it was, Joyce, an American by birth, was convicted and hanged solely because he held a current British passport in 1945–46.

With the help of comedians on the wireless, Lord Haw-Haw's

broadcasts to England during the Second World War were turned into a joke. But at the time of the Blitz they were frightening, with the accuracy of some of the things he said terrifying. Among other things, he seemed to know much about the clocks in England. His remark over the German radio that the town clock at Banstead was a quarter of an hour slow on a particular day was said to be right, and he was reported to have stated correctly that the town hall clock at Gosport was two minutes slow. The Old Bailey itself, built at a time when architecture lacked imagination, never charming, was now scarred and ugly, parts of it sliced away by German bombs.

The unlovely commercial buildings that had once claustrophobically beset the Central Criminal Court had been wiped away entirely by the Blitz. Aesthetically it was in a way pleasing and refreshing, but a city nevertheless abhors space just as nature does a vacuum, and the new and beautiful desert would soon disappear. Blackened churches stood here and there, birds flying in and out of the dark sockets of their glassless windows, their altars soon to be decorated by long grass and ugly weeds.

The Old Bailey itself had turned full circle. The much appreciated brightness of the new building had reverted to the dark dinginess of the bad old days. There was no manpower available to remove the heavy black-out, the bombed areas had been sealed off, and the halls and passages and stairways were back in the perpetual dusk of yesteryear. The glass dome through which daylight had once streamed, was now boarded up and Joyce was brought up into a Court No.1 that was illuminated only by harsh electric light.

In the dock, small and surprisingly nondescript, sat the best of the Nazi broadcasters in English, the man whose imitations of Winston Churchill, at a time when Britain was under siege by the Luftwaffe, were masterly. William Joyce had been granted legal aid by the senior Metropolitan magistrate, Sir Bertrand Watson. Joyce had secured the services of Mr C.V.B. Head, an experienced solicitor of the firm of Ludlow & Co, which had offices adjacent to Bow Street. Head chose a strong team of counsel for the defence, headed by G.O. Slade KC.

Although the legal arguments were both lengthy and complex,

the gist of the case for the prosecution was that as Joyce possessed a valid British passport he was under the protection of the British Crown, and therefore owed a corresponding duty of allegiance even though he was not a British subject, while the defence contended that to convict Joyce it would have to be satisfactorily proved that he owed allegiance at the time he had made the broadcasts.

Mr Justice Tucker, the trial judge who had four years earlier, at the trial of Anna Wolkoff, already decided that William Joyce was a traitor, ruled as a question of law that the duty of allegiance continued until the passport expired. Lord Porter was not alone in disagreeing with this. He believed that Mr Justice Tucker's ruling was a misdirection and that a reasonable jury properly directed might have considered that the allegiance had been terminated before 18 September 1939, the date of Joyce's first broadcast for the Germans.

Mr Justice Tucker asked and answered questions that rightly were a matter for the jury, when he said: 'Against the mere receipt of the passport there has to be set the fact that its possession was at least desirable, to enable the accused man to proceed to Germany from this country; the fact that it was not found in his possession again or anything further known of it; his statement as to his intention of becoming naturalised in Germany; and his acceptance of a post from the German State.'

William Joyce, a man whom people found it easy to like, was motivated by love for an England of long ago which he desperately wanted to recreate, but which had only ever existed in his imagination. His conduct in pouring scorn on England, whose defeat by Germany he never ceased to prophesy, was despicable, but was he guilty of treason?

In his opening speech, the young and charismatic Attorney-General of the new Labour government, Sir Hartley Shawcross, told the jury that only those owing a duty of loyalty and faithfulness to the British Crown can be convicted of treason, saying: 'The basis of this allegiance is that so long as the Prince affords protection to his subject, so long that subject owes a debt of allegiance to the Prince. Protection by the Prince, by the Crown, by the State. Protection on the one hand and allegiance on the other are reciprocal.'

This argument was seriously challenged by the fact that William Joyce was a citizen of the United States of America. Nevertheless, he was found guilty of treason and sentenced to death, his appeals to the Court of Appeal and the House of Lords being dismissed, in the latter case with Lord Porter being the sole dissentient. Joyce was hanged at Wandsworth Prison on 3 January 1946, four weeks before the Lords delivered their judgement on his appeal.

There were two legal innovations in the conviction of William Joyce. It proposed that a British court has jurisdiction to try an alien for an offence committed abroad, and established that anyone under the protection of a British passport owes in return, even though the circumstances are such that it cannot be exercised, a duty of allegiance to the British Crown.

When Joyce's appeal was heard in the Court of Criminal Appeal, Sir Hartley Shawcross said that the 'incalculable advantage of the whole system of British law is that its principles are capable of adaptation to the new circumstances perpetually arising'.

Ever since there has existed an uneasy feeling, not just among those in the legal profession, that in the case of William Joyce this 'adaptation' went too far; that the law was stretched beyond acceptable limits to get a conviction for treason.

There were other treason trials from the Second World War held in the Old Bailey. Thirty-three-year-old John Amery, the black sheep of a distinguished English family, who pleaded guilty in order to avoid bringing them further shame, was hanged at Wandsworth Jail on 29 December 1945. Norman Baillie-Stewart, a Seaforth Highlander subaltern, who pleaded guilty, was sentenced to the incredibly short prison sentence of five years. Margaret Frances Bothamley, a sixty-seven-year-old woman who broadcast for the German radio service, was sentenced to a year's imprisonment, in the first division (a suspended sentence) – which in itself was surprising for that era.

Another radio announcer for the Germans was Elsa Gertrude Brietzman, a Brighton woman who was at the Old Bailey bound over to be of good behaviour for two years. Thomas Haller Cooper, a London clerk aged twenty-six, was charged with high treason and sentenced to death, but later reprieved. Patrick Joseph Dillon was part of the German propaganda system. Pleading guilty at the Old Bailey to offences against the Defence Regulations, he was sentenced to ten years' penal servitude. Gerald Percy Sandys Hewitt, charged at the Old Bailey under the Defence Regulations with assisting the enemy, was sentenced to twelve years' imprisonment. Nineteen-year-old Dennis John Leister was sentenced at the Old Bailey to three years' penal servitude for joining the British Free Corps. Channel Islander John Lingshaw, aged twenty, was sentenced to five years in prison for broadcasting on German radio.

Pearl Joyce Vardon pleaded guilty at the Old Bailey to assisting the enemy by broadcasting. A Jersey schoolteacher, Pearl fell in love with a German officer in the forces occupying her island, then went to Germany with him. The sentence of death for two offences under the Treachery Act was quashed at the Court of Appeal for Dorothy Pamela O'Grady from Sandown, Isle of Wight, but she was sentenced to fourteen years' penal servitude for offences against the Defence Regulations. Ship's engineer George Johnson Armstrong, aged thirty-eight, was sentenced to death by Mr Justice Lewis at the Old Bailey on 8 May 1941 for two offences under the Treachery Act, and was hanged. Frances Dorothy Eckersley, aged fifty-one, and her son, James Royston Clark, aged twenty-two, pleaded guilty at the Old Bailey to aiding the enemy, contrary to the Defence Regulations. The mother received a sentence of one year's hard labour, while the son was bound over for two years.

A long list of British servicemen was dealt with by courts-martial, but others sentenced to prison at the Old Bailey were Reginald Arthur Humphries (five years), Alfred Vivian Minchin (seven years), Herbert George Rowlands (two years), Ronald David Barker (two years), Kenneth Edward Berry (nine months) and Walter Purdy (sentenced to death but sentence commuted to life imprisonment).

So they passed through the dock at the Old Bailey: the not-so-good, the bad and the ugly. Some had excuses, such as being of German blood; others simply wanted to improve their personal lot in the war; while those who acted out of hatred for Britain remained arrogant throughout their trials.

John Amery was the 'black sheep' playboy son of a distinguished English family. In the 1930s his love of fast cars and the high life had him in trouble with the police. He went to Spain at some time during the Civil War, and arrived in France in 1940. He went on a recruiting drive for the Germans, touring prisoner-of-war camps asking British servicemen to join the 'Legion of St George', a British force that would fight for Germany. He also broadcast over the radio for the Germans. When tried at the Old Bailey on 28 November 1945, Amery saved his family from further shame by saying 'I plead guilty to all counts'. He was sentenced to death and hanged at Wandsworth Jail on 29 December 1945.

The traitor with perhaps the weirdest story of all was Norman Baillie-Stewart, who was doing deals with the Germans before Hitler came to power. A Seaforth Highlander subaltern, he was in 1933 court-martialled and sentenced to five years' penal servitude for selling military secrets to the Germans. During the Second World War he openly broadcast for the Germans in Berlin and elsewhere. At the Old Bailey in January 1946, he was charged with high treason and with offences against the Defence Regulations. The treason charge was dropped and the judge, Mr Justice Oliver, gave Baillie-Stewart the opportunity to go back to Germany. The Allied Control Commission objected to this, and Baillie-Stewart was sentenced to five years in prison.

The strange leniency afforded Baillie-Stewart has been the subject of much conjecture, both at the time and since. One legal reason given to explain the unusual and unexpected clemency at the Old Bailey was that Baillie-Stewart had abjured his British citizenship long before the war. This didn't explain why at the same Old Bailey William Joyce, who had at no time been a British subject, was sent to the gallows. The truth hasn't appeared yet, and doubtless it never will.

There were many other traitors, too, all less significant than those detailed above. But none of them achieved so prominent a place as William Joyce in the history of the Second World War.

8. THE 'OLD' TRIALS

It is claimed that the law is no fairer now than it once was. Only the presentation has changed, say the critics; the anomalies and injustices remain, but are now better concealed. Certainly the sordid practices of long ago bear no relation to the dignified demeanour of My Lords the Queen's Justices in recent times. Any fundamental differences should show when the carefully selected cross-section of cases in this chapter are compared with the 'new' trials in the following chapter.

The murder of magistrate Sir Edmund Berry Godfrey was included in Chapter Seven. The depositions sworn before him by the perjurer Titus Oates resulted in an illogical anti-Catholic panic. When Sir Edmund was found dead it was immediately claimed that those of the Roman faith had killed him to ensure his silence. Yet the truth was that the magistrate had not believed Titus Oates, and therefore intended to take no action on the declarations made to him. A more likely motive for his murder would be vengeance on the part of Protestants.

Three Catholic men, Green, Berry and Hill, all servants at Somerset House, the Queen's residence, were charged with the murder, and a young man named Atkins, who was in the service of Samuel Pepys, was accused of being an accessory. The Whigs were decorating the hustings with 'No Popery' banners, the nation was outraged by the killing of Sir Edmund, who had been strangled, with his own sword thrust through his chest, and Lord Shaftesbury found it convenient to fix responsibility for the mysterious murder on the four young men. There is not a single historian of substance who doesn't believe that the conviction and executions that followed were deliberate judicial murders.

The four had been arrested on information given by a Catholic silversmith by the name of Miles Prance. Prance himself had been suspected of complicity in the murder and had previously been arrested. While in custody and under pressure, he had admitted to having kept watch while the murder was perpetrated.

When Prance subsequently withdrew this statement, he was tortured in the 'condemned hole' at Newgate until he reaffirmed that his accusation was true. Two other witnesses for the prosecution were the infamous Titus Oates and William Bedloe. The latter advised Prance, 'You had better confess than be hanged', which had Prance decide to turn King's evidence.

Atkins was a Protestant, but Sir William Jones, the Attorney-General, told the court that he was a Catholic, and called a young witness to prove it. An astute Atkins questioned the witness before anyone else could, and proved that he was indeed a Protestant. Sir George Jeffreys, one of the three sitting judges, intervened quickly to say: 'We will proceed to other evidence.'

All four accused had cast-iron alibis, but only Samuel Atkins, who had proved himself to be Protestant, was permitted to establish his innocence. Robert Green, Henry Berry and Lawrence Hill were sentenced to death. As they were being taken back to Newgate, the tipstaff, an officer of the court, jumped on them and stripped them of their upper clothing, claiming that these garments were his fee according to custom.

The tipstaff was brought before the bench. Lord Chief Justice Scroggs and the vicious Sir George Jeffreys saw little wrong with the court officer's act, but the third member of the bench, Justice Dolben, admonished the tipstaff, saying: 'This seems a very barbarous thing, to take the clothes off their backs, and they must be restored.'

So the three men, victims of a disgrace to justice, were at least decently dressed when they were hanged at Tyburn in February 1679. By eerie coincidence, the area where the magistrate had been found dead had formerly been called Greenberry Hill.

Just over one hundred years later, the events leading up to one of the most dramatic trials ever held at the Old Bailey, from which ensued a horrible execution, were taking place off the coast of Africa.

Joseph Wall, a brave and distinguished military man, who was also something of a soldier of fortune, fell in love with a Dublin girl. In fact, he loved too well but not wisely. A man accustomed to violence, Wall's courting of Miss Gregory was so physically enthusiastic that he was fined and ordered to pay damages for assaulting her.

Gallant as a soldier, Joseph Wall proved himself ungallant as a lover when he fled to England to avoid paying up. There he applied for, and was granted, the governorship of the island of Goree off the West African coast at the tip of the Cape Verde Peninsula.

Never a likeable man, Wall's quarrelsome nature and fiery temper were exacerbated by the cruelly hot climate. He was a sadist who, it was claimed, had blown men from a cannon. In 1784, already greatly disliked, he incurred the wrath of some men of the Africa Corps by stopping money from their pay. It is not clear whether this was done for personal gain, but it did result in a deputation coming to see him on the matter. The spokesman for the disgruntled group was a man named Benjamin Armstrong, who put his case across with polite respectfulness.

Even so, Wall was enraged and called a parade of the men under his command. Ordering a gun carriage to be brought out, Wall had six black slaves tie Armstrong securely to it. Wall next ordered eight hundred lashes to be applied.

Armstrong writhed in agony as ropes with ends an inch thick bruised rather than cut into his flesh. Each slave administered twenty-five lashes, then was relieved. This ensured that weariness didn't cause the punishment to slacken.

While it was taking place, with Wall watching with relish, he cried out: 'Lay on, you black beasts. Lay on, or I'll lay on you. Cut him to the heart; cut his liver out.'

Just five days after Wall had left the island to return to England, Benjamin Armstrong died from the awesome beating he had received. Governor Wall was a wanted man, but two years went by before he was arrested in Bath. At Reading he somehow gave his escort the slip. Fleeing to France, he lived there under an assumed name.

Then, in 1801, perhaps influenced by the false hope that comes with a new counting of one hundred years, Wall returned to England and wrote to the Secretary of State, offering himself for trial.

His submission was quickly seized upon and at the Old Bailey Wall denied that he had ever treated his men badly, and he cited Benjamin Armstrong as the leader of an open mutiny. Yet even in the dock his manner was such that the jury wasn't fooled. Seeing the sixty-five-year-old Wall as a brute, they found him guilty and he was sentenced to death.

Joseph Wall was to die in a manner that possibly even he didn't deserve. In attendance was Dr Ford, one of Newgate's most notorious chaplains, who took J.T. Smith, formerly Keeper of the Print Room at the British Museum, along with him. Smith left the following description of the visit:

> As we crossed the press yard a cock crew, and the solitary clanking of a restless chain was horrible . . . The prisoner entered. He was death's counterfeit, tall, shrivelled and pale; and his soul shot so piercingly through the portholes of his head, that the first glance of him nearly terrified me . . . His hands were clasped and he was truly penitent. After the yeoman had told him to stand up, he 'pinioned' him, and tied the cord with so little feeling that the governor, who had not given the wretch the accustomed fee [a bribe to be as gentle as possible], observed, 'You have tied me very tight,' upon which Dr Ford ordered him to slacken the cord, but not without muttering.
>
> Then, turning to the doctor, questioned him, 'Do tell me Sir: I am informed that I shall go down with great force; is that so?'

A new drop was being put into use, and after the chaplain had explained the working of it, Wall joined him in prayer and displayed a deep contrition. Then Kirby, the Keeper of Newgate, asked the customary question of whether the victim-to-be had any last wish.

Wall brought a frown to the face of hangman James Botting, who took the condemned man's reply as a criticism of his skill, when he replied, 'I most earnestly desire that I be not pulled by the legs and that the cord be properly adjusted.'

When Wall made his appearance on the scaffold, there was not a trace of sympathy to be detected on the multitude of faces looking up at him. Botting, used to being hissed, as were all executioners, was surprised to be cheered as he adjusted the noose around the neck of Joseph Wall. Dr Ford fared worse when his hackneyed prayer was constantly interrupted by crude remarks shouted by the crowd.

Botting, either nervous or, more likely, drunk, had bungled fixing the noose. When the trap opened, the knot slipped round to the back of Wall's neck. Instead of dropping, he spun round in the air, his head grotesquely awry, his legs kicking and body jerking as he fought for breath.

A contemporary reporter wrote: 'The condemned man was seen to struggle much more than has been the case with any other sufferer. At the expiration of eleven minutes it was found necessary to pull his legs; and not till then did he finally cease to breathe.'

So Joseph Wall had met his end horribly and in the way he had feared and pleaded for it not to happen.

Even though he had botched the hanging, it was business as usual for James Botting, who, minutes later, was selling pieces of the rope he had used. He was charging one shilling an inch, while Rosy Emma, reputed to be the hangman's wife, was selling a similar rope at twopence a piece, and was doing good trade with some people who had come from Epping to sell butter at Newgate Market, and had taken the opportunity to witness the hanging.

These executions of old make grim reading, but before leaving the subject, an astonishing story of Tyburn comes from Silas Todd, the eighteenth-century Wesleyan minister who did marvellous work in Newgate Prison.

On a day when ten men were being transported to Tyburn for execution, Silas Todd was rewarded for his teaching when one of the men, named Lancaster, beseeched the unruly crowd to 'come to the Throne of Grace', promising that, as he had, they would find a merciful God.

The story takes a supernatural turn when there was nobody to claim Lancaster's body after he had been hanged. The eager men who sought bodies for surgeons to cut up quickly grabbed it and took it to Paddington. Eight sailors came on the scene then. Annoyed that they had arrived too late for the executions, the sailors heard what had happened to the unclaimed body, and decided to have some fun. Before letting Silas Todd relate the rest of the tale, it has to be stressed that the sailors had absolutely no knowledge of Lancaster, when he was alive or dead.

'When the sailors had obtained the body,' says Silas Todd, 'two of them cast it on their shoulders and carried him round by Islington. They being tired, two others laid themselves under the weight of the body and carried it thence to Shoreditch. Then two more carried it from Shoreditch to Coverley's Fields. At length after they were all rendered weary, and unable to carry it further . . . there was unanimous assent to lay it on the first doorstep they came to. They did so and went their way! This gave birth to a great riot in the neighbourhood which brought an old woman downstairs. When she saw the corpse lie at the step of the door she proclaimed with an agitated spirit, "Lord here is my son John Lancaster".'

Silas Todd plainly believed that his work with John Lancaster, and that man's turning to God before he was executed, had resulted in a mini-miracle that had the body taken home. Maybe there is an alternative explanation, but it isn't easy to find.

Heavenly justice to one side, earthly injustice is ever present in the story of the Old Bailey, as the following case shows.

Although one looms large in history and the other is largely forgotten, Abraham Lincoln, President of the United States of America, and Spencer Perceval, Prime Minister of England, had something in common. Both dreamt of their assassination the night before it happened. Perceval has the distinction, to date, of being the only British prime minister to have been assassinated, while Lincoln is one of several American presidents to die in this way.

Aged fifty, Spencer Perceval was married with six sons and six daughters. On the morning of 11 May 1812, a shaken Perceval told his family of the dream in which he had entered the lobby of the House of Commons where a man wearing a green coat with brass buttons had fired a shot at him. In the dream, the Prime Minister had been hit in the chest and everything had gone black.

Having been Chancellor of the Exchequer since 1807, and retaining that title on becoming Prime Minister and First Lord of the Treasury in 1809, Perceval was devoted to politics. Nevertheless, he gave way that day when his family pleaded that, because of the ominous dream, he should not go to the House. Yet he was forced to change his mind when a messenger arrived with an urgent appeal requesting his presence because the government was in trouble in a debate on the Peninsular War.

That same afternoon a man named John Bellingham was brooding on an imaginary injustice. Once a Liverpool merchant whose principal business was with Russia, Bellingham had been imprisoned in that country for debt. His appeal to the British ambassador couldn't be entertained because under Russian law he had been lawfully convicted.

The court decision had been a correct one, but Bellingham remained aggrieved, refusing to recognise the legality of his trial and punishment in Russia. Back in England he appealed to the British government to put right the wrongs he believed himself to have suffered.

Receiving no redress, he took the unusual step of writing a letter to the magistrates at Bow Street. Although this was a strong letter in which he threatened to take the law into his own hands if he wasn't given help, Bellingham had included both his name and his address.

He then turned his attention to the House of Commons, keeping the place under observation, watching every Member go in and out for some days. His intended target was Lord Leveson Gower, the former ambassador to Russia and the man Bellingham was convinced had let him down in his time of dire need.

Bellingham's opportunity came on the afternoon of 11 May 1812, when, wearing a green coat with brass buttons, he gained entry to the House of Commons. Armed with a handgun, he concealed himself behind some folding doors in the lobby of St Stephen's Chapel.

Shortly after 5 p.m., Prime Minister Spencer Perceval, his terrifying dream either forgotten or pushed to one side, hurried into the House, eager to join the debate that was going on.

He never made it. Bellingham, presumably mistaking Perceval for the former ambassador to Russia, stepped out to fire a pistol at him from close range.

Hit in the left side, Perceval reeled back, exclaiming, 'Oh, I am murdered!' Just minutes later he was dead.

Bellingham made no attempt to flee. Not resisting arrest, he made a statement to the police that instantly cast doubt on his sanity. 'I could gain no redress at the public offices and was told to do my worst,' he said. 'I obeyed them. I have done my worst, and I rejoice in the deed.' He did not disclose who the 'them' were that he had obeyed, and the police were too wise and experienced to enquire.

There was an almost obscene rush to bring this odd-thinking man to trial. Only four days later he stood in the dock at the Old Bailey upon a charge of murder. Not unexpectedly, an application was made for a short postponement of the trial to permit evidence of insanity to be called. This was overruled once it had been opposed by the Attorney-General in a vicious and discreditable speech.

Nevertheless, clear evidence was given that the accused's father had died mad, and there were witnesses willing to testify as to Bellingham's insanity, but time was not allowed for them to be called. In a crazy speech in his own defence, which lasted two hours, he expressed his regret at killing the Prime Minister, when it was Lord Gower who deserved to die. Right to the end he maintained that the act he had carried out had been inevitable, and that he had merely been an innocent agent of a power greater than himself.

The jury convicted Bellingham without the slightest hesitation, and he was whisked to the gallows with the same unseemly haste that he had been tossed into court.

On 18 May, just one week after firing the fatal shot, John Bellingham was hanged outside Newgate Prison at eight o'clock in the morning. He was unlucky in having been born at least a generation too early. Thirty years later, in a similar situation, the McNaughton Rules were established (see Chapter 1).

There is no suggestion of any miscarriage of justice in the trial of Eleanor Pearcey at the Old Bailey, but it is an intriguing story of an eternal triangle of yesteryear, made remarkable by the accused's peculiar attitude towards her defence.

The mistress was Mrs Eleanor Pearcey, who was also known as Mary Eleanor Wheeler. Despite an over-long face with a receding chin above an abnormally long neck, she was a striking woman and of refined appearance. She also had a dark secret. Ten years earlier, on 29 November 1880, her father, Thomas Wheeler, had been hanged at St Alban's Prison for the murder of a farm labourer named Anstree.

Mary lived at 2 Priory Street, Kentish Town, in a house she rented from her lover, Frank Hogg. Hogg, who had once managed his mother's provisions shop, had changed his occupation to furniture dealing when the family business had closed down. He had met Mary about the same time as he started courting Phoebe, who was to become his wife. Hogg lived not far away, in Prince of Wales Road, with his wife, their baby daughter Phoebe Hanalope, Hogg's mother and his sister Clara. It was a convenient arrangement that was devoid of suspicion, as Mary and Phoebe were friends, while as her landlord, Frank Hogg had excuse and reason to call at Mary's home.

Although close – Mary having nursed Phoebe through a lengthy illness, and the two of them exchanging regular visits – Phoebe did not know that her friend was having a sexual relationship with her husband, although there is a possibility that Frank Hogg suffered some misgivings about what went on between his wife and his lover.

All in all, it was the kind of situation that could run for as many years as those involved wished it to. The problem came when Mary Pearcey became dissatisfied with her part-time relationship with Frank. Though she outwardly continued to show Phoebe Hogg affection, Mary had begun to resent the person she regarded as the 'other woman'.

One day in October 1890, Mrs Pearcey called a neighbour's son and paid him a penny to deliver a note to Mrs Hogg. It invited Phoebe to take tea with Mary at her house. Showing the note to the others in her house, Phoebe put her baby in a pram and started off happily to her friend's house. She arrived there, and two people who were passing separately saw her go into Mary Pearcey's house. They were the last to see Phoebe alive in public.

When Frank arrived home that night he was surprised to find that his wife and infant child were out. She had left a note which said 'Won't be long', and the fact that Phoebe had timed the note 'quarter past three' alarmed him.

His so-far-contained suspicions about the relationship between his wife and his mistress came to a head, and he hurried to Priory Street, letting himself in with his own key as he did when arriving for extra-marital sex. The house was deserted and dark, except for a dim light in a back bedroom which was Mary's signal to him that she was out and would not be back until late. He waited for a while, then left a note on the table, reading 'About twenty past ten. Cannot stop longer.'

Incredibly, Frank Hogg then returned home and went straight to bed. Although he might be expected to believe there was a perfectly innocent reason for his wife's absence, it is difficult to understand how he could rest easy about the baby.

He did again become alarmed in the morning, but being aware that Phoebe's father, who lived not a great distance away, was seriously ill, he decided that his wife had gone to visit him. Before setting off for his father-in-law's house, he asked his sister to go to Mrs Pearcey's home to see if she could find out anything.

Filled with anxiety at discovering that his wife was not with her father, Frank Hogg hurried home to tragic news. The newspaper had a sensational story of how a clerk named Macdonald had, soon after seven o'clock the previous evening, been walking along Crosfield Road when he had seen the body of a woman lying across a pathway leading to a partially completed house. It was covered by a dark jacket, and when he lifted the garment, Macdonald was shocked to see that the head of the woman was almost severed from her body. He had called a police constable from the Swiss Cottage Railway Station, and a doctor was sent for. Eventually, the body was taken to the mortuary. There was a detailed description of the body that had convinced Hogg's sister, who had seen the newspaper much earlier, that it was Phoebe.

Clara had found Mary Pearcey at home that day when she had called on her. Reluctantly, after Clara had persisted, Mary Pearcey said that Phoebe had visited her on the previous evening. She said that the other woman had tried to borrow money that Mary didn't have to lend, and had then left Priory Street, and Mary hadn't seen her since.

When Clara said she was going to the mortuary with the intention of viewing the body, Mary Pearcey said she would go with her. A clear-headed Clara Hogg first went to the Hampstead police station. There they met Inspector Bannister, who was in charge of the murder enquiry, and a Dr Bond accompanied them to the mortuary.

There a dramatic scene took place. Clara Hogg stared down at the mutilated body which lay on the slab, the blood that partly covered the face making it unrecognisable. Mary Pearcey looked at the corpse, too, but in an oddly detached manner.

'I cannot recognise the face,' a shaking Clara said, 'but I am sure that the clothing is Phoebe's.'

Asking Dr Bond to wash the blood from the dead woman's face, Inspector Bannister took the two women out into the corridor to wait. When Dr Bond called them back in, Clara was in no doubt. 'That is Phoebe!' she exclaimed.

A transfixed Mary Pearcey clutched Clara, gasping, 'Oh, that is not her!'

'Oh, yes it is,' the sobbing Clara said, reaching out to touch one of the dead woman's hands.

'Don't touch it!' Mary Pearcey cried, in a terrible state now as she clutched at Clara, her whole body trembling.

Disengaging herself from the other woman's grip, Clara told her to go, as she wanted to stay a while with her sister-in-law. The watching Inspector Bannister was very suspicious. Mrs Pearcey's behaviour was that of a guilty person, but she expressed her willingness when the policeman asked if he might search her house.

Bannister went back to Prince of Wales Road with Clara, sending two detectives, Parsons and Nursey, home with Mary Pearcey. There they found nothing unusual in the front room, but the kitchen was in darkness. Nursey tried to raise the blind to let daylight in, but it was stuck. With Mrs Pearcey in the front room idly running her fingers over the piano keys, he pushed the blind aside to find that two panes of glass in the window had been broken. There were bloodstains on the broken glass and also on the walls and ceilings. Going to the front room, he questioned Mary Pearcey about the bloodstains. Without turning her head from the piano or ceasing her playing, she replied absently, 'Killing mice. Killing mice!'

She had previously told Nursey that she hadn't seen Phoebe Hogg for some time, but when he now challenged this she altered her previous statement, saying, 'I believe I saw her yesterday!'

At this stage she became agitated. Nursey, now convinced that the murder had been committed in the house, called Inspector Bannister. When the senior officer arrived, a more thorough investigation of the premises was carried out. While this was going on, Mary Pearcey sat in the front room in an armchair, quietly whistling a tune.

The police officers discovered the following incriminating items, all of which were bloodstained: two carving knives, a poker, a black skirt and apron, the latter having been washed, and some lace curtains in a bath.

When Bannister questioned Mrs Pearcey, who was still whistling, on these items, and she couldn't give a satisfactory answer, he told her, 'I am going to arrest you for the wilful murder of Mrs Hogg last night, and also on suspicion of the wilful murder of the female child of Mrs Hogg.'

The whistling stopped and Mary Pearcey jumped up, exclaiming, 'You can arrest me if you like, I am quite willing to go with you. I think you have made a great mistake.'

When taken to the station and formally charged, her self-confidence began to wear thin. At half past ten that same night, PC John Roser found the missing pram standing against the wall of a house in Hamilton Terrace. The handle was broken and bloodstained, while inside the pram was a waterproof apron, a length of string, and a piece of butterscotch wrapped up in paper. Not long afterwards, a hawker by the name of Smith found the body of the Hogg baby lying in some nettles on a piece of building land at the side of the Finchley Road.

This was apparently a premeditated murder in which Mary Pearcey had rid herself of a rival in love. At one point she was heard to observe, 'We were having tea. Mrs Hogg made a remark I did not like. One word brought up another . . . '

Breaking off there, she said no more. She appeared at the Old Bailey before the sedate and old-fashioned Mr Justice Denman. If anyone facing a murder charge can be described as lucky, Mary Pearcey was, for she came to the Central Criminal Court when the old intimidating, bullying style of barrister was giving way to a new breed who behaved in a gentlemanly way.

For the prosecution was Mr Forrest Fulton, who was to become Sir Forrest Fulton and Recorder of London. Tall and elegant, with a blonde moustache, he had the looks of a matinée idol, and a quiet, reassuring manner. Matching him in impressive style was Mr Arthur Hutton for the defence. With a monocle seemingly fixed permanently in one eye, Hutton had to that time defended more murder cases than any other member of the Criminal Bar. Like the prosecutor, he relied upon silver-tongued eloquence rather than aggressive rhetoric. Hutton made a determined effort to have the charge reduced to that of manslaughter on the supposition that the death of Phoebe Hogg was the result of a quarrel between the two women.

The accused woman sat in the dock, despair on her face, a vacant look in her eyes. Her long neck had veins that stood out like cords, and the blood could be seen pulsing through them. Dubbed by the press as the 'Long-necked murderess', she was charged under her real name of Mary Eleanor Wheeler. Although known at the time as Mrs Pearcey, she had never married, and had taken that surname from a man with whom she had lived for a time. Having no occupation, she was quaintly described in court as 'living under the protection of a gentleman'. There was, of course, no doubt that the 'gentleman' was the husband of the murdered woman.

The astute Arthur Hutton had prepared a defence, as he later explained to author Hargrave Lee Adam. 'She was certainly a strange woman,' Hutton recalled. 'Yes, one of the most mysterious clients I have ever had . . . I never understood her or quite why she committed the terrible murder, of which she was undoubtedly guilty . . . The line of defence I wanted to adopt was to the effect that a quarrel suddenly arose between the two women, words led to blows, and that in the heat of the combat Mrs Pearcey struck Mrs Hogg an unlucky blow that proved fatal. Then, scared at what she had done, she tried to dispose of the body, as most murderers usually do. The killing of the child, I maintained, was incidental.

'But, would you believe it, she flatly refused to agree to such a defence! Absolutely refused to my adopting that line at all. She would give no reason for her objection, nor could all the eloquent persuasion I was enabled to bring to bear upon her induce her to alter her mind. Why did she adopt such an attitude? I am quite unable to say. A most mysterious woman, more baffling in fact, than is usual with her mysterious sex. At all events and much to my regret and chagrin, I had to abandon that line of defence. And as, failing that, there was little or no defence to put forward, the ultimate outcome of the trial was merely the confirmation of a foregone conclusion.'

That foregone conclusion saw the sad-faced jurymen file back into the box to deliver the fateful guilty verdict that Mary Wheeler seemed to have deliberately engineered. It was a strange case indeed, for she was known to be a kind-hearted woman, fully trusted by birds that would come to her windowsill and permit her to feed them breadcrumbs by hand.

With the black-draped figure of the chaplain already beside the judge like the Angel of Death, Mary Wheeler stood at the front of the dock. Face ghastly pale, eyes staring into an eternity created by her imagination, she swayed her body from side to side. Surrounded by warders, she didn't seem to hear the solemn, terrible words of the sentence. A deep silence followed the concerted gasp from the public gallery.

In that silence, Mary Wheeler started slightly at a light touch on the shoulder from a warder. Casting a despairing look around the court, she turned slowly. Then she disappeared below in the confused shuffle of the feet of her escort.

At the time, something stronger than a rumour persisted that Mary Wheeler had a male accomplice. This was supported, and the mystery exacerbated, when she had her defence counsel, Arthur Hutton, insert a three-word announcement in a continental newspaper: 'Have not divulged.'

Only Mary knew what that message meant and why she had published it. She took that, and all her other secrets, with her just two days before Christmas 1890, when she was hanged in Newgate Prison by executioner James Berry. She met her death in the same way her father had just over a decade earlier. It may be that murder was in the blood.

That was one of the most puzzling trials in the history of the 'old' Old Bailey, and what must rank as one of the most horrific cases took place in the final years of the old building. The story begins in Wyndham Road, Camberwell. This was then a low-class thoroughfare, drab and dirty, which ran from Walworth through to Camberwell New Road, coming out not far from the Kennington end. It had known better days as part of the old Surrey gardens, but the brightness and the prettiness had long ago faded away to leave the whole street grey, grimy and depressing.

A young business couple, John William Darby and his pregnant wife, Beatrice, sold up their glass and china shop at Leytonstone to take possession of a shop at 22 Wyndham Road in May 1902. The baby, the Darbys' first child, was born in the rooms above the shop that the couple lived in. The birth caused the Darbys to change their plans, for Beatrice's health was so poor following the confine-ment that the doctor recommended a change of scene. John Darby had taken a three-year lease on the premises, and after explaining his position to the landlord, a Mr Knight who lived in Camberwell Road, he decided to sell the whole concern, including stock, fittings and furniture.

After John Darby had placed an advertisement a man named Louden came to view the place and said that he would like to buy the business. The landlord was informed of this by the Darbys, and when he received a communication from a Mr Edgar Edwards regarding purchasing the business, Mr Knight assumed that Edwards was an agent acting for Mr Louden.

While negotiations were going on, Beatrice Darby visited her sister, Mrs Baldwin, and invited her to the baby's christening. A delighted Mrs Baldwin accepted, and her sister said she would send the date of the ceremony. But a day or two later, Beatrice's sister received a letter from her saying that the baby had been taken ill and that the christening had to be postponed. The letter ended by asking Mrs Baldwin over to tea.

Not knowing how the sale of the business was progressing, Mrs Baldwin expected John, Beatrice and their baby to be at 22 Wyndham Road when she arrived. She was surprised to find a man she didn't know behind the counter, and she asked him where Mrs Darby was.

'Oh, she has gone out,' the man replied. 'But she is not expected to be long.'

Waiting outside of the shop for some time, a puzzled Mrs Baldwin eventually went home when her sister failed to put in an appearance.

She was not the only one surprised to find a stranger in charge of the premises. There was some rent due, and Mr Knight called to collect it from John Darby, but was told by the man behind the counter that the Darbys had gone.

After that, a man named Edwards turned up in another place at another time. The place was 89 Church Road, Leyton, a private house which was to let, and the time was December of that same year. Edwards applied to the agents for the key to view the house with a view to renting it. He furnished them with two references, which the agents took up. Both proved satisfactory. Subsequently these references turned out to be forgeries. One came from the address of 22 Wyndham Road, Camberwell.

It was agreed that Mr Edwards would rent the house at ten shillings a week, and he employed a man to dig the garden at the back before he moved in. Then Edwards moved to the house, bringing furniture, crates and many boxes. He also did some digging in the back garden himself. The next door neighbour saw him dig a deep hole, which was later filled in.

Around this time a Mr John Garland instructed Messrs Duggan & Co, trade valuers of Devonshire Chambers, Bishopsgate, to sell the good-will and stock-in-trade of his grocer's shop of 1 Jodrell Road, Victoria Park. Mrs Garland, an elderly lady, was anxious to retire. John Garland, aged about forty, was a tall, well-built man.

Through the agents, Edgar Edwards arrived to view the premises and left without making any decision about purchasing the place. A few days later Garland received a letter from Edwards which said that he would pay a deposit of twenty pounds to Messrs Duggan, and inviting Mr Garland to Edwards' home, from where they could go to the agents together to complete the transaction.

Consequently, John Garland went to 89 Church Road, Leyton, on 23 December 1902, and there saw Edgar Edwards, who said he was waiting for workmen to arrive to do some work in the house. Promising that they would go to the agents as soon as the men turned up, Edwards chatted to Garland about the business he was in the process of buying. He showed Garland around the house, at all times carrying what appeared to be a roll of wallpaper in his hand. With the workmen still not showing, he took John Garland to the local public house, where they drank a few beers before going back to the house.

There was still no sign of the workmen, and an impatient Garland said he could delay no longer, they would have to go to the agents. He had turned to open the door of the room they were in, when he received a mighty blow to the head from behind, felling him.

Lying on the floor, semi-conscious, Garland saw Edwards coming at him again, wielding the roll of wallpaper, which concealed an 8lb lead weight from a sash-window. He pleaded with Edwards not to hit him again, asking why he was doing it. Edwards made no reply, which left Garland with no alternative but to fight back.

Protecting himself fairly well, while a demented Edwards delivered blow after blow, John Garland was able to reach the front door, crash his fist through a glass panel and shout 'Help!' and 'Murder!'

A passing man on a cart jumped down to run to his aid, sending a boy to fetch a policeman. PC Matthews arrived to find Garland sitting on a chair outside the house, bleeding freely from wounds to the head. He told the officer that he had been attacked by Edwards, who was then standing inside the door.

Matthews told Edwards that Garland had made a complaint, and that he must accompany him to the station. Edwards replied that Garland had first assaulted him, and that he had defended himself with the first thing to come to hand. 'I am sorry for what happened,' he added.

Appearing before a magistrate the next morning, with a hospitalised John Garland too ill to attend court, Edwards again apologised for what had occurred.

In an attempt at finding out what it was all about, the police examined the house at Church Road. They came across a lot of letters with the address of 22 Wyndham Road, Camberwell, and went there to find a shop that was closed. Inquiries told them that the occupant had packed up and moved away, so they forced the front door and went in. The place was empty, but upstairs they found what appeared to be bloodstains on the walls and floor. An attempt had been made at washing some away, while ink had been poured on others. They found a heavy sash weight that had blood and human hair adhering to it.

It was plain that an investigation into attempted murder was about to include murder, and Chief Inspector Collins of Scotland Yard was called in. He contacted Mrs Baldwin, the sister of Mrs Darby, and took her to Edwards' house in Leyton. There she was able to identify furniture, jewellery and other property as belonging to John and Beatrice Darby. What she couldn't place was a number of empty boxes.

Having heard about the hole that had been excavated and then filled in the back garden, the police started digging. They found a sack that contained human remains, and when they had dug a hole as big as the neighbour had previously seen, they found John and Beatrice Darby and their baby, all cut up into pieces. The empty boxes were explained. Edwards had brought the Darbys from Camberwell in them, cut up and in sacks.

Further enquiries told the police that Edwards had employed a couple named Goodwin to run the shop at 22 Wyndham Road. They didn't live in, and were not allowed upstairs, where the rooms were kept locked. Eventually Edwards had Goodwin hire him a van, which he used to move everything above the shop to the house in Leyton.

It was learned that the tall, fairly well-dressed and respectable-looking Edwards, whose real name was probably Owens, was an 'old lag'. He had not been out of prison long before embarking on this murderous campaign. Possessed of terrific strength and great cunning, Owens/Edwards wasn't the brightest, for it was estimated his net gain from battering the Darbys to death and strangling their baby was no more than five pounds. He had been so hard up at the time he was pretending to buy the shop from the Darbys that he had pawned his umbrella for one shilling and sixpence. He had redeemed the umbrella immediately after killing the couple and their baby.

He said nothing at police court hearings, which were attended by John Garland, his head swathed in bandages. It became clear that Edwards had intended to murder John Garland at Leyton, then go to Victoria Park and kill Mrs Garland.

When brought to trial at the Old Bailey, all of the quiet confidence Edwards had displayed in the police court deserted him. There was such a huge crowd outside that even many of those who held tickets couldn't get into the court. He began to behave like a madman, shuffling his feet and looking vacantly around. For some time he refused to reply when asked how he would plead, but then he screamed out, 'You have no business to ask me such a question!'

'Enter a plea of not guilty,' the judge, Mr Justice Wright, said quietly, and the case was proceeded with.

It was said that Edwards had barricaded himself in his cell that morning, and that it had taken considerable time and effort to remove him forcibly and get him to the court. Right from the start of the trial it was obvious that he was trying to be regarded as insane. He sometimes turned his back on the judge and tried to engage the warders with him in conversation. The defence stressed that many of the accused's relatives suffered mental illness, and at times Edwards would roar with maniacal laughter, treating the whole trial as a joke.

There were other unsolved murders that the police might have tied Edwards in with, but his behaviour in court made it seem pointless to do so. He had spent fifteen years in prison, and while at Pentonville he had shown great ingenuity in making items for an escape, including a portable ladder. At one time it was feared that he had used the ladder to escape, but he was found still in the prison, lying in the guttering of an outhouse, close to death from exposure.

Edwards laughed uproariously when the jury returned a verdict of guilty, and when the clerk tried to ask if he had anything to say as to why sentence shouldn't be passed on him, Edwards continually interrupted with, 'Come, come! Get along with it – get it over quickly! Bring them along! Get along with it, I say, get along!'

The judge had equal difficulty when he tried to pass sentence of death, with Edwards interrupting, saying things such as, 'I wish you would get along with it as quickly as possible!'

' . . . hanged by the neck until you are dead,' said Mr Justice Wright solemnly.

Edwards gave an awful grin, saying, 'That's all right. Good – good – get along!'

'Amen,' said the chaplain.

'And all I can say is, ha ha,' Edwards exclaimed loudly.

He was still laughing when five warders took him down. Long

after Edwards had disappeared he could still be heard laughing. It was something that left everyone in the court unsettled.

When later told that the Home Secretary had declined to grant a reprieve, Edwards replied, 'Thank you. I did not ask for an appeal, and it is best to end it all now.'

When hangman William Billington came to Edwards' cell for him on 3 March 1903, the condemned man leapt to his feet saying, 'Now get on with it as quick as you can.'

'I've been looking forward to this,' Edwards remarked to the chaplain as he stepped onto the trap door.

Edgar Edwards, or Owens, was not the last person to be tried at the 'old' Old Bailey, but he truly represented all the madness and the horror that had gone on since it was established.

9. THE 'NEW' TRIALS

The history of the 'new' Old Bailey begins in 1907, when the first Sessions to be held there were presided over by Lord Alverstone, the Lord Chief Justice. Change in any shape or form is always unsettling, sometimes frightening, and at the time there were those who complained that they missed the 'cosiness' of the old court. Yet the opening ceremony differed little from that of the old days. The Lord Mayor headed a procession of sheriffs, sword-bearer, mace-bearer and the gaudily attired City Marshal. On the bench in Court No. 1, Lord Alverstone spent some time looking around, the grandeur of the huge, high-backed oak chairs, their olive-green leather covering stamped in gold with the City Arms, devalued to some degree by the shabby look of the Sword of Justice that was now affixed to the carved oaken walls at the back of the judge's seat. Everyone felt a little strange in the new surroundings, and this showed.

His lordship then made a short speech regarding the dignity of legal procedure, and the purity of British criminal law. He spoke of his trust that the new courts would uphold the high standard of justice for which the old courts were famous. This departure from historical reality was forgiven due to the sense of occasion, although an army of ghosts doubtless made a silent protest. Then it was business as usual.

The first big murder trial at the new courts was that of Horace George Rayner, who was also the first prisoner to be condemned to death in the new building.

Rayner was charged with the murder of William Whiteley, known far and wide as the 'Universal Provider'. Whiteley was an ambitious businessman with premises in Westbourne Grove, and, despite his grand nickname and reputation as a do-gooder, he was widely hated. Blamed for being the cause of many small shopkeepers failing, he had at one time been burnt in effigy. Many believed that, if Rayner had killed Whiteley, he had done the world a great service.

Yet Whiteley's death was unconnected with his trading principles, or lack of them. Rarely does a man expand his business interests without an accompanying widening of his sexual horizons. Whiteley was no exception, and this was his undoing.

Rayner, young, tall, handsome and neatly dressed, called at the home of William Whiteley in Porchester Terrace on an afternoon in January 1907. He asked for Whiteley, but the butler who answered the door advised him to go to the business premises in Westbourne Grove, as his master never saw anyone at home. Polite and pleasant to the butler, Rayner carried a small bag in which there was a loaded revolver that he had bought the previous day from the shop of Cogswell and Harrison in the Strand.

'Does Mr Whiteley expect you, or have you an appointment?' a clerk named Goodman asked when Rayner entered one of Whiteley's shops in Westbourne Grove.

Rayner shook his head. 'No, but if you say I come from Sir George Lewis, Mr Whiteley will see me.'

This worked – Lewis had previously acted for Whiteley as a solicitor. Going into Whiteley's private office, Goodman returned to ask Rayner to follow him. Whiteley was standing by the open door, which he closed on Goodman once Rayner was inside. This puzzled Goodman, for there was such a lack of recognition on the face of his employer that he was sure Whiteley had not previously met Rayner. Even so, Rayner was in the office for more than half an hour. This was highly unusual, for Whiteley was a very busy man with little time to spare.

Goodman and his fellow employees spun round in surprise when an agitated Whiteley emerged from his office to call to one of the workers, 'Jules, fetch a policeman for me.'

Having said this, Whiteley, who had left his office door open, stood at the end of one of the counters. After a few minutes had passed, Rayner came out of the door.

'Are you going to give in?' Rayner asked Whiteley.

With a dismissive wave of his hand, Whiteley replied, 'No.'

'Then take this. You are a dead man, Mr Whiteley,' Rayner said as he produced a revolver from his bag, pointed it at Whiteley's head, and pulled the trigger twice.

As Whiteley fell dead, Rayner turned the revolver to his own temple, and fired. He fell to the floor, and the frightened staff were convinced they were looking at two dead men. But Rayner was taken to hospital and eventually recovered. He had, however, lost an eye, and one side of his face was now horribly mutilated.

The tragedy was initially inexplicable. It was plain to everyone in the shop that neither of the two men had known each other, so what had made Rayner seek out the 'Universal Provider' and kill him? It was a complicated situation, and can only be outlined here. Rayner was illegitimate. Carnal carelessness would seem to have run in the family, for his mother's sister had a baby boy, of whom William Whiteley was the father. This boy actually took the name of his father, being called Cecil Whiteley. On one occasion Rayner had met his cousin, and had learned of the father/son relationship. Working on the basis that one bastard was as good as another, Rayner devised a plan in which he would pass himself off as cousin Cecil, and blackmail William Whiteley. On the surface it seemed a stupid idea, but Rayner had done his homework. Although William Whiteley financially supported his illegitimate son, he had not seen him since he was a baby. Consequently, Whiteley, and many other people, had no reason to believe that Horace Rayner was not Cecil Whiteley.

Rayner was a married man, although he was totally unreliable as a husband because he had never really settled into any kind of work. So the idea of using blackmail to get money fits the situation, but doesn't explain why Rayner needed to carry a loaded gun. If intimidation was required, although this shouldn't be necessary in blackmail, an empty revolver would have served the purpose. It is possible that Rayner, who was in a desperate financial state, intended to kill himself if his extortion scheme failed. But, if so, why had he shown such determination to kill Whiteley, firing two shots?

Horace Rayner, horribly disfigured, first appeared at the police court in Marylebone. Remanded in custody for trial at the Central Criminal Court, the affairs of both Rayner and the man he had killed were thoroughly investigated. Whiteley had been a 'Universal Provider' in more than one sense, and the possibility that he was the father of Horace Rayner had a bearing on the case. It was established that Whiteley had probably never met Rayner's mother, and if he had he certainly had had no intimate relationship with her.

Nevertheless, it was a juicy story as far as the public was concerned, and the trial brought the first big crowd swarming into the new building. Many had to stay out in the street, where they awaited the verdict. It wasn't a long wait. The hearing lasted just one day. The case for the prosecution, headed by A.H. Bodkin, who was known as Sir Archibald Bodkin when he afterwards became Director of Public Prosecutions, was concisely put by Mr R.D. Muir, who told the court: 'Blackmail is my suggestion to you the clear object of that journey, but murder not necessarily the object. The prisoner must have contemplated the possibility of failure. He may not have known to the full of what firm character the late William Whiteley was, but he must have realised that a man like Mr Whiteley was not a child. He must have recognised the possibility of resistance and refusal to be blackmailed, and in such circumstances what would be the prisoner's position? Prosecution, conviction, imprisonment, the probable result of a man attempting to blackmail and failing – a man of the prisoner's deliberate temperament and calm resolution you would think may be a man to blackmail and succeed, or to fail and commit suicide, but not necessarily to commit the crime of murder. Now there was a document found on the prisoner, consisting of leaves torn from a small notebook. On it were written the following words:

> To whom it may concern. – William Whiteley is my father, who has brought upon himself and me a double fatality by reason of his own refusal of a request perfectly reasonable. RIP.

'That may have been written before he went to William Whiteley's office at all,' continued Muir, 'or it may have been written while he was there. But whenever it was written it shows a determination formed at the time it was written to murder Mr Whiteley, and in my submission to you it matters not whether that resolution was formed on 23 or 24 January. It shows deliberation. It shows intention. Here is no outburst of sudden and uncontrollable passion induced by either insult or injury, but a determination formed to murder William Whiteley either in anticipation of a refusal or because of a refusal actually given. In my submission to you there is, therefore, no grounds upon the facts as I have opened them for finding that this crime is a crime other than one of deliberate, wilful murder. If you are of that opinion it is your painful duty to find the prisoner guilty of the crime with which he is charged.'

As Rayner had given the name of Sir George Lewis as a kind of passport to Whiteley's office, Lewis was called as a witness. He declared that Rayner had no authority to use his name. Sir George Lewis added that he had previously had something to do with Whiteley's matrimonial affairs, but claimed his professional privilege as a solicitor, and this was allowed. Other witnesses were called, but their collective testimony did nothing to improve the position of the prisoner.

In the box himself, Rayner gave his version, the only version, of what had happened in Whiteley's office. As calm and unruffled as ever, he said that he had always been under the impression that Whiteley was his father. He had nothing other than gossip and chance remarks he had overheard to support this claim. Rayner, who had lived at Brighton, Eastbourne, Barnet and Soho, and had gone to Russia for a short time at the age of seventeen, had, when a child, met Whiteley on several occasions. Never having had a regular job, Rayner had been unemployed most of the time, and was in a poor state of health due to malnutrition.

Living at Rowton House, he had often contemplated shooting himself, but hadn't been able to afford a gun. He had somehow got over that obstacle, as well as being able to afford to drink a considerable amount of brandy before going to the office of Whiteley, a man he hadn't seen for twenty-five years. He said that his purpose was to try to get a job working for Whiteley, and being aware that Sir George Lewis had some involvement in Whiteley's affairs, had used the name to gain access to the private office.

With the only person able to contradict him dead, Rayner's account of his meeting with Whiteley began with the businessman asking, 'What is it I can do for you?'

Rayner answered, 'I think I am right in stating that your son is speaking to his father?'

Whiteley had said, 'Is that so? When did you see me last?'

After a short discussion on this subject, Rayner had described the desperate straits he was in, and brought in the all-important question, 'Can you assist me in any way? I shall be pleased if I can only obtain employment.'

Whiteley's reply had been less than helpful, 'I don't intend to get involved with what is past.'

Rayner felt a surge of hope when Whiteley asked him if he would like to go abroad, thinking that the man he believed to be his father was considering funding him. But then he had become really annoyed when Whiteley suggested indifferently that he seek the help of an organisation such as the Salvation Army. That, and an ensuing reiteration from Whiteley that he would not help in any way, brought the situation to its tragic climax.

Two psychiatric experts testified that they had examined Horace Rayner and had failed to detect any traces of insanity in him. All that was left to Mr George Elliott, defending, was to base a plea on sentimental grounds, describing Rayner as 'a degenerate, whose mental heritage was tainted, defective, weakened by the indulgence – in drink – of two generations.'

It was weak compared to the strong prosecution case, the closing speech of which was of short duration. The judge summed up in less than half an hour, while the jury weren't out for ten minutes before coming back with a verdict of guilty. The black cap appeared, and Rayner declined in an almost inaudible voice when asked if he had anything to say.

Then Lord Chief Justice Alverstone delivered the first sentence of death at the 'new' Old Bailey: 'Horace George Rayner, I will not harrow the feelings of those who hear me or yourself by any reference to this terrible crime of which you have been convicted on the most conclusive evidence, a crime which showed deliberation and a determination to revenge yourself upon a man if you could not succeed in obtaining from him the assistance you hoped he would give you. I cannot hold out to you the slightest hope that the sentence of the law will not be carried into effect, and I call upon you most earnestly to spend the time that may be allowed to you in earnest communion with your Maker.'

This advice from the judge was not needed. Although declared sane at the Old Bailey, Horace Rayner was reprieved and sent to Broadmoor Criminal Lunatic Asylum. Released in 1919, he died shortly afterwards.

In 1911 the Old Bailey saw the first capital case in which a conviction was quashed. It is unfortunate that those involved – the man who had killed, the principal witness, and, sadly, the victim – were unpleasant characters. Charles Ellsome was a young labourer who lived with Rose Pender, a nineteen-year-old prostitute. Ellsome found it easier to live off Rose's earnings than to work for a living.

But the flow of immoral earnings that kept him in comfort suddenly dried up. Rose had left him, and an angry Ellsome was more than once heard to mutter that he would 'do her in'. Had this been a young man's attempt to rescue his ego after being deserted by a prostitute, it would have merely been stupidity. But in the circumstances it was suicidal, for this was a public announcement of his intention. Ellsome did plan to murder Rose. He quite openly bought a long chef's knife.

A friend of Ellsome's was Jack Fletcher, who had gone one better by living with two prostitutes. Early one morning, Fletcher was awoken by the hoarse voice of Ellsome outside his bedroom window, shouting his name. When a bleary-eyed Fletcher opened the window to look down into the street, Ellsome told him, 'I've killed Rosie stone dead.'

The dead body of Rose Pender was found lying on the pavement with several stab wounds. It didn't take a Holmesian-style investigation for the police to discover who the killer was. Ellsome was arrested, and Jack Fletcher 'helped the police with their enquiries'.

Fletcher made two separate statements to the police, but only one of these was used in evidence at the trial of Charles Ellsome before Mr Justice Avory at the Old Bailey.

In the witness box, Fletcher displayed the particularly obnoxious type of arrogance that stems from a low intellect. He impressed no one, least of all the jurors, and made things even worse by declaring, 'I thieve for my living and I am proud of it.'

Though he was the principal material witness, it was clear to all that anything he said would require corroboration. Neither was the testimony given by Ellsome in his own defence of a much higher standard. He denied murdering the girl, but the alibi he gave melted away early in the heat of cross-examination, and his evidence carried no conviction.

Noted for his fairness, Mr Justice Avory, beset by liars, warned the jury in his summing-up that Fletcher's evidence could not be accepted unless corroborated, and stressed that it was corroborated by the statement that Fletcher had made to the police immediately after the murder.

The judge was in error. He had seen both statements, and in his summing-up had referred to the first statement made by Fletcher, which had not been produced at the trial and was therefore 'not in evidence'. It was the second statement that had been 'put in', and in this there was no corroboration of the verbal testimony Jack Fletcher had given in court.

At the time Mr Justice Avory was not aware of his mistake, and neither was the jury, who in due course returned their verdict of guilty.

The red-robed judge spoke of the degraded life of Charles Ellsome, ending his short speech with, 'For the crime of which he has been convicted, he must die.'

But Ellsome's legal team had spotted the flaw in the summing-up. They went to the Court of Criminal Appeal, where Mr Justice

Darling had no alternative but to set aside the conviction. There could be little doubt that Ellsome had stabbed Rose Pender to death, but he left the court a free man.

A companion story to the one that got away is the one who could have got away – but didn't. This was Frederick Field, who twice stood in the Old Bailey dock on charges of murder. In both instances Field had been arrested and brought to trial *on his own confession* that he had committed murder.

Field worked for a firm of sign-board erectors, and on the morning of 2 October 1931 he and his foreman discovered the body of Norah Upchurch, a prostitute aged twenty, in the passageway of an empty shop in Shaftesbury Avenue. As Field had been at the premises the previous day to take down a To Let board, he was questioned by the police. He was regarded with suspicion, for the door had to be forced that morning because Field claimed that he had the previous day given the key to a man he assumed to be the owner. He described him as 'a man in plus-fours, with gold fillings'.

At the inquest on the girl, Field behaved oddly and identified another man there as the person to whom he had given the key of the shop. The coroner had the jury join him in inspecting the man, and it was discovered that he had not one gold tooth in his head. The coroner deemed that Field was a compulsive liar. That he was a liar was easy to prove, but there was nothing to place him as the killer, and no action was taken against Field.

In July 1933 Field walked into the offices of the *Daily Sketch* at Kemsley House and announced that he had murdered Norah Upchurch. He made a lengthy, detailed statement describing how he had lured her into the shop. There he had strangled her and made off with her handbag, which he had left in a ditch at Rose Hill, Sutton.

Chief Inspector George Cornish of Scotland Yard was called and he arrested Field, who stepped chirpily into the dock at the Old Bailey. Lithe, fair-haired and good-looking, he faced Mr Justice Swift, who was fat, somewhat pompous, and who appeared to have an easy trial ahead of him. Field had confessed that he'd had possession of the keys of the shop at the material time. In court the confession he had made to the police was read out. In the course of his statement Field had said: 'I lost my temper and gripped her round the throat . . . she seemed to faint away and fell back out of my hands on to the floor. She did not scream or speak. I knew that something was seriously wrong when she fell back, and I lost control of myself, and cannot remember exactly what happened afterwards . . . '

At the end of the statement, he declared: 'The reason I have come to the police to give myself up is because I am fed up. My outlook is bad, and through arrangements I have made my wife and child will be better off without me.'

In court, however, he denied the killing, and instead repeated his story of having given the shop keys to a man in plus-fours who had gold teeth, and stated that he had lied to the police.

He said that the finger of suspicion had been pointing at him since the time of the inquest on the girl, and he had made the untrue statement to the police so that he could be brought to court, where he would prove his innocence.

Field swore that he had not seen Norah Upchurch on the night she had been murdered, and neither had he known her, or even seen her, before that.

'It is a peculiar way of proving your innocence to say you are guilty of murder,' Mr Justice Swift commented drily.

'It was the only way,' came Field's prompt reply.

Even the man prosecuting for the Crown, Eustace Fulton, was made uncomfortable by the situation. Field's reason for confessing to murder seemed an incredible one, but for what other purpose would a man more or less volunteer to have the hangman's noose put round his neck?

Struggling to appear casual in the extremely unusual circumstances, the judge conversationally enquired of Fulton: 'Do you think it possible to convict upon the evidence?'

'I do not think so, my Lord,' the prosecutor replied.

Mr Justice Swift then explained to the jury the exact position in law. The only evidence against Field was his statement. Plainly the man was a liar, but they could not convict him of murder because he was more than careless with the truth. The judge directed that they should return a verdict of not guilty, and he then discharged Field, who soon afterwards joined the RAF as an aircraftman.

Five years went by in which Field never crossed the path of the police. But then, on the night of 4 April 1936, a middle-aged widow, Mrs Beatrice Sutton, was murdered in her Clapham flat. She had died from suffocation, and was found with two pillows over her face. There were no clues to the identity of her killer.

Field hadn't settled in the RAF, and at this time he was posted as a deserter. He had a regular woman friend at that time, who feared there would be trouble if he didn't surrender himself to the RAF, and she tried to persuade him to do so. But he was adamant that he would not go back, which resulted in her ending their relationship.

But he didn't leave her alone. On the night of Beatrice Sutton's death, he called on his woman friend in a wild, desperate state. He gabbled that she would read 'something' in the newspapers, and was so frightening that the woman's mother, who happened to be there at the time, sneaked out to telephone the police to say where they could collect Field, who was a deserter.

Neither the woman, her mother, nor the police connected Field with the murder of the widow. But while he was in a police cell awaiting an RAF escort from Hendon, Field once again had the urge to confess. In a statement he gave a detailed and accurate description of the room in which the murder had been committed, the position the body had been lying in, and other things that showed he had an intimate knowledge of the murder. When the statement had been completed, Field signed it without hesitation.

It was obvious that he planned to get away with the second confession as he had the first. Back in the Old Bailey he went through his earlier routine to retract the confession. With a military bearing he related how, while on the run as a deserter, he had spent two or three nights sleeping in cupboards under the stairs of the block of flats in which Mrs Sutton had lived. On the night of the murder he heard voices raised in anger, and saw a man coming out of a flat, leaving the door open. Field had looked in to see the woman dead with a pillow over her face.

This time, however, his confession contained too many

accuracies to be unconnected with the murder. He said that he had later decided to confess to the murder because he wanted to commit suicide due to his woman friend having finished with him. He thought by standing trial and being convicted, the public executioner would take his life, which was what he wanted.

Eustace Fulton was once again the prosecutor, and he looked sagely over his glasses at Field to ask: 'If you wanted to confess to a murder you had not committed, what would have been more convincing than to have put your head out of the window and called the police?'

A shaken Field took some time in answering, and when he did he stumbled over his words and lacked conviction. 'At that time I had not definitely decided to confess to the murder,' he replied.

'Why did you describe pressing her throat in your statement?'

'I assumed that was what had happened.'

Fulton was on the final stretch of the prosecution. 'And you explained it in a way the doctors say she was murdered?' he asked.

'It was pure supposition,' Field stammered.

The trial was just about over. There was no defence other than his confession being false, but the facts in it fitted the crime exactly. His woman friend was in court, and her sobbing accompanied the pronouncement of the sentence of death, during which Field stood to attention in the dock.

Frederick Herbert Charles Field, the strange man who had made one confession too many, was hanged at Wandsworth Prison on 30 June 1936.

*

Although murder cases have in the main been used here to tell the story of the Old Bailey, the court did, of course, deal with other crimes. With the outbreak of the First World War, spy-mania gripped Britain. Anyone with a German name or the hint of a guttural accent was viewed with great suspicion, even those who were friends, workmates or neighbours of long standing. There was no call for alarm, as the British government was firmly in control of the German spy situation. With one or two minor exceptions, the officers of the British Intelligence Department were in possession of the names and addresses of all foreign agents trying to learn naval and military secrets.

Yet just a few years earlier things had been very different. With a coming war a certainty, the hard work of the police was often negated by some ambiguity about the Official Secrets Act of that time. The Germans were seen to be much more efficient. First two British officers, Captain Trench RMLI and Lieutenant Brandon RN, were accused of espionage on the Isle of Borkum. Tried at Leipzig, they were sentenced to four years in prison.

A further sensation was caused by the arrest at Bremen of Bertrand Stewart, a London solicitor and young Yeomanry officer of great promise. Convicted at Leipzig of attempting to obtain information injurious to the interest of Germany, Stewart received a prison service of three years and six months.

An indignant cry went up. Why weren't the German spies in Britain arrested? How they came to be is a story that begins in Portsmouth and ends at the Old Bailey.

In 1911 a man who called himself Captain Grant lived in a private hotel in Green Road, Southsea, Hampshire. He was a German who spoke English remarkably well. Stockily built, Grant had a jovial face and a disarmingly charming manner. He told his landlord that he was the son of a judge, had received a university education and had travelled the world extensively before coming to England to research and write a book about coal. After completing this work, Grant added, he would like to settle down in Southsea as a teacher of German. He was an affable, harmless kind of man who had a passion for fishing during the day, and a devotion to solving newspaper competitions in the evenings.

But the police knew that 'Captain Grant' was really a clumsy German spy named Heinrich Grosse, and they had him under observation. As a secret agent Grosse was so inept that he wasn't aware that the British police knew his name, or that he was under continual surveillance.

When a naval pensioner named William Salter, a telephone

operator on HMS *Vernon*, tried setting himself up as a private detective by inserting an advertisement in a local newspaper, Grosse, using the name of Grant, wrote to him asking that they meet. When they did, he told Salter that he wanted to know the amount of coal, for government purposes and for shipping, in different ports, and also how many men would be in the Portsmouth naval barracks that Christmas.

'Some people,' Grosse said, giving Salter a smile of innocence, 'would call this spying, but it is not spying from a war point of view. It is nothing to do with the army and navy. It is spying for commercial purposes only.'

Seeing the proposal as suspicious, Salter pretended to go along with it but reported his meeting with Captain Grant to the Admiral Superintendent of the Portsmouth dockyard. From that time onwards Salter was acting under police instructions. With his help, Grosse was followed to a shipping office in Southampton, where he asked about a passage to Berlin. Fearing that he was intending to escape to his own country, the police arrested Grosse when he returned to his rooms at Southsea.

They found letters in code that, when deciphered, proved conclusively that Grosse was a spy employed by the notorious Steinhauer, the Kaiser's master spy. Grosse had been sending messages to Steinhauer through a go-between agent named Petersen, who was based at Rotterdam.

The police found a sketch of Portsmouth harbour under Grosse's blotting pad, and a loaded six-chambered revolver was in a chest of drawers, together with a box of cartridges.

One of the letters, signed by Petersen, read:

> Portsmouth and the immediate neighbourhood is the spot that I am keenest about. Kindly let me have your address as soon as possible and let me know whether to send registered letters there. You will then receive the remaining five pounds. I do not want to send the whole amount to the hotel. Mr Stein [Steinhauer] has informed me of your idea of sending me a short diary. I shall be glad to get it.

Another letter by Petersen revealed the full range of Grosse's activities. It said:

> I hope you received the registered envelope which I sent you the other day with its enclosures. One of my friends told me that your recent information was accurate and without any personal embellishment. I hope you will take trouble to make our joint business a good one in future.
>
> You will see from the newspapers that there is a special interest at present about things relating to England and Germany. This happens most opportunely for you, and you can see that the field of operations will be a valuable one. I do not want to hurry you too much, but I am now giving you some questions, the answers to which I consider will be very useful to me.
>
> 1. Is it really true, as stated in the newspapers, that the new submarines are being fitted out with guns? How and where are they mounted?
> 2. Where are the guns stored for arming merchant ships in time of war?
> 3. What sort of guns have the mine-laying cruisers *Naiad*, *Thetis* and *Latona*?
> 4. Have these got wireless telegraphy?
> 5. How much coal is there on shore? Is there no more coal in the dockyard than what is stated?
> 6. More details are required about the system of range-finding. The information about a floating conning-tower is surely imaginary.
>
> There is, therefore, work and stuff enough. I wish you every success in my branch of work. P.

With war imminent, the Official Secrets Act was amended to allow stricter control over foreign nationals, and Grosse was the first to be accused under its new provisions. His trial, before Mr Justice Darling at Winchester in February 1912, was regarded as being so important that Sir Rufus Isaacs (Lord Reading), who was then Attorney-General, conducted the case for the Crown.

When he gave evidence in his own defence, Grosse was fairly confident, but he fared badly under cross-examination. He appealed to Petersen for money towards his defence, but a spy under arrest is of little use to his masters, and Grosse had the following reply delivered to his prison cell:

> According to your wishes I will send your solicitors eighty pounds for your defence. I must confess that this amount for your defence seems to me to be very high. I fear the benefit is out of all proportion to the expenditure. In no circumstances can I do more for you.

It was money wasted, for the jury returned a verdict of guilty. The Attorney-General then revealed to the court that Grosse had, in 1898, been sentenced to ten years' imprisonment when he tried to utter forged notes in Singapore.

As a direct consequence of the arrest of Heinrich Grosse, the Special Intelligence Department was able to discover the structure of the German spy network in Britain, and destroy it. They moved in on a colleague of Grosse, Karl Gustav Ernst, who ran a hairdresser's business in Caledonian Road, King's Cross. Ernst proved to be the medium through whom Steinhauer made contact with all his agents in England. Bundles of letters to the agents, complete with English postage stamps, were sent under separate cover to Ernst, who then posted them in various parts of London.

On the day war broke out, Ernst was the first of twenty German spies to be arrested. He had been interned with two hundred other suspected German spies. In addition, some nine thousand Germans and Austrians, who were of military age but still in England, were held as prisoners of war.

Ernst protested, claiming that he was a British subject, born in Hoxton, although his parents were German. This was a bad move, for he had been arrested under the Official Secrets Act. In November 1914 he was tried at the Old Bailey on an indictment charging him with inciting another man to communicate to Steinhauer information relating to the movements, armaments and dispositions of British vessels which was calculated to be useful to the enemy.

Sir Archibald Bodkin, who prosecuted for the Crown, told the court that Steinhauer held a high position in the secret service of the German government. He revealed that, since 1911, Post Office officials had been opening letters addressed to Ernst, not only in his own name but also those of Walters and Waller, copying the contents, sealing them up again and forwarding them to Ernst. As Steinhauer's forwarding agent, Ernst received a payment of twenty shillings a month, which was later increased to thirty shillings.

In the witness box Ernst denied having attempted to procure any information about Royal Naval ships. He admitted that he had been working for Steinhauer since 1910, and that some two hundred letters had been exchanged between them, and he had forwarded about the same number of letters to addresses in England. All of this the British Intelligence Department already knew, but the arrest and conviction of Grosse led to twenty German spies being caught when the war began.

'You are a mean, mercenary spy,' Mr Justice Coleridge said in sentencing Ernst to seven years' penal servitude. 'You were ready to betray your country to the enemy for money, and equally ready, I dare say, to betray Germany to us for an increased reward.'

Ernst was lucky, for in the First World War twelve German spies were shot at the Tower, while a thirteenth committed suicide. In the Second World War the Old Bailey was kept busy with German spy trials. A total of fifteen were hanged, either at Pentonville or Wandsworth Prisons. The only exception was in the case of Josef Jakobs, whose military rank had him tried by court-martial and executed by firing squad.

*

Perhaps because it happens rarely, escaping the gallows is always newsworthy, as a sensational 1932 trial at the Old Bailey proves. The Permissive Society came about in the 1930s, was put on hold during the war, and revamped in the 1960s. Aged twenty-seven, Elvira Dolores Barney belonged to the wild social set of that era that was popularly known as the 'Bright Young Things'. Most of them were well-off and able to afford to drink too much, drive around town too fast in sports cars, wear brightly coloured clothes and indulge in riotous parties at which promiscuous sex was the norm.

Elvira came from a wealthy family, her parents being Sir John and Lady Mullens, who had an impressive house in fashionable Belgrave Square. Lloyd George, something of a purveyor of honours, had knighted old Etonian John Mullens for his generous donations to political party funds. To Elvira, who lived in a mews flat off Knightsbridge, a good time was much preferable to a good name. She had married, but her husband had left her, going to America to try his luck in show business as a singer.

Left alone, Elvira found her ideal lover in Michael Scott Stephen. As is often the case, their relationship swung between mind-blowing sex and screaming arguments. Stephen was a man of wild and extravagant habits. Living in a bedsit in the Brompton Road, he described himself as a dress designer, but got his money from sleeping with women. In the spring of 1932 he was being totally supported by Elvira Barney.

In the early hours of 31 May that year, Dr Thomas Durrant, a well-known London physician, went to 21 Williams Mews, Knightsbridge, in response to an urgent call by Elvira. He found Michael Stephen lying dead in an upstairs bedroom. Fully clothed, Stephen had a loaded revolver close to his left hand. Elvira was in a hysterical state, crying out, 'He can't be dead. I love him so . . . he wanted to see you to tell you it was an accident.' She made a dive for the gun, saying, 'Let me die, let me die. I will kill myself.'

Placing his foot on the revolver so that she couldn't pick it up, the doctor managed to calm Elvira sufficiently for her to tell him in a garbled way that she and Stephen had quarrelled. He had brought the revolver out from behind a cushion on a chair. They had struggled, the gun had gone off, she didn't know how, and Michael Stephen had lain dying, asking her to call a doctor.

Dr Durrant called the police. Detective Inspector Winter arrived

and discovered that the revolver had five chambers, three containing live cartridges, and two which had been discharged. The
policeman looked into the bedroom and noticed a bullet hole in the
wall. When he went to question Elvira she flew into a violent rage,
refusing to accompany him to the police station until her parents
arrived. 'I'll teach you to try to put me in a cell, you foul swine,' she
yelled at a disconcerted Winter.

This spoilt-brat behaviour was common in Elvira Barney's social
circle, but when her parents arrived they managed to persuade her
to go to the police station where she made a statement saying that
the shooting had been an accident, the gun having gone off when
she and her lover had been quarrelling over another woman. She
was charged with the murder of Michael Stephen.

Elvira Barney was in a dire situation, but a form of justice can
always be bought. That is not to suggest that any illegality took
place in this case, but the accused woman's parents were wealthy
enough to engage the services of Sir Patrick Hastings, one of the
most brilliant advocates of the day. Hastings specialised in civil
actions and rarely appeared in a criminal court. He had, in fact,
turned down this brief, but his wife, who felt sorry for Sir John and
Lady Mullens because of the disgrace that the daughter's conviction
for murder would bring on them, pleaded with Sir Patrick, and he
eventually agreed.

The trial began at the Old Bailey on 5 July 1932 before Mr Justice
Humphreys. Sir Percival Clarke led for the prosecution, which
began with the testimony of Mrs Hall, the wife of a chauffeur, who
lived in the house opposite Elvira's in the mews. She spoke of
hearing Elvira and Stephen rowing at two o'clock in the morning.
She heard Elvira Barney twice say, 'Get out. I'll shoot!'

In her written statement to the police, Mrs Hall had said, 'I'll
shoot *you*.' It was odd that Clarke didn't pick her up on this, for the
first version favoured the prosecution more.

'Did you hear any answer?' Percival Clarke asked.

'No, I only heard a shot,' Mrs Hall replied. 'It appeared to come
from Mrs Barney's front room. After the shot I heard Mr Stephen
shouting, "Good God, what have you done?" Mrs Barney then

screamed. "Chicken, chicken, come back to me. I will do anything I can for you." Mrs Barney was crying and very hysterical. The doctor arrived shortly afterwards.'

Upon further questioning, Mrs Hall said Elvira had done some shooting three weeks previously. On that occasion Michael Stephen had been outside and Elvira had been screaming at him to go away otherwise she would call the police. He had gone off in a taxi, but had soon come walking back. Mrs Hall then saw Stephen walking away, when Elvira looked out of her window, naked, and shouted 'Laugh, baby, laugh for the last time!' Elvira had then fired the gun.

When Sir Patrick Hastings cross-examined Mrs Hall, he asked if Michael Stephen had spoken to her after Mrs Barney had fired the gun.

'Yes,' Mrs Hall replied.

'What did he say?' Hastings asked.

Not surprisingly, Sir Percival Clarke jumped up to object that the answer to Hastings' question was hearsay and would be inadmissible as evidence. Hastings submitted that it was always admissible to give evidence of a statement accompanying an incident such as this. This wasn't correct. Hastings knew this, just as Mr Justice Humphreys must have done, but the judge overruled Clarke's objection. Sir Patrick Hastings subsequently wrote on this incident in his book *Cases in Court*: 'Sir Percival stoutly objected to the evidence as inadmissible, and he was probably right, but Mr Justice Humphreys, straining the laws of evidence in favour of the defence, allowed the question.'

The last sentence of Mrs Hall's reply, 'He [Stephen] said he didn't want to leave Mrs Barney *because he was afraid that she might kill herself*', was of cardinal importance for the defence, for when the accused took the witness stand she was to claim that she had fired the revolver on the first occasion to induce Stephen into believing that she was going to commit suicide.

As Mr Justice Humphreys was a most experienced criminal lawyer, he is not likely to have made a mistake in allowing hearsay evidence. But this would seem to be the only possible reason, for 'second-hand' evidence was invaluable to the defence. Witnesses on the night of the killing testified that they had heard two shots, which would account for the bullet hole that Detective Inspector Winter had discovered in the bedroom wall. Defence counsel proved the witnesses to be unreliable with regard to the number of shots, and Elvira Barney said that the hole in the wall was a result of her attempt at suicide on the night which a neighbour claimed she had fired the gun at Michael Stephen.

She was supported in this by Inspector Winter when he was cross-examined by Hastings. The policeman revealed that no trace of any bullet had been found in the mews, despite a thorough search.

This corroboration from Winter seemed conclusive until he was questioned about the fingerprints found on the gun, and his answers showed his police methods to be somewhat sub-standard.

Having already testified that fingerprints on the gun were likely to be blurred if two people had fought to gain possession of it, he was asked: 'Was it found that the marks on the gun were so blurred that no fingerprints were decipherable except one?'

'That is so,' Winter replied.

'Whose was that one?'

Inspector Winter hesitated uncomfortably before admitting: 'Mine.'

Sir Bernard Spilsbury, who had carried out the post-mortem, dismissed any notion that Stephen had shot himself, as in the position the body was found it would have been impossible for him to have bent his wrist with enough power to have fired the gun.

Another concession made to the defence came when Hastings was permitted to have the doctor who had examined Elvira Barney testify without the physician being regarded as a witness for the defence. Had the doctor been a proper defence witness, then the rules of court procedure would not have allowed Hastings the right to make a closing address to the jury, which depends on the only material witness being the accused person.

The doctor reported that he had found fairly extensive bruising on Elvira's arms and on her right thigh that might have been caused by fingers. There were also cuts and abrasions on one of her hands.

Seizing on this, Hastings asked the doctor, 'If she had been struggling with the revolver in her hand, would the marks be consistent with that?'

'Yes.'

Aware that he was risking the advantage he had gained, perhaps even the life of his client, Hastings, with considerable apprehension, had Elvira Barney take the witness stand.

He skilfully succeeded in creating at least some sympathy for her with the jury by coaxing his initially very nervous witness into talking about her marriage to a man who ill-treated her, but whom she could not divorce because he was in the United States. She said she had been devoted to the dead man, and had become his mistress, supporting him 'almost entirely'.

Michael Stephen had other failings apart from being kept by a woman. He had an obsession with gambling and, using Elvira's money but taking another woman with him, often went on gambling excursions. At times Elvira had been frightened of him, and had once called the police to her flat.

She told the court that Stephen had been kind to her at first when they had returned to her flat on the night of the shooting. But then his manner had altered. 'He made love to me,' Elvira said, 'and he was very angry because I did not respond in the way that he wanted me to.'

Embarrassment causing her to falter, she went on: 'He said perhaps my feelings had changed, and I told him it was only because I was unhappy and could not forget what he had said to me. Then he said that he was not pleased with the way in which things were going and he wanted to go away the next day and not see me at all. That made me very unhappy. He got up from the bed and dressed. I asked him not to leave me and said that if he did I should kill myself.'

Snatching the revolver, saying, 'Well, you won't do it with this', he ran from the bedroom to the spare room with Elvira following him. They struggled as she tried to take the revolver from him, and then the shot was suddenly fired.

When Sir Percival Clarke thoroughly and doggedly cross-examined her, Elvira did not change one word of her testimony. At one stage, he asked: 'Did you genuinely intend to commit suicide?'

'The last time I genuinely intended to do it,' Elvira replied.

That she had loved Stephen was very evident, and Dr Durrant had testified that while her lover was lying dead in her flat, Elvira had kissed him several times. She denied ever threatening to shoot him, as more than one witness had testified they had heard her doing, but had said, 'Don't leave me. If you do, I shall shoot myself!'

Elvira swore that she didn't know whose finger had been on the trigger when the gun had gone off. There was nothing to say that her account of events in the flat was not true, and had the police not blundered in picking up the revolver, there might well have been evidence on it to prove her story. Against her was her hedonistic way of life. Her kind generally made nuisances of themselves, and as an obviously spoilt child of rich parents she wasn't likely to have made a good impression on the jury.

But she was afforded great help by Sir Patrick Hastings' speech made in conclusion, and the praise Mr Justice Humphreys heaped on that speech in his summing-up. It was, said the judge, 'One of the finest speeches I have ever heard at the Bar.'

In his summing-up, the judge put a hitherto unraised point to the jury. This was that if the accused woman had been attempting suicide, an illegal act at that time, and her lover had died while struggling to take the revolver from her, then it was open to them to convict of manslaughter.

The jury was out for two hours, returning with a verdict of not guilty of either murder or manslaughter. Mr Justice Humphreys then ordered that Elvira be discharged. She left the dock to run to her wealthy parents and her friends, the type satirised by Evelyn Waugh in early novels such as *Vile Bodies*.

Sadly, Elvira's acquittal in the Old Bailey didn't free her from narcissism. Sir Patrick Hastings learned this when he met her again in frightening circumstances as described in a paragraph from his book: 'I only saw her once more in her life. A few days after the trial, term having ended, I was driving my car up the steep hill from Boulogne on the Paris road when a long, low car, driven by a woman, dashed round the corner on the wrong side, nearly killing me and my chauffeur who was sitting beside me. As he indignantly picked up his cap he said: "Did you see who was driving that car, sir? It was Mrs Barney!"'

This is certainly a case of truth being stranger than fiction, with Elvira Barney coming close to ending the life of the man who had saved her from death on the gallows.

She did, in fact, settle, in the loosest use of that word, in Paris. It was in that city that Elvira Barney died, still young, and reportedly consumed by regrets.

10. THE WAR YEARS

Far from uniting the criminal fraternity and the law-abiding section of society against a common enemy, the Second World War had the opposite effect. Firearms were readily available, deserters supported themselves by illegal means, women were made vulnerable by the black-out, and the Blitz constantly hampered those involved in combatting a considerable increase in crime. The Old Bailey, stretched to the limit by a high number of cases, its north-west corner hit by bombs on the night of 10 May 1941, killing two employees fire-watching on the roof and destroying Court 2, still had the 'ordinary' crimes of peacetime to deal with.

One murder trial had its origins two decades back. In 1920 Harry Dobkin married Rachel Dubinski. The marriage was a brief one, lasting just three days, but presumably it was consummated because Rachel gave birth to a child nine months later. Harry didn't want to know, but Rachel kept pressure on him to pay maintenance, and when he failed to pay, as he did on several occasions, she saw to it that he spent some time in prison.

With her husband obviously failing to support his child, there can be some sympathy for Mrs Dobkin, but this won't survive the fact that she was still harassing Harry, often creating ugly and abusive scenes in public, in 1941, when their offspring would have been around the age of twenty. In addition, Rachel Dobkin knew of something in Harry's past which allowed her to blackmail him.

At the time of the London Blitz, Rachel Dobkin disappeared, although no suspicion fell on Harry. He was doing his bit for the war effort at that time as a fire-watcher, although the police had reason not to rate him highly when he failed to report a fire in the crypt of a Baptist church in Kennington, when he had been on duty next door.

Time passed, and Rachel Dobkin had been missing for fifteen months when demolition workers found what they took to be the remains of an air-raid victim in the crypt. The police weren't sure, and Home Office pathologist Dr Keith Simpson was called in. He said that the bones were those of a woman who had been dead for a year or eighteen months. A clumsy attempt had been made to remove all identifiable parts of the body. The head had been severed from the body, by hand and not a bomb, but the killer had foolishly left it behind. By the use of dental records, and the presence of an untreated fibroid growth, the mutilated body was identified as being that of Rachel Dobkin. A blood spot, so minute that it was difficult to discern, was found on the voice-box, and further examination proved that the woman had been strangled.

An astute policeman looked up the file on Harry Dobkin's failure to report a fire in that crypt, and he was questioned. Arrested and charged with the murder of his wife, Dobkin, a man who had been persecuted by a shrew of a woman, did not go for a plea of manslaughter, neither did he offer much in mitigation.

On 27 January 1943, Harry Dobkin, aged forty-nine, was hanged at Wandsworth Prison.

If any killer could claim justification, it was Harry Dobkin. It was very different in the case of Leading Aircraftman Gordon Cummins. Aged twenty-eight, Cummins, an aircrew trainee in the RAF, was a latter-day Jack the Ripper. In the early hours of Sunday, 9 February 1942, the body of Evelyn Hamilton, a forty-two-year-old school-teacher was discovered in an air-raid shelter in Montagu Place, Marylebone. She had been strangled and her handbag, known to have contained the sum of eighty pounds, had been stolen, but there was no sign of sexual assault.

The next day the body of Evelyn Oatley, a thirty-five-year-old part-time actress and prostitute, was found in a room she rented in Wardour Street. Her throat had been cut, and her vagina savagely mutilated with a tin-opener. Clear fingerprints had been left both on the tin-opener and on a mirror in the room. Pathologist Bernard Spilsbury examined the woman's body and gave the opinion that she had been strangled before her throat had been cut.

On the following day, Tuesday, forty-three-year-old Margaret Lowe was strangled with a stocking in her flat in Gosfield Street in the West End. Her body, which had been mutilated with a razor blade, was discovered some time later by her fourteen-year-old daughter.

On Wednesday of the same week, at a hotel not far from the air-raid shelter where Evelyn Oatley had been killed, Doris Jouannet, who also called herself Doris Robson, a thirty-two-year-old, was found dead. She had also been strangled with a stocking, and her genitals were horribly cut about.

The news that a sadistic maniac was on the loose terrified the prostitutes of London. One who could consider herself fortunate was Margaret Hayward, who was picked up by a man in a pub close to Piccadilly Circus on Friday of that week. She was being throttled in a dark doorway when her attacker was interrupted by a delivery boy doing his rounds. The man fled, but left behind his gas mask, on the back of which was marked RAF No. 5259878. The police had a definite lead, but before they could act on it, another woman was attacked.

She was Mrs Mulcahy, or Kathleen King, who lived in Southwick Street, Paddington, and when she was approached while street-walking, she took the 'john' to her flat in a taxi. Once there he gripped her by the throat with both hands and squeezed. But he had no easy victim here. The prostitute screamed and kicked. Panicking, the man gave her an extra five pounds on top of what he had already paid, and ran off.

On Sunday, a week after what was then believed to be his first victim had been discovered, Gordon Frederick Cummins was arrested in his billet in St John's Wood. Superintendent Cherrill of Scotland Yard found a silver cigarette case belonging to Evelyn Oatley, together with other items stolen from his victims, in Cummins' possession.

It was likely that Cummins was linked with two unsolved murders – that of Maple Church, aged nineteen, who had been found dead on a bomb site near Euston Station in October 1941, and Mrs Humphries, whose body had been discovered in Gloucester Crescent near Regents Park.

At the Old Bailey he was charged with the murder of Evelyn Oatley (aka Nita Ward). Cummins refused to admit to any of the crimes, but the evidence, including the clear fingerprints left in his victim's room, was enough to convict him. The trial didn't come up to the usual Old Bailey standard, however. While Superintendent Cherrill was on the stand giving evidence about the fingerprints found on the tin-opener, the photograph of an impression left at the scene of one of the other murders was mistakenly passed to the jury.

This jury was discharged and a new trial ordered. All this meant for Gordon Cummins was some more time on earth, for he was found guilty and sentenced to death. Cummins appealed, pointlessly, and was hanged, during a fierce air-raid, at Wandsworth Prison on 25 June 1942.

This trial was one in a tightly packed schedule at the Old Bailey. The strain was too much for Lord Chief Justice Hewart, who was forced to retire through ill health. He was replaced by Lord Caldecote, who, as Attorney-General, had led in the doubtful Bywaters–Thompson case, and who would, a few years later, together with Mr Justice Humphreys and Mr Justice Lynskey, make up the Court of Criminal Appeal that would hear the appeal of William Joyce.

Regarded by most of those around him as inferior to his predecessor, Caldecote was a more compassionate man. Possibly the fact that he achieved little, not even recognition, during his six years of office, was due to his long spells of incapacity due to poor health. At these times, Mr Justice Humphreys, well into his seventies, wizened and withered, yet still as sharp as a tack, deputised for him.

It was said at the time, and has been said since, that the Old Bailey in its hour of need lacked good leadership. Nevertheless, the show went on, as it were, with two young murderers, Sammy

Dashwood and George Silverosa, passing through the court system to the gallows.

Thursday was early-closing day in Shoreditch, and as pawn-broker Leonard Moules, aged seventy-one, came out of his shop to put the shutters up on 30 April 1942, the two ex-Borstal boys were waiting. Dashwood, twenty-two, and Silverosa, one year his senior, had eaten a midday meal in a Bethnal Green café, where Dashwood had covertly shown Silverosa a .45 revolver and announced his intention of 'doing a job'. Silverosa went along with the idea.

Following the old man when he went back into his shop, they beat him about the head mercilessly, using the handgun as a club. They then robbed the safe, inside which they left a clear palm print. Leonard Moules died nine days later in Bethnal Green Hospital, not having regained consciousness.

A police investigation found a soldier who had seen two men with a gun in the café on the day of the fatal assault on the old pawnbroker. The soldier said that, to the best of his recollection, one of the men had been named Sam, the other George.

Their Borstal records meant that Dashwood and Silverosa were known to the police, who set out to look for them. The two may have been good pals when everything was going all right, but it was very different when the chips were down. The police found George Silverosa first, and he at once admitted to the robbery, but said that the violence had been done by Sammy Dashwood. The palm print on the inside of the safe belonged to Silverosa.

At the Old Bailey the attitude of the brutal pair, who had killed without compunction, showed that they had served an apprenticeship of callousness in Borstal. They were hanged at Pentonville Prison on 12 December 1942.

Soldiers charged with crimes at the Old Bailey, at a time when their comrades were fighting and dying on the front-line, were viewed with contempt. Many people connected with the courts had lost a loved one in battle, with two judges, Mr Justice Hodson and Mr Justice Cassels, each having lost a son on active service. Yet this undoubted animosity did not buckle the wheels of justice, as the case of soldier Dennis Leckey confirms.

Leckey, who served with the Royal Artillery, looked the part of a war hero. The young gunner was a fine physical specimen, and as handsome as any film star. He was charged with the murder of redheaded Caroline Trayler, a pretty and promiscuous cinema usherette from Folkestone. Deprived of 'love' because her husband was serving in North Africa, Caroline, who was just eighteen years of age, was easy game.

On the evening of Whit Sunday, 13 June 1943, Caroline finished work at the cinema and went for a drink in the Mechanic's Arms. Leckey was there in uniform, and he began a conversation with her. After a while she told him she must leave because she had a date, but Leckey persuaded her to stay with him. They left when the public house closed at 10 p.m., and were seen together in the nearby streets by three separate people.

That was the last time Caroline Trayler was seen alive. The following Thursday a policeman found her body lying face down on the floor of a small, disused shop. She had been strangled soon after violent sexual intercourse had taken place. Death had occurred late on the previous Sunday evening.

Identifying Caroline was no problem, but all the police could discover about her companion was that he was a soldier in an area, a world, at that time, filled with soldiers.

A tour of the district's military establishments took the police to a camp at Acrise, some five miles out from Folkestone. There they found that Gunner Dennis Edmond Leckey had gone absent without leave the day after Caroline's body had been found. Leckey had taken with him the paybooks of gunners Melia and Latham, together with a number of leave passes. A police watch was kept on his Manchester home, but he was able to pay his wife a visit and get away without being noticed.

When the landlady of the Mechanic's Arms was shown a photograph of Leckey, she instantly identified him as the man who had been with Caroline Trayler on Whit Sunday evening. Police nationwide were asked to look out for him, but, as so often happens, it wasn't the cleverness of the police but the stupidity of the criminal that resulted in the capture of Leckey. A Metropolitan

Police constable named Briggs was called to a public house close to Marble Arch, where a man had stolen an American soldier's wallet. The man gave the name of Latham, and had a paybook in that name. But Briggs recognised Leckey and took him into custody.

When officers from the Kent County Constabulary arrived at Marylebone police station, Leckey admitted being with the girl on the night of her death, but refused to say more until he could have the advice of a solicitor.

It was later learned that Leckey had been with a soldier named Knight on Whit Sunday. They split up when Leckey had met Caroline, agreeing to meet up again at eleven o'clock to get back to the camp at the proper time. Leckey failed to keep that appointment. Late that night he met a young WAAF officer walking along the road to Acrise, and carried her bag for her until they parted. Arriving back in camp late, he told an unusually obliging sergeant of the guard that he had met a girl, and his late return wasn't reported.

Leckey appeared before Mr Justice Singleton at the Old Bailey on 19 September 1943. Scientific evidence was produced to the court by Dr Davidson, Director of the Metropolitan Police Laboratory at Hendon. He had compared pubic hairs cut from the dead girl's body with a short length of hair found on Leckey's trousers. The hairs were of similar texture, thickness and auburn colour. Any defence planned for Leckey must have been shaken when Dr Keith Simpson, the pathologist who had examined Caroline's body, said that some rust-coloured wool fibres he had taken from under the girl's fingernails were identical to the fibres of the shirt Leckey had worn on the night of the murder.

A total of thirty-four witnesses gave evidence, testifying in the main to his movements while AWOL. Among other things, he had slept with a woman he had met at a railway station, convincing her that he was a sergeant-pilot in the RAF, and had stolen two wallets and a watch from two US soldiers he had shared a room with after passing himself off as an American.

In the witness box Leckey said that after leaving the Mechanic's Arms, Caroline Trayler had agreed to having sexual intercourse, and had actively co-operated in an alleyway between two houses. They had parted on good terms. He explained that he was late back to camp because he had been sick from mixing drinks that evening. The next morning he was depressed at having been unfaithful to his wife for the first time, and letting down his two children. He ran off from the camp with the intention of going home to confess his infidelity to his wife. He had stolen the paybooks, some with money in them, for various reasons.

These, and the other thefts, seemed to be out of character. Leckey had a clean record up to that time. Having joined the Territorial Army in May 1939, he had been called up two days before the war began.

On the debit side of his testimony was the fact that his wife could only learn from him that he had been unfaithful, and therefore there was no urgency to tell her. If he was so distraught over the breaking of his marriage vows, why did he then spend a night in bed with Mrs Woolley, the woman he had travelled to Birmingham with on a train?

He said that on the Saturday evening of his absence, he was returning home from his mother-in-law's with his wife, when he had seen a police car outside his house. He had run off to the London Road railway station, where he had slept the night in the waiting room before catching a train south. Had he told his wife about having had intercourse with Caroline Trayler, which was his purpose for going home without a pass? Leckey admitted that he hadn't. His intention was to go back to camp, but when he saw a newspaper with his photograph on the front page as wanted in connection with Caroline's murder, he had panicked completely.

Leckey was the sole witness for the defence, and his counsel, J.D. Casswell, was left to make a closing speech that, considering the evidence against Leckey, was little more than an exercise in futility.

There could be little doubt of Dennis Leckey's guilt, which must have been clear to the judge, but in his summing-up, Mr Justice Singleton three times laid emphasis on the fact that when cautioned and arrested, Leckey had replied. 'I do not wish to say anything until I have seen someone, a solicitor.' Leckey had, in fact, exercised the right to remain silent that is included in the police caution. But the judge, rudimentarily wrong in law, had commented to the jury that if Leckey hadn't committed the murder, why hadn't he replied to the police 'I did not murder the girl; when I left her she was all right'?

The jury, being laymen, were not aware of this blunder by Mr Justice Singleton. After half an hour they delivered a verdict of guilty, and Leckey was sentenced to death.

At the Court of Criminal Appeal two months later, the Lord Chief Justice, Viscount Caldecote, said there was a great deal of evidence on which the jury, properly directed, could have convicted Leckey, but the remarks by Singleton on the accused man's silence were a misdirection. The appeal was upheld.

A lucky Dennis Leckey walked from the Appeal Court a free man, saved from the gallows by a judge who had made three successive slips of the tongue.

Another serviceman in serious girl-trouble in those middle years of the war was Private August Sangret, a French-Canadian. Sangret, aged thirty, became friendly with Joan Wolfe, a teenage runaway who spent time with soldiers from nearby training camps. She lived rough on Hankley Common close to Godalming in Surrey, and Sangret had used his experience, or instinct, as a descendant of Cree Indians, to build wigwams for her out of branches and grass. This had Joan known to most people in the area, including soldiers and the police, as the 'Wigwam Girl'.

True love, or whatever it was between the Cree Indian and the English girl, mustn't have run smoothly, for on 7 October 1942, soldiers on a training scheme on the Common discovered a shrivelled arm protruding from an earth mound on some high ground. The police were called to discover that the arm was attached to a decomposed body, which was swiftly identified as that of Joan Pearl Wolfe.

Sangret was the immediate suspect. The girl had been killed some four hundred yards from where the corpse had been found and her body dragged to the hilltop for burial in keeping with Cree tradition. Just before being questioned by the police, Sangret hid a clasp-knife with an unusual hooked tip, which, when discovered, a pathologist later told the court had to be the weapon with which the girl was stabbed before being bludgeoned about the head and killed.

No real motive for the killing was ever established, but forensic evidence proved the guilt of August Sangret. Even so, the jury deliberated for two hours before returning a verdict of guilty which, surprisingly, was accompanied by a recommendation for mercy. This was not taken up by the Home Office, and Sangret was hanged at Wandsworth Prison on 29 April 1943.

A wartime case that was a threat to Anglo-American relations was dubbed 'The Cleft Chin Murder' by the press due to an unusual facial feature of the victim, taxi-driver George Edward Heath.

The story begins with Private Karl Gustav Hulten, a twenty-two-year-old American serving in England with the 501st Parachute Regiment, United States Army. From Massachusetts, where he had a wife and child, Hulten was Swedish by birth, going to America with his mother as a young child. It is a story that demonstrates the incredible laxness of the US Army that permitted Hulten, absent without leave for several weeks, to drive around Britain in a stolen ten-wheel US Army truck, calling in at various camps to fill the petrol tank when it was running low, with no questions asked.

Carrying out various robberies, Hulten made Hammersmith in London his 'headquarters', sleeping there at night in the stolen truck. He was one of the frustrating type of liar who always attaches his lies to something of the truth, so that what he has to say cannot be totally ignored. He was dressed as a US Army officer in a Hammersmith café where he met eighteen-year-old Elizabeth Marina Jones, an out-of-work striptease dancer who used the professional name of Georgina Grayson. She was to become 'Bonnie' to his 'Clyde' in a partnership that went on a crime spree and ended in murder.

She was so deeply attached to her father that when he was called up into the army she left home to hitch-hike to his camp. When she was brought back home her mother took her to a magistrates' court to complain that the girl was out of control. An order was made, and the girl who had gone in search of love from her father was abandoned to an approved school, one step removed from a Borstal institution, by her mother. On leave from the school at the age of sixteen, she married an older man, a soldier, with the approval of her relatives. This had nothing to do with love, or whatever it is that leads to matrimony, but was a disastrous move by the girl to avoid going back to the approved school, which didn't accept married women. Her new husband was violent to her on their first night, and they parted.

The story has been spiced up with claims that there was a sexual relationship between her and Hulten, and a film that romanticised their story had the fact that they were lovers as its theme. In truth, Hulten, who believed that back home he had been a gangster acquainted with Al Capone, and who carried a US Army issue revolver in England, was probably incapable of performing at that time. On the occasion that it did cross his mind when he was sharing Jones's room with her, he was put off by the ugly rash on her lower abdomen. The rash was responsible for her redundancy as a stripper.

On their first meeting Hulten asked Jones if she would like to come for a ride. Expecting an officer like him to have a car at best, or a jeep at worst, she accepted the invitation, agreeing a place and a time they would meet later that evening. Hulten didn't keep the appointment, and Jones was walking unhappily back to her room when a huge truck pulled up beside her and he called, 'Hi!'

This wasn't the kind of transport she had expected, but Elizabeth Jones climbed up into the cab nevertheless. Hulten drove them through the semi-deserted streets of blacked-out London to take the road to Reading. It was a great adventure for the girl, who was thrilled when Hulten told her he was a paratrooper. When she said that she would 'like to do something dangerous', Hulten surprised her with the information that he had been a gangster in America, and was now part of a London gang.

The American, boosted by her interest in him, bragged: 'I'm on my way now to hold up a hotel near Maidenhead.'

When they passed a girl on a bicycle, and Hulten stopped the truck to walk back, knock the cyclist down and rob her, Jones assumed that this was just a small bonus along the way to robbing the hotel. When he was back in the truck and they were once more on their way to Reading, she was so excited that when they pulled up outside of a small hotel near Maidenhead, she asked in awe, 'Is this the hotel you are going to rob?'

'No,' Hulten shook his head, wondering how to save face in a situation bravado had got him into. Knocking a defenceless girl off a bike was about his limit. 'I think we are being watched. We'd better not carry on.'

He drove a disappointed Jones, who preferred her middle name of Marina when she was not being called 'Georgina', home on that Tuesday night, but called for her again in the truck on Thursday. Hulten drove to the West End, telling Marina that he was going to rob a taxi-driver. He followed a cab until it stopped, then jumped down and pointed his pistol through the window at the driver. But Hulten's crimes were never well planned, and this one had two defects. First, the driver had just come on duty and had little money on him, and secondly he had a US Army officer for a passenger. The officer shouted, Hulten took off like a scared rabbit, clambered up into the truck and drove away.

Recovering from that failure, he used the truck to follow a prostitute wearing a fur coat, intending to rob her of it. But the street-walker picked up a client and went off, the coat Hulten had prized going with her.

Giving up on the West End, Hulten headed the truck towards Reading once more. He stopped the truck beside a girl struggling along carrying a suitcase.

The girl was from Bristol, and had come to London to stay with a man she believed wanted her. But the girl's and the man's interpretation of 'wanting' differed. When she arrived he threw her straight out, a reaction probably caused by the fact she was having her period at the time. Having discovered there was no train back home that night, the girl was alone and frightened in the capital.

'Where are you heading?' the American called down to her from the lorry.

'Bristol,' the girl replied.

'We can take you as far as Reading, and you'll get a train easily from there,' Hulten offered.

The relieved girl saw this as the end of a nightmare. Given confidence by the presence of another woman in the truck, she climbed in.

She suspected nothing when Hulten stopped the truck in a deserted place between Maidenhead and Reading, close to the waters of the River Thames, complaining bitterly that they had a flat tyre. All three got out and Hulten, announcing that he would have to change a rear wheel, asked Marina to fetch an iron bar from the back of the lorry. When he had the bar he caught the unsuspecting Bristol girl a vicious blow across the head with it. Although stunned, she was still conscious to some extent, so Hulten grabbed her throat and half-throttled her until she blacked out.

Marina went through the unconscious girl's pockets and robbed her of all the money she had – just five shillings. They then dragged the girl, who was bleeding badly from the head, down to the river-bank and dumped her half in and half out of the water. There they abandoned her, driving off with their erstwhile passenger's suitcase and handbag.

Fortunately, the girl was found and taken to hospital, where she recovered.

Hulten and Jones spent most of the rest of the day in her room going through the contents of the suitcase they had stolen. Apparently he had abandoned the stolen truck that he had used for weeks, due to it having a flat tyre. He went out in the afternoon, returning at half past one the next morning to say, 'Come on, let's go and get a taxi!'

Marina said later, 'I knew the meaning behind those words, that he wanted me to go with him to rob a taxi-driver.'

They waited in a Hammersmith doorway opposite Cadby Hall, and when a grey Ford private hire came along, Hulten sent Marina out into the road to shout, 'Taxi!'

The car stopped and Hulten came out to tell the driver to take them to the top of King Street, where Jones lived. The driver said this would cost ten shillings, an extortionate charge for so short a journey, but Hulten didn't argue. They then passed King Street, and the driver mentioned this, asking, 'Where do you want to go?'

'It's farther on. I don't mind paying more,' Hulten replied.

They drove on, out through Chiswick onto the Great West Road. Hulten leaned forward to instruct the driver to go slowly. A few hundred yards further on he said, 'We'll get out here.'

Having previously heard a click and seen the automatic in Hulten's right hand, Marina knew that he was about to scare the driver into giving them money. As the driver stretched back over his seat to reach for the handle of the near-side back door of the car, there was a bang and a bright flash. The driver flopped sideways, moaning, and Hulten got out and went to the front of the car, pushing the driver over into the passenger seat, and getting behind the wheel.

Hulten drove the car away, ordering Jones to go through the driver's pockets. She leaned over the back of the seat and did so. Among the items she found was an identity card with the name George Edward Heath. Then Hulten stopped the car on some open ground. Pushing the driver out into a ditch, he turned the car and drove back toward London. Marina found the bullet on the floor of the car and passed it to Hulten. He then got her to drive while he went through the driver's property, tossing what he didn't want out of the car window.

Leaving the car in the park at the rear of Hammersmith Broadway, they went to Marina's room. She was in a state because she knew that the taxi-driver was dead, but Hulten took an it's-all-in-a-day's-work-for-a-gangster attitude.

The following morning, 7 October 1944, an electrician's apprentice named John Jones found George Edward Heath's wallet, identity card and other items on the grass verge of the Great West Road just outside Staines. The boy took them to the nearest police station. An hour later an auxiliary firemen taking a shortcut home from night duty found the body of a man lying in a ditch just off the same road.

In a short time the police had identified the body as that of George Heath. It was determined that he had been shot from behind, the bullet passing right through him to exit at the front of the body. Paralysis would have occurred within thirty seconds of the shooting, and death within fifteen minutes.

The marks on the verge showed that a car had driven up on it for the body to be thrown out, and the police discovered that Heath had been driving a private hire car that had been reported as missing. The car was a grey Ford V8 saloon, with the registration number RD8995. This was broadcast to all police forces with the hope that finding the car would possibly lead to the killer.

At eight o'clock in the evening of Monday, 9 October, PC William Waters saw the car parked in Lurgan Avenue, a turning off Fulham Palace Road. His torch, which had illuminated many odd sights in the black-out, confirmed for him that the licence plate read RD8995. A stake-out was swiftly organised, and when a man came out of the house outside which the car was parked, the headlights of a police car were switched on, and he was apprehended as he was getting into the vehicle. In a style that fitted in with Hulten's American gangster image, he was pulled from the car and unceremoniously slammed face-first against a brick wall.

'Is this your car?' Inspector Read, the senior officer present asked.

'No,' came the reply in an American drawl.

The captive was wearing the uniform of a US Army officer. In one of his pockets was a loaded automatic pistol with the safety-catch off, while in another pocket was a six-round clip of ammunition. Taken to Hammersmith police station, Hulten gave his rank and name as Second-Lieutenant Richard John Allen of the 501st Parachute Regiment, US Army.

This meant that the prisoner came under the provisions of the United States of America (Visiting Forces) Act, 1942, that was agreed between John G. Winant, the US Ambassador to England and Anthony Eden MP in August of that year. A pre-eminent clause stated 'no criminal proceedings shall be prosecuted in the United Kingdom before any court of the United Kingdom against a member of the military or naval forces of the United States of America (subject to certain exceptions)'. As will later be explained, Karl Gustav Hulten was the only GI in the Second World War to be an exception.

But initially the Metropolitan Police had to abide by that Act and Hulten was passed into the custody of the Criminal Investigation Department, United States Army, where he was interrogated by Lieutenant Earl de Mott.

Hulten continued his disregard for the truth, first saying that he had found the car abandoned close to a camp at Newbury on Sunday afternoon. Then he changed the story to say that he had stolen the vehicle from a Hammersmith car park the morning before his arrest. He also had two versions of his movements on the night of the murder. In the first he claimed that he had been sleeping in a truck outside Newbury, and in the second, which he insisted was the true account, he had spent the night in Hammersmith with a girl named Georgina Grayson. He offered to show de Mott where the girl lived.

With a US Army Escort, Lieutenant de Mott, and two British police inspectors, Hulten led the way to a drab-looking house in King Street, Hammersmith, where he pointed out the window of Georgina Grayson's room. This was around noon, but when the police went to the room they found the girl still in bed. She was taken to the police station and questioned. There she revealed that she had given Hulten only her stage name, and told the police her real name. She had no need to feel guilty about fooling Hulten with her name, for the police discovered that she knew the young GI as 'Ricky Allen'. The policemen from both sides of the Atlantic realised, with some trepidation, that they were looking into a dream world created by Hulten, who lived there with Elizabeth Jones. But there was nothing at that time to connect her with the Heath murder, and she was allowed to return home.

Releasing the girl brought the police some amazing luck. She met a friend who was a War Reserve policeman, who remarked that she looked tired and worn. Marina's reply at first said nothing that she hadn't told the police, which was that she knew the man involved in the murder and was aware that he couldn't have done it because he was with her all of that Friday night. Then she make the mistake of remarking: 'If you had seen somebody do what I have seen done you wouldn't sleep at night.'

The War Reserve policeman reported this at once, and Inspector Albert Tansil paid a return visit to Jones in her room, where she greeted him with an honesty she hadn't previously shown, saying, 'I'm sorry I told you lies at the police station. I'll tell you the truth now.'

Tansil took her back down to the station where she gave a full account of how she had met Hulten, and the series of petty but often brutal crimes they had committed together. She concluded by reciting the facts of the shooting of the taxi-driver, saying that when she and Hulten returned to her room she had said, 'He's dead, isn't he?' Hulten had answered 'Yes', and she had exclaimed, 'That's cold-blooded murder then, why did you do it?' Hulten's reply was like a line straight out of a gangster movie: 'People in my profession haven't the time to think what they do.'

The British police took a long and detailed statement from the girl, which was then handed to de Mott, who used it for further interrogation of Hulten. The accused American admitted that Marina's statement was correct, but he showed a vindictiveness towards her that would alter the procedure that had existed up until then in the United Kingdom during that war.

Normally, Hulten would have been court-martialled and Jones brought before a British criminal court. But the attitude Hulten had shown toward Marina made the English and American authorities recognise the advantage of having them tried together. It was anticipated, and later proved to be correct, that the two accused would condemn each other. Home Secretary Herbert Morrison was asked for, and granted, permission for Hulten and Jones to be tried together.

Hulten had made a statement to the police saying that he had at no time intended to harm the taxi-driver, but merely to 'shoot through the car' (an Americanism for firing a pistol in a cab to frighten the driver into handing over his takings). He stated that Jones had hailed George Heath's car in Hammersmith without any prompting from him, adding verbally, 'I would not have been here but for the girl. If it had not been for her I wouldn't have shot Heath.'

While in custody, Marina did her own share of sniping by asking to see the police inspector in charge of the case, telling him, 'I merely wanted to tell that I lied to you because Ricky threatened me.'

Jones wrote Hulten a letter from Holloway Prison on 9 December, saying that if she was convicted it would kill her mother, and continuing with:

> So you see, Ricky, you must tell the truth . . . Don't you think I have suffered enough, being in Holloway on remand only? You promised me in court you would tell the whole truth. Do not go back on your word, Ricky.
>
> What the police have against me is going through the man's pockets. Had you not ordered me to do so, I could never have done it. But as my own life was in danger, I did so. I could not believe you had done it, Ricky. You know the condition I was in for hours afterwards – I was dazed, and still you threatened me, even when you knew I was too scared to go to the police.
>
> And there is another thing you must tell the police, as you promised, the truth about the body. I did not help you carry him to the ditch. You know that. Ricky, for God's sake tell the truth. You and God are the only two who know of my innocence. Half of this case is fresh to me. The gun, for instance – I did not know it was stolen . . . I did not know you were married and had a child. I did not know you had deserted the Army.
>
> Why did you do it, Ricky, and why have you got me into this? You are making me pay for a nightmare which I can't believe has really happened . . . If you have any respect, and honour, or pride, left, you will speak the truth, Ricky.
>
> Sincerely,
>
> Georgie

Marina didn't know at that time that Hulten had had an association with another girl in the six weeks or so that he had been on the run.

This was Joyce Cook, a young assistant in a bakery shop, who was totally ignorant of the fact that Hulten was absent without leave. He had, in fact, absconded from the stockade in his camp, where he had been placed for a minor military offence. It could be speculated that Hulten had deliberately first gone against authority, then absent without leave, to avoid going to France and into combat with his unit. His pretend heroics in England, with his victims always unarmed, often female, were certainly preferable to the real thing.

The trial of Hulten and Jones commenced on Tuesday, 16 January 1945, in Court No. 1 at the Old Bailey. There was already an outcry in the United States, with protests going as high as the President. The American people didn't take kindly to one of their boys being judged in a British court.

Newspapermen came from the United States to report the case, swelling the already crammed ranks of British journalists. A newspaper had paid the fare from Wales of the parents of Elizabeth Marina Jones so they could offer their daughter moral support by being in court.

The judge was the tetchy Mr Justice Charles, while L.A. Byrne and Gerald Howard prosecuted for the Crown. Defending Hulten were John Maude KC and T.K. Edie, while appearing for Jones were Mrs Lloyd Lane and J.D. Casswell.

The first morning was largely taken up with the opening speech of the prosecution, then the jury was locked away in a room for the afternoon while legal arguments were settled. Most important of these was Maude's attempt to persuade the judge that Hulten's statement not be tendered in evidence because the accused man complained that Lieutenant de Mott had subjected him to 'third-degree' methods to obtain it. Justice Charles refused with the words: 'I tell you frankly I do not believe that man.'

Although the jury wasn't in court to hear Hulten condemned in such a way before the trial had really begun, the newspaper journalists were. The jury was able to read the unfortunate remarks of the judge in the morning papers before the second day of the trial began.

The evidence for the prosecution lasted for two and a half days, which built up the atmosphere so that there was a hushed air of expectancy when Elizabeth Jones took the stand. It was strongly rumoured that she was a prostitute, and she emphatically denied this. Her short, violent marriage had never been consummated, and both Hulten and she had affirmed that no intimacy had ever occurred between them. Marina admitted sleeping with one man, a Canadian flying-officer who piloted a bomber plane. They were very close but, shortly before she had met Hulten, her lover had not returned from a bombing raid. He was reported killed, and she was devastated.

At the commencement of her time in the witness box she was so nervous that even her own counsel couldn't hear her replies. She was asked by her representatives to speak up, and Justice Charles brusquely ordered her to do so. The judge interrupted so many times that he came close to cross-examining the prisoner. As she gained some slight confidence, she reiterated that she had been under threat from Hulten, and was frightened of him.

When he testified, Hulten stated for the first time that Marina had urged him to go out and rob a taxi-driver. When he refused, she asked him to give her the gun and she would go alone. He told the court that the only reason he had the gun in his hand when they reached the Great West Road was because the 'jauncing around' in the moving car had pushed it out of its place in the belt of his trousers.

Changing the story of the shooting, having told de Mott that he had deliberately fired the gun to intimidate the driver, Hulten told the court: 'After we got to the roundabout I told him where we wanted to stop. The driver of the car stopped, and, as I was getting up, my arm, my right arm, was leaning on the arm-rest on the right side of the car. As he stopped he reached over the back to open the door, and as he was reaching over the back to open the door, Miss Jones was up, and I started to get up. At the same time my right sleeve caught on something on the right-hand side of that door. What it was I don't know, and as I went to go the door just jerked me and the gun went off at that time.'

Hulten insisted throughout that Jones was always a consenting party, and at times was the instigator. Yet although he went to great lengths to incriminate the girl in the dock, Hulten had admitted not telling her that he intended to use the pistol. Maybe this is indicative of his intelligence, for if Hulten had not continued to use the car involved in the shooting, even being stupid enough to park it outside the home of his second girlfriend of that time, where he was arrested, there is every likelihood that he would have got away with murder.

Mr Justice Charles did Marina no favours in his summing-up, constantly stressing to the jury that little reliance could be placed on her plea that she had been terrified of Hulten and had acted under the compulsion of threats from him. As to her complicity in the shooting, his direction was: 'Where two people concert and agree upon the commission of a felony, like robbery, that is a felony that must involve violence – for a man of thirty-four years of age does not allow his body to be stripped and pillaged without resistance – then both of these people are guilty of murder if death results in the way that I have indicated to you.'

The jury returned a verdict of guilty on Hulten, and one of guilty with a recommendation for mercy on Jones, who was led below sobbing. Both appealed to the Court of Criminal Appeal, and while this was happening there was a fight going on in the United States to have Karl Gustav Hulten, at the very least, brought home for the US judiciary to deal with. The people of America were appalled that a British judge could sentence an American subject to death.

There was outrage when it was eventually learned that, while the campaign to save Hulten had been in full swing in America, the British executioner, Albert Pierrepoint, had hanged him at Pentonville Prison at eight o'clock on the morning of 8 March 1945. Despite still being a serving soldier in the United States Army, Hulten chose not to wear his uniform when he took the short walk to meet the hangman.

There was little evidence of female solidarity in Britain at that time, for during the six weeks that Marina was in the condemned cell at Holloway, the women employees at a factory in Scotland threatened to strike if she was reprieved.

History doesn't record whether that threat was carried out when Marina was reprieved, just thirty-three hours from the time set for her execution.

Believing that a reprieve was another word for a pardon, Marina expected to leave Holloway Prison for home at once. But she had to serve a custodial sentence that lasted until 1954. On release from prison she changed her name and returned to live in her native Wales. She died relatively young. In what was a sad life from start to finish, her ultimate misfortune had been to meet the wrong man at the wrong time.

11. THE POST-WAR YEARS

The post-war period of the history of the Old Bailey must begin with the story of the suave, handsome killer Neville George Clevely Heath. This Walter Mitty with fangs lived in a make-believe world in which he used false names and bogus military ranks to be larger than life in order to attract women for his sadistic practices. As an officer in the RAF, he was twice court-martialled and then dismissed from the service for conduct prejudicial to good order and for unlawfully wearing military decorations. In spite of this he rose, under the name of Armstrong, to the rank of captain in the South African Air Force.

Did he know the truth, or was he completely befuddled by his own lies? At his trial for the brutal murder of thirty-two-year-old Margery Gardner, both a Broadmoor psychotherapist and a medical officer in the prison service were of the professional opinion that Heath was aware of what he was doing – but not aware that what he was doing was wrong.

Heath's own counsel perhaps made the best assessment when he told the jury that the accused wouldn't be taking the witness stand, adding: 'You probably wouldn't believe a word he said if he did.'

In the summer of 1946, 'Colonel' Heath booked himself into the Pembridge Court Hotel, Notting Hill, London, and in his room murdered Margery Simee Brownwell Gardner, an actress who was separated from her husband. Mrs Gardner's body had been horribly mutilated, plainly the work of a sexual maniac.

A statement issued by the police named Heath as a man they

wanted to include in their enquiry, and his strange state of mind was exhibited in a letter he wrote to them, in which he said he had lent his Pembridge Court Hotel room key to Margery Gardner as she had 'met an acquaintance with whom she was obliged to sleep'. The letter continued with a description of Mrs Gardner's companion, and ended with the advice that he could be contacted through the Personal columns of the *Daily Telegraph*, '. . . but at the moment I have assumed another name.'

In his book *A Lance for Liberty*, J.D. Casswell, who was to defend Neville Heath when he was eventually tried at the Old Bailey, makes two revelations – that Mrs Gardner was a masochist who enjoyed being whipped, and that this was not her first encounter with Heath. Casswell wrote: 'It is almost certain that a month before her death she had been with Heath to another hotel bedroom and had only been saved then from possible murder by the timely intervention of a hotel detective. She had been heavily thrashed, and Heath was standing over her in a fiendish fashion.'

Heath travelled to Bournemouth then, booking a room at the Tollard Royal Hotel in the name of Group Captain Rupert Robert Brooke. Sadly, his arrival in the seaside town coincided with that of twenty-one-year-old Doreen Marshall, a Middlesex girl who had been ill and had come to Bournemouth to convalesce. Miss Marshall checked in at the Norfolk Hotel, which was no great distance from the hotel where Heath was staying.

The first indication that the two had met came on 5 July, when the manager of Miss Marshall's hotel telephoned the manager of Heath's hotel to say that she had been missing since the previous Wednesday, and the last known of her was that she had ordered a taxi to take her to the Tollard Royal Hotel. Mr Ivor Relf, the joint manager, remembered that Group Captain Brooke had entertained a young lady to dinner on Wednesday evening. The following morning he politely enquired of Brooke if Miss Marshall had been his dinner guest on the previous Wednesday.

Denying this with a laugh, Heath said of his guest, 'Oh no, I have known that lady for a long time . . . '

Some fifteen minutes later, Heath, still using the name of Brooke, telephoned the police to say that he believed he could help with their enquiries. Soon after this, Doreen Marshall's concerned father and sister arrived at the police station in Bournemouth. Continuing his odd behaviour, Heath arrived at the police station at a quarter past five that evening, and met the missing girl's relatives, giving them, and the police, an account of his dinner-date: 'We left the hotel at 11.30 p.m., and sat on a seat overlooking the sea. We walked down the slope towards the Pavilion . . . Miss Marshall did not wish me to accompany her but I insisted on doing so – at least some of the way . . . '

Although the police had come under fierce criticism for not issuing a photograph of Heath to the press after the Margery Gardner murder, they had circulated one to police stations. At Bournemouth an astute detective constable named Souter was struck by the similarity between Group Captain Brooke and Colonel Heath. Strenuously denying that he was Heath, Brooke was held at Bournemouth to await the arrival of Metropolitan police officers. But he complained of feeling cold in the evening air.

This was a mistake on the part of Heath, for he was permitted, under police escort, to collect his sports jacket from the Tollard Royal Hotel. In the pocket of that jacket the Bournemouth police found a cloakroom ticket and the return half of a London–Bournemouth railway ticket, the latter subsequently being proved to belong to Doreen Marshall.

On Monday, 8 July, a Miss Evans was taking her dog for a walk in the Branksome Chine area of Bournemouth when she became puzzled by flies swarming heavily in one particular spot. She called her father who, with the missing girl in mind, alerted the police. They found the body of Doreen Marshall, naked apart from one shoe, but with a black dress and a yellow coat of the 'swagger' style fashionable at the time, thrown over it. Beads from a broken necklace were spread around. This spot was in a gorge leading down to the sea, and no more than two miles distant from either the Norfolk or the Tollard Royal hotels. Miss Marshall had been bound and gagged, her throat cut and her body horribly mutilated.

Having been satisfied that they had arrested a murderer for

another police force, the Bournemouth police found that they, too, wanted Heath for murder. In his hotel room they had found a knotted handkerchief that was stained by earth and blood.

In London Heath was picked out at an identity parade as Mrs Gardner's companion on the night she had died, by the receptionist at the Pembridge Court Hotel and by a taxi-driver who had been hailed by Heath outside the Panama Club, where he had been dancing with Margery Gardner. Shortly afterwards he was identified by a jeweller to whom he had sold Miss Marshall's watch, and the pawnbroker with whom he had pledged the dead girl's ring.

Many guests and employees at the Tollard Royal Hotel averred that he was the man they had known as Group Captain Brooke. The police at Bournemouth used the cloakroom ticket found in Heath's jacket to redeem his luggage. In a suitcase they found a riding-whip, the criss-cross thongs of which corresponded with the lash marks found on Margery Gardner's body.

At the end of July 1946, the twenty-nine-year-old Heath was charged with the murders at West London Court, and committed for trial at the Old Bailey on a charge of having murdered Mrs Margery Gardner.

Heath's trial at the Old Bailey began on 24 September 1946 with Mr Justice Morris as the judge. There was so much evidence against Heath that his guilt couldn't be doubted. Even he was prepared to plead guilty, but his counsel persuaded him against doing so. Married in February 1942 to the daughter of a well-known Johannesburg family, Heath, who was divorced by his wife Elizabeth in 1945, had been in Borstal and, though it couldn't be disclosed in court, had a history of sexual violence.

Giving evidence at the trial was Miss Yvonne Symonds, who was aged nineteen and must have considered herself to be the luckiest person in the world. Meeting Heath at a dance in Chelsea on 15 May that year, she had slept with him in Room 4 at the Pembridge Court Hotel, the very room in which, just four nights later, he murdered and mutilated Margery Gardner. In Worthing, her home town, with Heath after the Gardner murder, she actually discussed the murder with him. Why hadn't Yvonne Symonds suffered the same fate as the other two women who had been with Heath at that time? That question will forever go unanswered.

Wanting to prove that Heath had been insane at the time he had killed Margery Gardner (the killing of Doreen Marshall being omitted because of the rule of law that only one murder can be included in an indictment), the defence employed Dr William Henry de Barque Hubert BA, MRCS, MRCP, without knowing that despite his impressive name and qualifications, the expert was himself a drug addict. His performance under cross-examination was described as 'appalling'.

It wasn't in the interest of the prosecution to have Heath declared insane, so they waited, ready to counter any medical evidence produced by the defence. Hubert was in something of a state in court, being prepared to say that Heath probably knew what he was doing when he had murdered Margery Gardner, but was so mentally abnormal that he thought it right to inflict cruelty because that was the only means by which he could obtain sexual satisfaction.

The defence decided to go for a plea of partial insanity, which the Homicide Act later brought into English law as the Scottish concept of 'diminished responsibility'. But it didn't work at that time and the defence had to accept what Heath had known all along – that he was on a loser.

During the trial, the move to have Heath proved insane had allowed the defence to refer to the murder of Doreen Marshall, and aspects of this killing were included in the judge's summing-up.

'The law of insanity is not to become a refuge for those who cannot challenge a charge that is brought against them,' said Mr Justice Morris, before going on to refer to the deliberate concealing of Doreen Marshall's body, which had been found under a rhododendron bush, Heath's denials of his real identity, and a ready explanation he had given for the return half of the railway ticket, and asking: 'Is that or is that not the mentality of a man whose mind is working so that he must have known what he did was wrong?'

The jury took only one hour to find Neville Heath guilty. No appeal was lodged, and he was executed at Pentonville Prison on 16

October 1946. In law Margery Gardner had been avenged, but Heath having paid the ultimate penalty was second-hand vengeance for Doreen Marshall, for whose death he had neither been charged nor stood trial.

*

A very different case that dominates that era, a veritable *cause célèbre*, has been written about so much, and is still being written about, that it is unnecessary to go into it at length here. On the night of 2 November 1952 Christopher Craig, aged sixteen and fascinated by gangsters as portrayed in Hollywood movies, and Derek Bentley, a mentally retarded and epileptic nineteen-year-old with the mental age of eleven, attempted a break-in at a confectionery warehouse in Tamworth Road, Croydon.

Three days previously, Niven Craig, Christopher's twenty-six-year-old brother, had been given twelve years' imprisonment for armed robbery. Following in his brother's footsteps, Christopher Craig was armed with a revolver and a knife. The illiterate Bentley, who had already earned himself a criminal record, had a brass knuckle-duster and a knife with him.

In a roof-top chase that followed when the police had been called, Bentley had been grabbed and held by a police officer. Craig had his gun out and Bentley is alleged to have shouted, though he constantly denied it, that now famous sentence: 'Let him have it, Chris!'

Craig fired several shots, one of which is said to have hit PC Miles between the eyes, killing him. Even this has been disputed, as apparently there were armed police present and several shots were fired. Whatever, at the Old Bailey, with the trial judge, Lord Goddard, continually interrupting witnesses as they testified, both Craig and Bentley were found equally guilty in law, the former, due to his age, being 'detained at Her Majesty's pleasure', and Derek Bentley sentenced to death.

A huge campaign was mounted to save Bentley from the hangman. Two hundred Members of Parliament pressed for a reprieve, which the Home Secretary refused to recommend. On the morning of 28 January 1953, when Derek Bentley walked to the gallows – crying all the way, it is alleged, although executioner Albert Pierrepoint denied that claim – an estimated crowd of five thousand people stood outside Wandsworth Prison, and the singing of the hymn 'Abide with Me' filled the air.

The campaign on behalf of Bentley wasn't stopped by his death, but given momentum. In one extreme incident a fourteen-year-old Salford girl whose hero was Bentley travelled down to Croydon in April of that year armed with a gun, a dagger, a knife and a razor-blade holder, carrying a handbag packed full of newspaper cuttings covering the execution. Her intentions were never discovered. Calling at the Bentley home, she was invited in and given a cup of tea, while Derek Bentley's father contacted the police. At Croydon Magistrates' Court the girl pleaded guilty to being in possession of a gun without a firearms licence.

Christopher Craig was released on licence after ten years, and in the wake of a special screening for MPs of the film *Let Him Have It*, which resulted in the Home Secretary ordering Scotland Yard to reopen the case, he appeared on television. In that programme Craig claimed that there had been a police conspiracy and that Derek Bentley had never said the words 'Let him have it, Chris!'

First Bentley's father kept up the pressure for a pardon for his son and when he died his daughter, Derek's sister, Iris, took over. Having reviewed the case, Home Secretary Kenneth Clarke published his findings on 1 October 1992, saying that although he would have recommended a reprieve at the time, he would not grant a posthumous royal pardon.

Iris Bentley has now died, but her own daughter has promised to carry on the fight to get Derek Bentley his long-awaited pardon.

It was in 1952 that Lord Goddard, the Lord Chief Justice, together with seventy-eight other judges, was awarded a tax-free salary raise of a thousand pounds a year. The eight thousand pounds that the Lord Chief Justice had been receiving up to then, was, despite having been fixed at that sum in 1851, the highest salary in the Supreme Court of England and Wales. Although the

Lord Chancellor was doing better with ten thousand pounds per year, four thousand of that came as salary as Speaker of the House of Commons.

The crime that led to the Old Bailey trial that produced the last double execution in Britain took place on the night of 9 March 1954. Kenneth Gilbert, aged twenty-one, and Ian Grant, aged twenty-four, set out to rob the Aban Court Hotel, Harrington Gardens, south London, where Gilbert worked as a porter. Both men lived in Harwood Road, Fulham.

They knew that fifty-five-year-old George Smart, the regular night porter, locked the front door of the hotel at midnight, so they gained entry through a coal cellar. When they came upon Smart in the servery, he put up a fight but they were able to overpower him. Tying his hands with his own tie, and his ankles with string, they gagged him before running off without touching the safe. All they gained from the raid was two pounds in cash and some cigarettes.

At a quarter to eight the following morning the hotel's head waiter found Smart. Although he had succeeded in getting his hands free, the porter had suffocated during the night.

Both Grant and Gilbert were totally inept criminals. On the day Smart was found dead, Grant told a workmate named Chapman that he and Gilbert had 'done a job the previous evening to get some cigarettes'. When the early editions of the London evening newsapers appeared carrying a report of the death of Smart, Gilbert told Chapman that he and Grant had 'done a man in'. As a result of this careless talk, and within 24 hours of the death of Smart, the police arrested Grant and Gilbert at their homes in Harwood Road, Fulham.

Coming up before West London magistrates, both Gilbert and Grant made statements admitting that they had hit Smart and tied him up. Consequently, when the trial of the two men began at the Old Bailey on 10 May, Mr Christmas Humphreys QC, prosecuting, told the court that even if Gilbert and Grant had not intended to kill the porter or cause him serious harm, if either of them had contemplated violence to further the robbery, then both were guilty of murder.

George Smart's injuries included a broken jaw, numerous bruises to his face caused by heavy blows, and bruises on the back of his head. The cause of death was asphyxia, caused by a gag. Both men stated that they had no intention of killing the night porter, and in the closing speeches for the defence, their counsel argued that at most this was a case of constructive murder, and they asked for a verdict of manslaughter to be returned. Surprisingly, although insisting that in law Grant and Gilbert were guilty of murder, Mr Christmas Humphreys made it plain that the Crown would not be opposed to a verdict of manslaughter.

The judge, Lord Goddard, didn't agree, and he told the jury that in his view the case was one of murder. Accepting this, the jury was out for just twenty minutes before coming back with a verdict of guilty with no recommendation to mercy.

As the sentence of death was passed, two prison warders had to support Grant as he came close to collapsing. The two men were hanged, side by side, by Albert Pierrepoint at Pentonville Prison on 17 June 1954.

This was the last double hanging in Britain. Following the Homicide Act 1957, when more than one prisoner was to be executed for the same crime, they would be hanged simultaneously at separate prisons. Double hangings often went horribly wrong, usually because of a collision at the drop.

In 1955, the era of the Teddy Boy with his quaint style of dress and grease-induced Elvis Presley hairstyle, rock'n'roll music, coffee bars and National Service, nineteen-year-old Londoner Donald Brown had an interest in all of those things. But Donald, of Chaplin Road, Wembley, had his problems. Called up at the age of eighteen, the army had placed him in the Royal Victoria Hospital at Netley, Hampshire, instead of putting him in a camp with other conscripts. He was an odd character of below-average intelligence, although he had a big-time attitude. When he did something wrong, which was often, he never showed the slightest remorse. After a medical report described him as having a psychopathic personality, he was quickly discharged.

Back in civilian life, Donald did a series of labouring jobs around

Willesden, while in the evenings he went to dances and chased after girls. His off-beat thinking including pondering on what it would feel like to stab someone. For a time he had considered trying it out by knifing a dog, but dismissed the idea because he was too fond of animals.

Yet he had only postponed finding out what using a knife would be like, and on 18 September 1955, Donald Brown was before Mr Justice Glyn-Jones at the Old Bailey. He was charged with having stabbed sixty-three-year-old Herbert Blades, who managed a small tobacconist's shop at 18 Hillside, Stonebridge, in Willesden, early in the afternoon of Saturday, 11 June 1955. Robbery was the motive, with forty pounds having been stolen, and the killer was known to be a Teddy Boy. Three days later Donald Brown was arrested in a hospital at Folkestone, where he had been taken after swallowing an overdose of aspirin.

Brown made a statement to the police that on the morning of the murder he had gone to visit a friend in Harlesden. 'I saw him in his bedroom,' Brown said, 'and told him that I was fed up with life in general. I told him that I was going to the shop and knife the old man in the back to get a few pounds to enjoy myself for a couple of days. He thought I was joking.

'We went for a walk and then to my place where I changed my shirt and put my duffel coat on. We came back to Hillside and had a cup of tea in the café opposite Reffells [the name of the owner over the tobacconist's door]. My mate then went home. He said, "I'll see you about two." When he had gone I went across the road into the shop. I knew Buster [Mr Herbert Sidney Blades] very well. I said, "Let's have a glass of beer."

'I was round the back of the counter with him. He went into the back room to wash his hands at the sink. I was behind him and let him have it with my bowie-knife. He didn't say nothing. I carried on sticking it in him. He was lying on the floor. I slung my duffel coat off and washed my hands. I tore a piece from a towel that was on the floor and wrapped it round my little finger.

'I stayed a couple of minutes and went into the shop where I knew the money was. It was in the tin behind the counter. I took a bundle of notes out and put 'em in my trouser pocket. I straightened myself up a bit and walked out of the shop. I said, "Goodbye, Buster!" and I shut the door.

'I then went round to my mate's house and I said, "Come to the pictures?" He said, "You haven't done what you said you'd do this morning?" I said, "Of course not." He said, "Your finger's bleeding pretty badly," and I said, "I've just cut it mucking about with my knife." On my way to the pictures I went into Boots and they done it up for me. I could see my mate thought I'd done it, and I told him not to worry.

'He went to search me and I told him to keep his hands off. He said, "I'll only go to the pictures with you." We went to a cinema in the Haymarket. The picture was called something about fire. I slung my knife under the seat. I told my mate I was going to get some new clothes and I left him in the pictures. I said, "I'll see you on Sunday night." I went to Shaftesbury Avenue and bought some new clothes. The man in the shop put my old clothes in a parcel for me. When I left the shop I threw the parcel away round the back of the shops in Charing Cross Road.

'I then went to Cecil Gee's shoe shop in Charing Cross Road and bought a pair of shoes. I told them to keep my old ones. I went and had a haircut in one of the side turnings in Shaftesbury Avenue. Then I went to a news theatre, and after to the Turkish baths in Russell Square. I stayed all night until twelve o'clock on Sunday.

'I then went to Tottenham Court Road and had some dinner, and after that I had a walk round to kill time until four o'clock. I then went to the Astoria Cinema in Charing Cross. I left there about ten to eight and went to the Lyceum Dance Hall in the Strand. I left there at about half past ten and went back to the Turkish baths.

'I left there at ten o'clock on Monday morning and caught a coach from Victoria to Folkestone. I got down at about two-thirty and walked around along the seafront. I booked a room at a hotel called Seaton House. I went out again and went on a boating lake. After that I went up to the cliff-top and sat down until about six o'clock. I then went to see a play called *The Gay Time*. I came out of there at ten o'clock and I went back to my room.

'I had seen the newspaper where it said that a Teddy Boy was wanted for questioning. I thought the other people would be reading about it. I got into bed. I had taken a cup of tea up with me. I then thought it was best to finish it. I put some aspirins I had bought into a glass. I thought, "Well, this is it," and knocked them back. Nothing happened at first and then I started to get a bit tired. I didn't want to cause an upset in the hotel, so I went downstairs.

'A man came up from the basement. I said to him, "Here's some money." I gave him seven pounds. I said, "I've killed for it and I'm going to die for it." He said, "Don't be silly." I said, "It's all right, I'll be gone in a few minutes." I felt weak. He took me downstairs and two men came in and took me away in a car to hospital. I made out nothing was wrong with me. The nurse wouldn't let me go to sleep. I said, "If I don't go now I'll go later, so why worry." The police came in later and took me to the police station.'

Mr Christmas Humphreys QC, who prosecuted, read this statement to the court. He added that the accused's friend in Harlesden said that in the cinema Brown had a thick wad of notes in his pocket, which he tried to pass off as a packet of crisps. He produced a knife and put it under the cinema seat after kissing it. When Brown had left the cinema his worried friend had lost no time in calling the police.

Detective Superintendent Webb told the Old Bailey that Brown had spent many years in institutions. He had never known either of his parents, but since his arrest the police had been successful in tracing his mother. Brown had two convictions, both for theft, in 1950 and 1951.

Probably wisely, Mr G.D. Roberts QC, who defended Donald Brown, didn't have him take the witness box, but he called Dr J.A. Hobson as an expert witness. In the doctor's opinion Brown was insane and did not know that what he had done was wrong. When he had interviewed the accused in September, Brown appeared to be calm and composed, but showed no remorse for what he had done. He claimed that his victim had made an improper suggestion, but Dr Hobson had dismissed that as a lie.

'I felt at last I was somebody,' Brown told the doctor when

relating how the newspaper reports of the crime had made him feel important.

Brown said that the thought of being hanged had excited him, but since he had been in prison he would prefer to go on living. His suicide bid at Folkestone was really a sham, in the opinion of Dr Hobson, no more than a bid by Brown to achieve the notoriety of being found guilty of stabbing the tobacconist to death. Electronic brain tests had shown Brown to be abnormal, and he was both emotionally and morally immature.

Mr Justice Glyn-Jones took this into account when summing-up, but stressed that being abnormal did not equal being insane, and Brown was sane in law.

After a short retirement of twelve minutes, the jury returned a verdict of guilty, adding a recommendation to mercy.

Brown kept his detached air of indifference when the judge sentenced him to death, saying, 'You have been properly convicted of the cold-blooded and cruel murder of a blameless old man.'

On 30 September 1955, just two weeks after he was sentenced, Brown was reprieved and sent to Parkhurst Prison on the Isle of Wight.

In the late 1950s and 1960s identical twins Ronald and Reginald Kray, together with older brother Charles, ran a violent London East End gang. Though they controlled many businesses and could afford to pay to have their dirty work done, the Krays liked to be involved. This was their undoing. Carrying out their own killing led to the Kray twins being sentenced to 30 years in prison when they appeared at the Old Bailey.

Other cases of violence in the 1960s were dealt with at the Old Bailey, including the murder of three Metropolitan police officers. Detective Sergeant Christopher Head, Detective Constable David Wombwell and PC Geoffrey Fox were having a much-needed quiet day on Friday, 12 August 1966. All three had been involved in the gruesome investigation involving a number of naked or partly clothed bodies of prostitutes being recovered from the Thames. As the case remained unsolved, and as the victims were prostitutes, it became known as the 'Jack the Stripper' inquiry. It was a most unpleasant series of crimes that affected even the most hardened policemen.

At three o'clock in the afternoon of that Friday, the three policemen were called upon to go to Marylebone to collect Detective Inspector Coote, who had been giving evidence there. In 'Q' Car Foxtrot Eleven, they left the Beaumont Arms in Uxbridge Road, where they had eaten lunch, and drove up Wood Lane to turn left into Western Avenue. As they approached Wormwood Scrubs Prison, along Braybrook Street, East Acton, they became suspicious of a battered Standard Vanguard estate car, and pulled it in for a routine check.

Driving the car was its owner, John Witney, a convicted petty thief of thirty-six years of age who was an unemployed lorry driver. With him was a partner in crime, hardman Harry Roberts, who had experienced jungle warfare while doing his National Service. Just out of prison after serving a four-year sentence, Roberts was put on edge by the car being stopped by the police. A third man, John Duddy, was the latest recruit of Witney and Roberts. Close to being an alcoholic, Duddy made up a threesome that used guns to frighten the rent collectors and staff of the betting shops they robbed. A canvas bag containing three guns was between the two front seats of the car.

The car had no tax disc on display, and Witney told DC Wombwell that he was waiting for an MOT certificate. Asking to see Witney's driving licence and insurance, Wombwell was making a note of the details while DS Head walked round to look at the rear of the car.

'Can't you give me a break?' Witney protested. 'I've just been pinched for this a fortnight ago.'

As Wombwell bent to reply to this through the driver's window, Roberts drew a gun and shot him through the left eye. Wombwell fell to the ground dead, and DS Head ran back to where PC Fox sat behind the wheel of the police car. Jumping out of the Standard Vanguard, Roberts and Duddy ran after the police sergeant, Roberts firing a shot but missing.

Head was attempting to crouch behind the police car when

Roberts fired another shot, hitting the sergeant in the back. Meanwhile Duddy, who had no record of violence, ran up to fire three shots through the window at PC Fox. One hit him in the left temple, and the policeman died instantly. Fox hadn't applied the handbrake of the police vehicle, and as he died his foot came up off the footbrake. This added to what was already a horrific scene, for the police car's rear wheels ran over Sergeant Head, who was dying, trapping him underneath.

Roberts and Duddy jumped back into the estate car and Witney reversed it down the road. Then, swinging the car round, he drove it away at speed. The Standard Vanguard startled a young couple who assumed there had been a breakout from the prison. They took the number, PGT 726, but soon realised they had been wrong about a prison escape when they came upon the bloody scene.

That was between three and half past in the afternoon. At nine o'clock that evening, the car number had enabled the police to take John Witney into custody. A description of the car was put out on both television and radio, and a man reported that it was parked outside a lock-up garage in Vauxhall.

The police found three .38 cartridges and Duddy's .38 gun on the back seat of the car. They charged Witney with the three murders. He confessed, naming Roberts and Duddy as the two who were really guilty of the crime. But that pair had split up and disappeared.

Several days later Duddy was arrested in his home town of Glasgow, and confessed to the shooting on his way back to London. The police called at the home of Mrs Margaret Perry, Roberts' common-law wife. He wasn't there, for he had bought camping gear in Tottenham Court Road and had reverted to his army days by living rough in Epping Forest.

In August the largest and most sustained manhunt in criminal history had begun. Roberts' photograph was released to the media, and 16,000 posters bearing his photograph were distributed. While the search went on, the three policemen were buried and Prime Minister Harold Wilson attended a memorial service held for them in Westminster Abbey.

The police were overwhelmed by information that was useless, and, possibly due to the thousand-pound reward on offer, there were more than six thousand sightings of Roberts. There could be no more delay, and the trial of Witney and Duddy was set down for 14 November at the Old Bailey.

But a gypsy, John Cunningham, came across Roberts living in a tent in Thorley Woods, Bishops Stortford. Whether or not Cunningham knew this was a wanted man, he had no reason to help the police. So Cunningham stayed quiet until a couple of days later when he was being questioned by the local police about another matter. He told them then.

The police surrounded the area, and although the campsite had been abandoned, Roberts gave himself up without a fight when found hiding in a disused aircraft hangar on the edge of Nathan's Wood.

With Roberts under lock and key, the trial of Witney and Duddy was held over so that they could be joined by Roberts in the Old Bailey on 6 December.

Before judge Mr Justice Glyn-Jones, and prosecuted by Sir Dingle Foot, the Solicitor-General, Witney and Duddy pleaded not guilty to all the charges, but Roberts pleaded guilty to the murder of DC Wombwell and DS Head, but not guilty of the fatal shooting of PC Fox.

All three were found guilty on all counts. Sentencing them to life imprisonment, Justice Glyn-Jones recommended that they should each serve a minimum of thirty years. All three men appealed, but their appeals were dismissed.

The three were 'lucky' in that they wouldn't be executed. For many years there had been a campaign to end capital punishment. One of the most energetic protesters was Mrs Violet Van der Elst, who held demonstrations against hanging outside prisons at the times of executions. She appeared to have been succcessful when the new Homicide Act received the royal assent in 1956. But murder during robbery was one of the few crimes for which the death penalty was retained in the new Act.

Mrs Van der Elst and others fought on. Finally, in 1965, the

Murder (Abolition of Death Penalty) Act declared that 'no person shall suffer death for murder'.

The last murderers to be hanged in Britain were Peter Anthony Allen and Gwynne Owen Evans. They were both hanged on 13 August 1964 at Walton Gaol and Strangeways Prison for the murder during robbery of John Allen West. Between that time and the passing of the above Act, others were condemned to death but reprieved.

The crimes of Roberts, Duddy and Witney were rightly regarded as abhorrent and, quite naturally, all sympathy was with the three dead officers and the forces of law and order. But six years later, the murder of a young homosexual prostitute and transvestite, Maxwell Confait, did neither the reputation of the police nor the image of the Old Bailey any good.

At close to half past one on the morning of Saturday, 22 April 1972, the fire brigade was called to 27 Doggett Road, Catford. The basement and ground floor were ablaze, and the fire was spreading rapidly upwards. In a locked, smoke-filled back bedroom, Station Officer Speed found Maxwell Confait's body. The police were called and arrived at a quarter to two, and divisional police surgeon Dr Angus Bain followed a quarter of an hour later.

Confait, who was of mixed race and in his twenties, had been asphyxiated by a length of flex having been tightened around his neck. There was no sign of a struggle in the room, and there were no fingerprints. The police doctor didn't follow the usual procedure of determining the time of death by taking the rectal temperature. Confait's profession and sexual inclinations, well known to the police, stopped the doctor from doing so, as it might interfere with a later post-mortem examination to look at the back passage for signs of recent sexual activity. When the pathologist, Dr James Cameron, came to the fire-ravaged house, he, too, avoided taking the rectal temperature for the same reason. He noted that the body was cool to the touch but that rigor mortis had only just begun.

The fire had been started deliberately, and the police interviewed Confait's landlord, a West Indian called Winston Goode, who had been the first person to discover the fire. Goode was a peculiar fellow who had first met, and become friends with, Maxwell Confait in the Black Bull at Lewisham in 1970. Goode began to dress in women's clothing like Confait, who liked to be called 'Michelle'. A married man with children, Goode had separated from his wife, but she and the children lived in the house, and Confait had taken a room there in February 1972.

Goode told the police that he had been awakened by the smell and sounds of a fire. He had alerted his wife before setting off for Catford Bridge station to phone the fire brigade. But Mrs Goode had been disturbed by the wild-eyed look of her husband, and had sent a neighbour after him. The neighbour found Winston Goode in such a state that he was unable to use the phone, so the neighbour called the fire brigade. During intensive questioning by the police, Goode let slip that 'Michelle' had been going to leave the house in Doggett Road to live with another lover. Goode admitted that he was jealous, but denied having a homosexual relationship with Maxwell 'Michelle' Confait. The police nevertheless took hair and semen samples from Goode before releasing him.

When they went back to Goode on the following Monday, he had lost his mind and couldn't remember anything about the fire or matters connected. He was admitted to Bexley Psychiatric Hospital.

That Monday there was an outbreak of small fires close to Doggett Road. One was at a semi-derelict house, 1 Nelgarde Road, and at twenty minutes past five that afternoon, PC Roy Cumming stopped Colin Lattimore in Nelgarde Road. Lattimore, an eighteen-year-old, but who was educationally sub-normal with a mental age of eight, immediately admitted being involved in starting the fires. Cumming asked him if he knew anything about the fire in Doggett Road the previous Friday, and Lattimore replied: 'I was with Ronnie. We lit it but put it out. It was smoking when we left.'

Ronnie was fifteen-year-old Ronald Leighton, and Lattimore accompanied police officers to his house. There the police found Leighton with fourteen-year-old Ahmet Salih, and all three boys were taken to the Murder HQ that had been set up in Lea Road. There, in breach of the Judges' Rules stating that, 'As far as is practicable, children (whether suspected of a crime or not) should only be interviewed in the presence of a parent or guardian, or, in their absence, some person who is not a police officer and is of the same sex as the child', they were interviewed alone and separately by Superintendent Jones and Detective Inspector Graham Stockwell.

Lattimore and Salih claimed that they had been hit at the interview by temporary DC Peter Woledge, one of the arresting officers. Lattimore's nose bled, and Salih had been made to cry. Leighton claimed that he had been pushed around.

Another irregular procedure took place later that evening when Lattimore's parents and Leighton's mother arrived at the police station. They were told that their sons were ready to make a statement, and they were asked to witness this. Both the boys confessed to the murder of Maxwell Confait and to starting the fire in Doggett Road.

The taking of Ahmet Salih's statement had to be delayed for a Turkish interpreter to be called due to the poor English of the boy's mother. He confessed to starting the fire at Doggett Road, but insisted that he had only watched the killing of Confait.

It was one o'clock on Tuesday morning when Salih's statement was taken, and a little later that day all three were charged with murder. It was a good result for Superintendent Jones, who had the whole case wrapped up in less than four days.

When the three boys appeared at Woolwich Magistrates' Court on 2 June 1972, the prosecution relied heavily upon their confessions and they were committed for trial at the Old Bailey. Salih was allowed out on bail, while Lattimore and Leighton were taken to Ashford Remand Centre.

The coming trial caused neither the parents nor their legal representatives any great worry. Dr Bain and Dr Cameron had at the Woolwich hearing restated that Confait had been killed between six-thirty and ten-thirty on Friday night, and all three boys had cast-iron alibis for this period.

When the trial opened at the Old Bailey on 1 November 1972, with Mr Justice Chapman as the judge, and Richard Du Cann (brother of Tory politician Edward) leading for the prosecution, the accused, their parents and their lawyers were devastated to find that the legal goalposts had been moved. The police surgeon and the pathologist were now saying that Confait's death could have occurred as late as one o'clock in the morning. The heat of the fire, strangulation and alcohol had all speeded up the onset of rigor mortis, the medical men were now claiming.

It was a one-sided trial. When the defence tried to introduce the odd behaviour of landlord Winston Goode, the judge quickly shut them up, and in his summing-up he put much emphasis on the hooliganism of young people like the three accused. After three and a half hours on Friday, 24 November, the jury returned verdicts that Colin Lattimore was guilty of manslaughter, on the grounds of diminished responsibility, and also guilty of arson. He was ordered to be detained under the Mental Health Act without limit of time and was sent to Rampton Hospital. Ronnie Leighton was found guilty of murder and arson, and was sentenced to life imprisonment. He was sent to Aylesbury Prison. Ahmet Salih was found guilty of arson and burglary, and, because of his age, was sentenced to four years in custody at the Royal Philanthropic School, Redhill.

The three boys, on 26 July 1973, were all refused leave to appeal. George Lattimore, the father of Colin, was incensed by the injustice. When he had complained that DC Woledge had assaulted his son, ranks were closed and his complaint was swiftly dismissed. He wrote to everyone he could think of, including the Queen, without success. Carol Johnson, the local Member of Parliament, of the male sex despite the name, took up the matter with the Home Office, asking for the case to be reconsidered because of misconduct by the police and a breakdown of the judicial system. The replies were typical examples of establishment evasion, but the gist of them was that new evidence would be needed for the case to be reopened.

It was the National Council of Civil Liberties who proved effective in the face of failure by the government. They engaged one of the most prestigious pathologists in the country, Professor Donald Teare, to examine the medical evidence. Discounting any appreciable effect on the onset of rigor mortis of the heat of the fire or anything else present at that time, he stated unequivocally that on the medical evidence presented to the court, Maxwell Confait had died between six-thirty and ten-thirty in the evening.

Another breakthrough came with the change of government brought about by the general election of February 1974. Roy Jenkins and Alex Lyons, the new Home Office team, were committed to reviews of miscarriages of justice. Christopher Price, the journalist who had become the new MP for Lewisham, brought the press in to help. Shortly after these big changes, Winston Goode, who had found a new job as a metal-stripper in Catford, committed suicide by swallowing cyanide. As he had been the original suspect in the Confait murder, there was immense pressure that brought about a police inquiry into his death.

Long and involved actions in various fields followed until at last, on 18 June 1975, Roy Jenkins announced in Parliament that the Confait case had been sent back to the Court of Appeal. Under Lord Scarman this was to be a very different hearing from the previous one.

On Friday, 17 October, Lord Justice Scarman read the judgement. The three boys, now young men, were exonerated from any involvement in the murder of Maxwell Confait. In addition, there was insufficient evidence for the main arson charge and other minor offences. Colin Lattimore, Ronald Leighton and Ahmet Salih were promptly freed.

*

The 1970s began with an incipient movement for reform in legal administration. Most judges had by then come to accept the Murder (Abolition of Death Penalty) Act of 1965, but alarm had been caused by the thirty-year sentences on some of those involved in the Great Train Robbery. A murderer could expect to be released in something like ten years, and these long sentences seemed to value money above human life.

Lord Parker, the Lord Chief Justice at the time, was a hard-liner. He became more and more intolerant of the protest groups accusing the police of using methods more suited to Hitler's Germany than a democracy, and was appalled at the soaring crime rate. A backlog of offences was causing delays that had prisoners held on remand for long periods, something which exacerbated the problem of overcrowded jails. Though ready to admit that change was necessary, Lord Parker would not join in with the popular call for shorter prison sentences and an increased use of parole to ease the strain on prisons.

In February 1971 Lord Parker was succeeded by Lord Widgery as a new era in legal administration dawned. From the West Country, Lord Widgery was a rarity as a Lord Chief Justice who had never attended university. A reserved, detached manner made him seem cold, but he was sharp-minded and more flexible than his predecessor.

The changes in the system included the introduction of Crown Courts in place of the old Quarter Sessions. The new courts were to be presided over by High Court judges in their scarlet robes, and circuit judges and recorders wearing dark blue. The Lord Chancellor was given the power to fire High Court judges for incapacity or misbehaviour, and a retiring age of seventy-two was fixed. The Act bringing about these changes also transferred the jurisdiction of the Old Bailey to the Lord Chancellor's Department. But this was the only break with tradition in that respect, as the upkeep of the building and the ceremonial Sessions openings by the Lord Mayor remained with the Corporation, as did the twice-a-day escorting of judges into court by the sheriff and under-sheriff.

Just under a year after the appointment of Lord Widgery, Mrs Justice Heilbron, the first woman ever to preside as an Old Bailey judge, took her seat in Court 7, while Widgery first presided at the Old Bailey as Lord Chief Justice in April 1972. Before him was a nasty case in which a youth had broken into Westminster Cathedral. Finding the choir school headmaster in bed, the youth had robbed him at knife-point. Lord Widgery said gravely, 'The time has come when the public must be protected', as he sentenced the youth to five years' imprisonment.

In September of that year, Lord Hailsham, the Lord Chancellor, formally opened the new extension of the Old Bailey. Before a celebration luncheon served in the marbled Grand Hall, the Lord Chancellor unveiled a marble plaque incorporating the City of London's coat-of-arms.

The new courts had superb acoustics, something which was long overdue at the Old Bailey, as well as air-conditioning, and were of a design that, as well as providing other advantages, offered much greater comfort to the jury.

Yet only some six months were to go by before the Old Bailey was attacked and damaged for the first time since being bombed by the Luftwaffe. The attack came on Thursday, 8 March 1973, the day Ulster voted on a border referendum.

Some four weeks previously the Provisional IRA had hijacked four cars at gunpoint in Belfast. After being resprayed and fitted with false number plates, the four vehicles were packed with explosives, detonators and timing devices and driven to Dublin. Breaking away from the practice of using sleeper units in England, the Provisionals sent an eleven-strong team across the Irish Sea, some of them women, all of them young and relatively inexperienced.

One group left Ireland with two cars aboard the ferry on 5 March, and the second group left with the remaining two vehicles the following day. All eleven met up again in London, and the team stayed at a number of different hotels in Pimlico.

Marion Price had come over with the second group, while her elder sister, twenty-two-year-old Dolours Price, who was to take charge of the operation, flew in from Dublin the morning before the bombing. That evening the two sisters went to the Royal Court Theatre to see the play *The Freedom of the City*, the theme of which was not unrelated to their cause.

Before dawn on the morning of 8 March the team were driving the cars from where they had been left in the underground car park in Dolphin Square to their four destinations. One was left outside the Metropolitan police headquarters at New Scotland Yard, while another was parked outside the Central Army Recruiting Office at Great Scotland Yard, Whitehall. The third car was taken to Dean

Stanley Street, near Smith Square, where it was abandoned outside the British Forces Broadcasting Services. By half past eight that morning, when the fourth car was parked outside the Old Bailey, all four were in position and timed to explode at three o'clock that afternoon.

The eleven members of the team headed for Heathrow Airport to fly back to Dublin. But the Metropolitan police had been alerted the previous day by an unspecified warning of an attack. This came from an informer via the RUC.

A policeman noticed something suspicious about the number plates on the car outside New Scotland Yard. Explosive experts were called and the bomb defused. All but one of the team were arrested at Heathrow, three when they were already on the plane. The detective who questioned Marion Price at the airport at ten minutes to three reported that she looked at her watch and gave a pleased smile. The bomb outside the recruiting office at Great Scotland Yard had exploded six minutes previously, and the one at the Old Bailey went off at three o'clock.

One man died and one hundred and eighty people were hurt in the blasts. It would have been worse at the Old Bailey but for two things – the great iron gates had been closed by a warning, and this IRA operation was not as slickly professional as those that came later. Even as it was, workmen toiled all night clearing up debris that filled fifty dustbins. The entrance to the main building was severely damaged, and for a while only one makeshift court was functional.

Dolours and Marion Price, both attractive, were student teachers at St Mary's, one of Belfast's most prestigious Catholic training colleges. They, together with six others of their team, were sentenced to life imprisonment. Security became a priority at the Old Bailey from then on, with the judges who dealt with IRA terrorists being given protection.

An off-shoot from the trials of IRA activists and others was a serious erosion of the respect that the Old Bailey once had. One instance involved six black defendants who had staged a six-day siege involving hostages when attempting to rob the Spaghetti House restaurant in Knightsbridge.

Turning their backs to the bench, they displayed Black Power banners, and when asked to plead refused to do so, with one shouting, 'We have been pleading for five hundred years.'

'This is not a trial. This is a lynching party,' shouted another.

The judge ordered them to be removed and pleas of not guilty entered on their behalf. The accused men were brought back while the jury was being sworn in, but protested so volubly that they had to be taken downstairs once more. Only one opted to testify in his own defence, but used the opportunity to begin a political-style speech, and had to be silenced by Judge Mervyn Griffith-Jones.

At the 1977 Old Bailey trial of Martin O'Connell, Harry Duggan, Edward Butler and Hugh Doherty, four young IRA men who had carried out the Balcombe Street siege, and faced charges of murdering nine people and wounding two hundred others, all the accused were given massive sentences. As they left the dock, one shouted 'Up the Provos!', while another gave the V-sign to the judge, Mr Justice Cantley, who had an armed guard in the court and at his home. Other bombers employed ridicule to mock the Old Bailey and belittle the judge chosen to try them.

Yet the Old Bailey recaptured its majesty with trials like that of serial killer Dennis Andrew Nilsen. The story begins modestly with a complaint of blocked drains at 23 Cranley Gardens, north London. The property had been converted to six bedsit flats in the early 1980s, and on Thursday, 3 February 1983, annoyed tenants called a plumber because their toilets wouldn't flush. Arriving on Saturday, the plumber admitted that the blockage was too serious for him to handle. So a tenant telephoned a specialist company who sent engineer Mike Cattran to the property the following Tuesday.

Cattran traced the problem to a manhole at the side of the house. The stench was awful, and he noticed what appeared to be flecks of blood in the slime. Not relishing the task, he climbed down to investigate further and found pieces of rotting white meat, some with hair still attached to the skin. All of the tenants, including Dennis Nilsen, a quiet man in his thirties who worked in the Denmark Street job centre, denied flushing meat down the drains.

Never having seen flesh like it, Mike Cattran considered calling the police. But he reported the matter to his supervisor, Gary Wheeler, who went with him to the house the following day. This time there was no offensive smell when the manhole cover was lifted, and the blood-flecked slurry that Cattran had seen was gone. Wondering if he had imagined it, Cattran climbed down into the manhole and reached into the pipe. He pulled out a chunk of flesh and four bones that sickeningly resembled human fingers. As the manhole cover was replaced, two distressed tenants came out to say that they had heard someone scrabbling about outside during the night. On investigating they met Dennis Nilsen, who made an excuse of having gone out for a 'pee'. Cattran and Wheeler called the police immediately.

The manhole was explored, and lumps of human remains were placed in plastic bags and taken to the mortuary. Nilsen showed as much shocked surprise as the other tenants, but when Detective Chief Inspector Jay, who was questioning him, said on impulse, 'Don't mess about, where's the rest of the body?' Nilsen shook him by replying calmly, 'In two plastic bags in the wardrobe next door. I'll show you.'

Nilsen was arrested and taken to Hornsey police station, where Detective Inspector McCusker asked him, 'Are we talking about one body or two?' Nilsen answered, 'Fifteen or sixteen, since 1978. I'll tell you everything. It's a relief to get it off my mind.'

Nilsen adopted a cold, apparently frank attitude in the charge room. When asked if he was really saying that since 1978 he had killed sixteen people, he replied: 'Yes, three at Cranley Gardens and about thirteen at my previous address, 195 Melrose Avenue, Cricklewood.'

This seemed to be a ludicrous claim, for the police believed it impossible that such a catalogue of killing had gone on for so long undetected. But 195 Melrose Avenue, which had been renovated since Nilsen had lived there, proved he was telling the truth. He said he had burned people in the back garden, and more than a thousand charred bone fragments were unearthed.

Nilsen, whose English mother and Norwegian soldier father were divorced, had become a heavy drinker and made the discovery that he was a homosexual while serving as a cook in the army. Strangely, for a man who lured his lovers to his home and used them before killing them and cutting up the bodies, he had left the army because he had been appalled at the way it was treating the people of Northern Ireland.

With Justice Croom Johnson presiding, the trial of Nilsen began at the Old Bailey on 24 October 1983. It was impossible to dispute that Dennis Nilsen had committed the horrible crimes, so the defence was narrowed to a plea of manslaughter on the grounds of diminished responsibility.

On 4 November the jury, after one and a half days' retirement, found Nilsen guilty on all six counts of murder and two of attempted murder. Sentenced to life imprisonment, he wasn't long inside when he was slashed across the cheek by a fellow-prisoner.

'Am I mad? I don't feel mad. Maybe I am mad,' mused Dennis Andrew Nilsen, a paradoxical personality which shows what the Old Bailey has had to cope with in the past, and what it faces in the future.

12. THE MILLENNIUM

The Millennium has come and gone. The promising liberalism of the 1960s has long since degenerated into too many acceptances. Licentiousness followed, standards have taken a nose-dive. No progress has been made, but there has been a sideways shift. Barbarity and sadism was once the prerogative of the judiciary, whereas today such wickedness lies largely with those offending against the law.

In the days of long ago, poverty was the principal motive for crime. At the Old Bailey on 28 June 1777, a boy named Joseph Harris, aged fifteen, was sentenced to death for the theft of two half-sovereigns and some silver coins. Joseph collapsed when the noose was put around his neck on leaving Newgate Prison, and his father had to help lift his son into the cart and hold him as he sobbed all the way to the gallows at Tyburn.

At the Old Bailey on 18 April 1997, Sir Lawrence Verney, the Recorder of London and the Old Bailey's top judge, sentenced seven boys aged between fourteen and seventeen to prison for a total of seventy-seven years for the horrific gang rape of an Austrian tourist. An eighth boy, the fourteen-year-old leader of the gang, received a severe sentence the following day. There were no tears and none of the convicted youths showed the slightest sign of remorse as they were taken down.

Joseph Harris can be forgiven because he stole when he and his loved ones were starving. Yet no right-thinking person could excuse the vile behaviour of the gang of rapists who chanted 'F*** the white bitch!' as they dragged their victim towards the Regent's Canal, into the murky waters of which they eventually threw her, not caring if she drowned.

For the purposes of this book, the parallelism of these two terrible cases is that the immense evil in the case of Joseph Harris lay with the drunken gluttons enforcing the 'law', while the comparable evil in the rape case belongs solely with the perpetrators.

Another change over the last two decades of the twentieth century has capitalism, which is nothing more than an idea the same as communism or any other system, accepted as truth. With those who govern bred in materialism, greed has largely replaced poverty as the motive for crime, albeit a different kind of crime. The love of money is no longer regarded as the root of all evil. During a 1980 television interview, Margaret Thatcher hi-jacked the biblical Good Samaritan parable. Perhaps God was grateful to Mrs Thatcher for editing the moral of His parable, but the old GS himself could not have been best pleased when she said, 'No one would have remembered the Good Samaritan if he'd had only good intentions. He had money as well.'

Though he didn't meddle with the Bible, US financier Ivan Boesky boosted the 'New Order' of grab-what-you-can when in 1986 he proclaimed, 'Greed is all right. Greed is healthy. You can be greedy and still feel good about yourself.' There is no record of how good Boesky felt about himself when he was later disgraced for insider trading.

Ranting such as Boesky's and distortions like that of Thatcher put a wide smile on the unacceptable face of capitalism. But that smile was wiped off at the Old Bailey on Tuesday, 9 June 1999, when Jonathan Aitken admitted that he had lied in a High Court libel case by testifying that his wife Lolicia had paid the bill for a weekend stay at the Ritz Hotel in Paris. In fact, it was paid by an old friend and business contact, Said Ayas, an adviser to Prince Mohammed, son of King Fahd of Saudi Arabia, and godfather to Victoria, Aitken's daughter. In a desperate attempt to salvage his libel action, Aitken drafted a false statement for Victoria, who was sixteen at the time, and had her sign it before he submitted it in the High Court action.

The girl was later arrested but the Crown Prosecution Service decided not to prosecute her.

Jailed for eighteen months for perjury and perverting the course of justice, Mr Aitken had been regarded as a potential Conservative Party leader, and his great uncle Lord Beaverbrook had once described him as 'a very bright boy with a very bright future'. But the future was dark when he left the Old Bailey cells for Belmarsh Prison in a custody van which he shared with six men facing murder charges, five accused of armed robbery and two on rape allegations. His plan to use the law against others had backfired, and the law had, in turn, been used against him. It had cost him his wife, his freedom, his job and his good name.

It was a humiliating exit for a man who had resigned as Treasury Chief Secretary in 1995 to fight allegations made by the *Guardian* and the television programme *World in Action*, pledging: 'If it falls to me to start a fight to cut out the cancer of bent and twisted journalism in our country with the simple sword of truth and the trusty shield of British fair play, so be it.'

Poor shakes as a latter-day St George, Aitken succeeded only in proving that it wasn't journalism that was 'bent and twisted'. He was no longer an MP, having lost the seat in South Thanet, Kent, in the 1997 general election and resigning from the Privy Council. In court he had the moral support of his mother, Lady Aitken, and his eighteen-year-old twin daughters Victoria and Alexandra. Both the girls, who had arrived at court hand in hand with Petrina Khashoggi, Aitken's illegitimate daughter, cried when he was sentenced. His wife, Lolicia, who had announced the couple's separation immediately after the collapse of the libel case, was suing for divorce and was living abroad and consequently was not in court.

In June 1997, Jonathan Aitken had taken a High Court libel action against the *Guardian* newspaper and Granada Television. The defendants alleged that Aitken had, among other things, procured prostitutes for Arab guests at a Berkshire health farm, concealed his links, while Minister for Defence Procurement, with a Lebanese arms dealer and was financially dependent on Arab contacts including Prince Mohammed, son of King Fahd of Saudi Arabia. They had claimed that while Aitken was a minister staying at the Ritz Hotel in Paris in September 1993, he had allowed the Saudi party to pay his bill for 4,257 francs (£480).

Aitken said that he had stayed at the Paris Ritz hotel over the weekend of Sept 17–20, 1993, when, he claimed, he had been in Paris for social and family reasons. He had repeatedly told the court that he, his wife, Lolicia, and their daughter Victoria had planned to spend time in Paris en route to Switzerland, where Victoria was due to start at a new school. In the witness box for eight days, being relentlessly questioned by George Carman QC, for the *Guardian* and Granada, Aitken denied everything. He gave a confusing and convoluted explanation of how his wife had settled the bill at the Ritz in cash. He blamed the Ritz for mistakenly allocating his bill to his Arab business colleague, Said Ayas. Said Ayas, fifty-six, was a friend of the Saudi royals and he and Mr Aitken were directors of Al Bilad (UK), the British investment arm of a Saudi company owned by Mohammed bin Fahd, a senior son of the Saudi king.

Aitken's case began to crumble when his Ritz bill showed that he had made a phone call to the Hotel Bristol in the Swiss village of Villars, where his daughter Victoria was going to school. The *Guardian* sent a reporter to Villars, but the hotel had since closed down. Undaunted, the journalist persuaded a caretaker to let him search through boxes of old records in the basement.

The *Guardian* man discovered that Mrs Aitken had stayed at the hotel and had paid the bill with her American Express card. The credit card company was subpoenaed to release her statement for September 1993 and it showed that she had also used her card to hire a car at Geneva airport.

Aitken's sworn testimony had said his wife arrived in Paris by ferry and train and then went to Geneva by train. The fact that she had hired the car at the airport made it a strong possibility that Mrs Aitken had travelled by plane to Switzerland. While Aitken was still in the witness box, British Airways was issued with a subpoena to check the records for the relevant days. The airline's internal investigator established that a Mrs L. Aitken and Miss V. Aitken had flown directly to Switzerland.

Rocked by this, Aitken was defeated by Budget Rent-a-Car documents proving that the car his wife hired was returned to Geneva airport at the time Aitken said she was in Paris. Aitken metaphorically fell upon his own 'simple sword of truth'. He left it to his Counsel, Charles Gray QC, to inform the judge the next day that the libel action was being withdrawn.

The collapse of his case had left Aitken facing a £2.4 million bill for costs. In his bankruptcy petition to the High Court Aitken said he had assets of less than £40,000 but owed creditors approaching £200,000. The court heard that the *Guardian* newspaper and Granada Television rejected his offer of £840,000 cash over the costs bill. Even though, unlike the Good Samaritan, he had no money, Jonathan Aitken will be remembered.

The next political high-flyer to bite the dust at the Old Bailey was Lord Jeffrey Archer, who was handed down a four-year jail sentence for perjury and perverting the course of justice following guilty verdicts at the Old Bailey on 19 July 2001. The charges related to his successful 1987 High Court libel case against the *Daily Star*. Archer, a multi-millionaire novelist, once a candidate for London mayor and a former Tory Party deputy chairman, won £500,000 at his libel trial over claims that he had slept with prostitute Monica Coghlan.

Things began to go pear-shaped for Lord Archer in November 1999 when he issued a press statement announcing his resignation from the race to be mayor of London after newspaper allegations by his former friend Mr Edward Francis. In the statement Lord Archer said he had asked Mr Francis to cover for him because he was with a woman, and led the press to believe it was his former mistress Andrina Colquhoun. In fact Miss Colquhoun was in Greece on the night in question.

At the Old Bailey, Archer had denied using a false diary and concocting a bogus story in his defence of the *Daily Star*'s claims in the libel action. The prosecution alleged that Lord Archer procured a false alibi from Edward Francis, who was his co-defendant in the trial and had ordered his personal assistant, Angela Peppiatt, to forge a diary on his behalf for use in the libel trial.

On Friday 13 July, the jury retired to begin considering its verdict on two counts of perjury and three of perverting the course of justice arising from the peer's 1987 libel case against the *Star*. It had also to consider a single count of perverting the course of justice against Ted Francis.

The jury of six women and five men was sent out at 12.55 p.m. after hearing twenty-four days of evidence. Archer was convicted on two counts of perverting the course of justice and two of perjury, but cleared on a third charge of perverting justice. Archer's former friend and co-defendant Ted Francis, who had been asked to provide a false alibi for the libel action, was cleared of perverting the course of justice. The jury took 23 hours and 31 minutes to reach unanimous verdicts.

The *Daily Star* alleged that Archer had paid Monica Coghlan £70 for sex in 1986. After Lord Archer had denied these allegations, a sting by the *News of the World* had Ms Coghlan pictured accepting cash at Victoria station from Michael Stacpoole, Lord Archer's friend. Though denying having slept with her, Lord Archer, in what he described as 'an error of judgment', acknowledged offering Ms Coghlan £2,000 to leave the country to escape reporters.

Monica Coghlan, the former prostitute at the heart of Lord Archer's 1987 libel action against the *Daily Star*, died in a head-on car crash in April 2001. One of seven children, she was born in 1951. Her childhood was troubled and her schooling ended at fifteen. Soon after leaving home she was sexually assaulted, and was working as a prostitute by the time she was seventeen. Giving birth to a son in 1985, she lived with her partner in a bungalow in her home town of Rochdale. When her partner died she looked after her son alone during the week. Travelling to London at weekends, she solicited in Shepherds Market and Mayfair. She said it was in Mayfair that Lord Archer first approached her.

Monica was driving her blue Ford Fiesta in Scammonden, West Yorkshire, in April 2001. Driving a stolen Jaguar in the opposite direction was Gary Day, thirty-four, who lived in Huddersfield. Day had shortly before used an imitation firearm to hold up a chemist's shop. Running from the shop, he stole a taxi but collided with a Land Rover. He then threatened the driver of the Jaguar and roared off in it. He had travelled only 500 yards when he smashed the getaway car into Ms Coghlan's Ford. Monica was airlifted to Leeds general infirmary where she died from her injuries.

Gary Day pleaded guilty to the manslaughter of Monica Coghlan, and also pleaded guilty to robbery and possessing a firearm when he appeared at Bradford Crown Court. Day was jailed for life.

On Monday 22 July 2002, Lord Archer launched a Court of Appeal bid to challenge his conviction for perjury and perverting the course of justice. Lawyers for the disgraced peer argued that Archer was the victim of an 'unbalanced' trial. Archer, who was also appealing against the length of his sentence, had waived his right to attend the hearing, but his two sons, James and William, were in the public gallery of the packed courtroom.

Nicholas Purnell QC, outlining the grounds of appeal, told Lord Justice Rose, sitting with Mr Justice Colman and Mr Justice Stanley Burnton: 'The submission that we make on behalf of Lord Archer is that the first and fundamental ground which interconnects with all the other grounds of appeal was that the learned trial judge wrongly exercised his discretion not to sever the trial of Edward Francis.' Mr Purnell said the decision of the Old Bailey judge, Mr Justice Potts, not to sever the trial of Francis had an 'unbalancing effect on the equilibrium' of the trial. Counsel argued that Mr Ted Francis was 'in a position effectively as a substitute prosecution witness and a substitute prosecutor'.

However, Archer's application for permission to appeal against the conviction was rejected within hours. Lord Justice Rose told Archer's QC Nicholas Purnell: 'For reasons we will give later in the day we are against you in relation to conviction.' As the decision was given, Archer's sons bowed their heads.

Offset against the liars appearing at the Old Bailey for sentencing in December 1997 was a man in trouble with the law for threatening to tell the truth. Thirty-four-year-old Richard

Tomlinson, a former MI6 officer, was the first person to be prosecuted under the 1988 Official Secrets Act and the first MI6 officer to be taken to court under official secrets legislation since the Soviet spy George Blake thirty-six years earlier. He was charged under Section 1 (1) of the 1988 Act that makes it an offence for any former intelligence officer to divulge sensitive information acquired by virtue of that role.

Tomlinson, from Milton Keynes, Bucks, was jailed for twelve months after admitting a synopsis of a book of his experiences in MI6 that would detail the agency's 'tradecraft' and operations, and even include agents' names, had been sent to an Australian publisher.

Pleading guilty, Tomlinson, who was born in New Zealand but has British nationality, a Cambridge graduate with a first-class degree in aeronautical engineering, joined MI6 in September 1992 and was sacked in August 1995. Owen Davis, for Tomlinson, said that he had soon found himself 'all on his own in the middle of theatres where his life was at risk'. During a posting to Moscow under diplomatic cover, he gathered intelligence to help the West to keep track of the former Soviet Union's nuclear missile armoury.

But the crunch came for Tomlinson when he was given a six-month posting to Bosnia, working with the SAS in trying to identify war criminals. At that time, his girlfriend was diagnosed with cancer. Torn between staying in Britain with her and going to Bosnia, he had decided his job came first. His girlfriend's death coincided with his posting back to London.

Tomlinson told his former employer that he planned to write a book about his time as an intelligence officer, and a series of injunctions was obtained, restraining him from publishing the book. But he continued in this enterprise and there were allegations made in the *Sunday Times*. A further set of injunctions was then obtained.

Known as Agent T after the *Sunday Times* articles, Tomlinson tried to take his case to an industrial tribunal. On advice from MI6 that this might lead to the release of sensitive information, the then Foreign Secretary Douglas, now Lord, Hurd refused to allow him to do so.

In May of 1997 it was discovered that he might be intending to write a book, and to give that book to publishers in Australia. Officers of the Metropolitan Police Special Branch were dispatched to Australia to interview a publisher, who was able to give direct evidence of Tomlinson's intention to publish his manuscript.

On 31 October, Tomlinson reported a break-in at his home. Special Branch officers who arrested him amid fears that he was about to travel to Australia accompanied the investigating police officer. They found a copy of his book on an electronic personal organiser and a computer disk containing a second copy.

There had also been concern that Tomlinson, who had an 'excellent knowledge' of the workings of the Internet, might attempt to publish his memoirs there.

With that novel case at an end, greed once again reared its ugly head at the Old Bailey on a massive scale in 2002 – although this time the defendants were not politicians. On Monday 18 February five men were convicted of attempting to commit what would have been the world's biggest ever robbery, had it not been foiled by the Metropolitan Police Flying Squad's 'Operation Magician'.

The five men were arrested in a massive police operation on 7 November 2000 as they tried to steal the De Beers Millennium Diamonds: eleven rare blue stones and the 777-carat flawless Millennium Star from the Millennium Dome in Greenwich, southeast London. Worth over £200 million, the diamonds are second in value only to the Crown Jewels. Armed with smoke bombs, ammonia and a nail gun, the gang crashed into the Dome in a stolen JCB and smashed their way into a high-security vault.

A speedboat had been moored close by for the gang's escape, but they were arrested virtually seconds before taking the diamonds. The gang had spent months meticulously plotting the heist, but so had the police operation codenamed 'Magician', the biggest undertaken in the history of the Flying Squad.

In summer 2000 the Metropolitan Police Flying Squad learned that a major armed robbery was in the planning. The police knew the identities of some of the robbers, but not the location of the projected heist. It was known that the gang was highly organised.

A major surveillance operation using officers from the Met's Directorate of Intelligence was launched. Within weeks police were sure they knew the venue of the robbery – the Millennium Dome in Greenwich.

On 1 September 2000 the police saw three of the suspects, William Cockram, Raymond Betson and Aldo Ciarrocchi, enter the Dome. They followed Cockram as he went straight to the Money Zone, entering the De Beers Millenium Diamond Exhibition to spend some time filming the vault with a camcorder. He then met up with Betson, and they videoed the surrounding river and jetty. Ciarrocchi joined them later, and the police then observed the three of them reviewing the videotape that Cockram and Betson had recorded earlier and studying a plan of the Dome. Members of the gang were also seen with a stolen yellow JCB mechanical digger at the Old Coal Yard in Whitehart Road, Plumstead.

Around 200 officers, including forty specialist officers, involved in Operation Magician gathered at the Dome in the early hours of 7 November 2001. Some were dressed as cleaners and had guns concealed in plastic bags and dustbins. Others patrolled there dressed as employees.

At 9.30 that morning the JCB, its cabin adapted to hold four people, crashed through a gap in the Dome's perimeter fence in Drawdock Road and rammed open the double locked gates at Gate 4. In the grounds of the Dome the JCB crashed through the side of the Millennium Dome and careered towards the Money Zone. Braking quickly outside the diamond exhibition, three men, all wearing gasmasks and body armour, jumped down from the cabin. Two of them entered the vault while the third kept watch outside.

Inside the vault, a loaded Hilti gun was fired into the glass of the cabinet containing the 777-carat Millennium Star diamond, and the cabinet was smashed with a sledgehammer. The gang then started on the second cabinet where the eleven rare blue diamonds were displayed. At this point the order was given to arrest the robbers. The man keeping watch outside threw a grenade in the direction of approaching armed officers. It exploded into a ball of blue smoke. He was swiftly overpowered and was found to be carrying further grenades, a firework and ammonia.

With the men outside the vault detained, the police used distraction devices to overpower and arrest the two men inside the vault. The driver, who was still inside the JCB, was arrested then, while other members of the gang positioned at various locations in the area were taken into custody.

At the Old Bailey, Robert Alvin Adams, Aldo Ciarrocchi, William Thomas Cockram and Raymond John Betson were convicted of conspiracy to rob and Kevin Peter Meredith was convicted of conspiracy to steal. Betson and Cockram were each jailed for eighteen years. Adams and Ciarrocchi were each jailed for fifteen years and Meredith was jailed for five years.

Judge Michael Coombe told them: 'You played for very high stakes and you must have known perfectly well what the penalty would be if your enterprise did not succeed.'

Two days later, on Wednesday 20 February, a sixth man involved in the robbery plot, Lee Wenham, aged thirty-three, was sentenced to four years in jail after pleading guilty to conspiracy to steal. At the same time he was sentenced to nine years after pleading guilty to an attempted robbery which took place at Ayelsford, Kent, in June 2000. Proceedings were dropped against another man, fifty-nine-year-old James Wenham, who had been charged with conspiracy to rob in relation to the raid on the Dome.

History was made in October 1997 when the first police officer to be charged with murder while on duty appeared at the Old Bailey. In February 1995, PC Hodgson, forty-nine, a firearms expert, was a member of the crew of an armed response vehicle that spotted a stolen sports car outside a shop in Barnes, south London. He shot David Ewin, thirty-eight, twice as he tried to drive the car 'like a maniac' in an attempt to escape.

PC Hodgson claimed that he had no other choice when he fired at Mr Ewin as he shunted backwards and forwards at high speed. Mr Ewin, a convicted criminal on licence from a five-year sentence for armed robbery, was high on a mixture of cannabis, cocaine, heroin and alcohol. John Bevan QC, prosecuting, said that as Mr Ewin tried to drive off, spinning the car wheels until they smoked,

PC Hodgson grabbed hold of his shirt and other vehicles boxed him in. There was a danger at this stage, said Mr Bevan, that Hodgson would be squashed between the cars. After trying to smash the windscreen with the butt of his gun, the officer moved to the pavement where he crouched down and fired two shots.

'The shooting of Ewin was unnecessary at a time when the physical risk to the defendant had passed because he was on the pavement and could have stepped back had he wished to,' Mr Bevan said. There were other options open to the officer, and by the time he pulled the trigger of his regulation issue Glock pistol, Ewin posed no threat to him or to bystanders. 'The only danger he posed was to the bodywork of the cars around him.'

Mr Bevan added that PC Hodgson's partner, PC Patrick Kelly, had never drawn his gun. He had described himself as 'very confused and shocked because at no stage had he perceived it as an armed incident'.

As Mr Ewin was hit, he shouted: 'You bastard, you have shot me in the stomach.' He was flown to hospital by air ambulance and was operated on, but died two weeks later.

PC Hodgson, who had been in the police firearms unit, SO19, since 1980, had denied murder and manslaughter, but he had already faced two trials. His first trial the previous December had aborted just before the jury was due to retire after an outburst from the public gallery. The second jury was unable to agree a verdict. At the Old Bailey on 14 October 1997, a jury acquitted PC Hodgson, but the incident led to a wide-ranging review of police firearms procedures. Outside the court, Detective Superintendent Aidan Thorne, of the Criminal Investigation Bureau, said, 'There are a large number of lessons to be learned and they are actively being considered.'

Mr Ewin's mother, Jean, described the verdict as outrageous. She said: 'People steal cars all the time – it's no excuse to shoot.'

In the autumn of 2002, the Old Bailey added a bewildering new dimension to its long and fascinating history. It was a trial that had as a backdrop a gift-giving culture within a royal world so strange that it seemed surreal to the average observer. Paul Burrell, former butler to Diana, Princess of Wales, faced three charges of stealing from the estate of the Prince of Wales and Prince William. Burrell, forty-four, of Farndon, Cheshire, denied stealing 310 items from Diana, Princess of Wales, the Prince of Wales and Prince William. Police officers who raided the former butler's home say the house was covered in royal memorabilia and photos. The presiding judge, Mrs Justice Rafferty, ruled that some evidence could be withheld to protect princes William and Harry.

One item deemed so sensitive by police that it was initially not identified in open court, but details about it written on a piece of paper and handed to the judge, was the signet ring belonging to her former lover James Hewitt that Diana kept in a locked box in her sitting room. Police who searched Mr Burrell's home did not find the ring.

Mr Burrell had made a thirty-nine-page statement to the police in which he had referred to a private audience with the Queen after Diana's death, in which he had told her that he had kept some of Diana's possessions for safe-keeping.

The detective who had led an investigation said to have cost £5 million, Detective Chief Inspector Maxine de Brunne, wrongly told Prince Charles and Prince William that there were photos of Mr Burrell and other royal staff dressing in Diana's clothes at parties. Less weirdly, but just as erroneously, the police told the princes that Mr Burrell had sold some of Diana's possessions abroad.

The trial sensationally collapsed on Friday, 1 November 2002, when it was confirmed, too late to save the taxpayer a small fortune and to prevent an Old Bailey trial from being labelled a fiasco, that Burrell had told the Queen he was keeping some of Diana's possessions. As the decision was announced, Mr Burrell sobbed in the arms of his defence lawyer, Lord Carlile.

Following closely at the Old Bailey was the trial of another royal butler, Harold Brown, who it was alleged stole property belonging to the estate of Diana and sold it on to Jan Havlik, who worked in the jewellery department at Spink and Son. The circumstances of the Paul Burrell trial had the prosecution conclude that there was no longer a realistic prospect of a conviction against Harold Brown on any counts of the indictment.

As ever with the Old Bailey, there was the barbaric as well as the bizarre. On 27 November 2000, Damilola Taylor, a refugee from Nigeria who had been in Britain only four months, bled to death in a stairwell on the notoriously rundown estate where he lived in Peckham, south-east London. He had been stabbed once in the leg, the knife severing his femoral artery. Four boys were charged with his murder but two were acquitted early in a three-month trial costing more than £7 million, which ended in April 2002 with the acquittal of the remaining two defendants. The Crown failed even to overcome a defence suggestion that Damilola was not murdered but could have died after falling onto a broken bottle. The verdicts left the Metropolitan Police greatly embarrassed after a £2.8 million investigation involving 120 officers. After the bungled inquiry into the murder of the black teenager Stephen Lawrence in 1993, the Metropolitan Police had been anxious to achieve convictions.

Another horror story was that of David Copeland, twenty-four, of Cove, Hampshire. He was the nail-bomber who had terrorised London in 1999, who was put on trial at the Old Bailey in June 2000. A racist with a hatred of homosexuals, Copeland had told Dr Philip Joseph, a psychiatrist called by the prosecution, that he had planted bombs in Brixton, Brick Lane and a gay pub in Soho because 'I knew it would piss everyone off, especially, like, Blair and Mandelson and them lot – Mr Boateng'. Copeland explained that he thought Mr Mandelson was homosexual and Mr Boateng was black. He admitted planting the bombs, including the one in Soho that killed three people and injured seventy. Though he denied murder, he admitted the manslaughter of Andrea Dykes, twenty-seven, who was pregnant, John Light, thirty-two, and Nik Moore, thirty-one, on the grounds of diminished responsibility. Copeland received six life sentences after being found guilty of three murders in an attack on a Soho pub in April 1999.

Another murder trial at the Old Bailey in 1996 was made all the more chilling by the youth of the accused. Earlier that year, sixteen-year-old Learco Chindamo, a school drop-out and leader of a gang of would-be Triads, had been questioned about the mugging of the husband of Barbara Mills, the Director of Public Prosecutions. Mr John Mills collapsed in his wife's arms after the attack near his home in Camden, north London. He had life-threatening wounds but was saved by emergency surgery. But the terrible story of Chindamo doesn't end there. On 17 October 1996, he was convicted of murdering the Roman Catholic school headmaster Philip Lawrence and ordered to be detained indefinitely. Mr Lawrence died after being stabbed as he tried to protect one of his pupils from a gang attack outside his comprehensive school.

These were really violent times and at the Old Bailey on 14 April 2000, Kenneth Noye, fifty-two, a key member of the gang behind Britain's biggest armed robbery in 1983, and who had escaped conviction after killing a police officer fifteen years previously, was jailed for life at the end of the M25 road-rage trial. Noye remained expressionless as the jury convicted him of murdering Stephen Cameron by stabbing him twice to end a roadside punch up.

Can the final pages of a book such as this profess to have registered any real change in criminality and the judiciary since page one? Sadly, the answer is no. New Labour in 1997 promised an effective system of law and order, but nothing has altered. Ours is still a class-driven society. If the laws of corruption were ever applied absolutely, it would probably be necessary to recruit the mugger and the burglar and the benefit-fraudster as jailers.

Neither, of course, are judges infallible. A century and a half ago, Macaulay wrote of the judiciary:

> The authority committed by our legal system to a judge is of such a nature that only the most humane and advanced among men can withstand the occasional temptation to abuse it. How many men or women are proof against the impulse to give vent to a feeling of irritation when out of health, or when nerves are in a state of tension? A few words spoken by defending Counsel may give offence to a judge, and at that instant the fate of the accused may be settled once and for all.

Some things may have changed since Macauley's day, but human nature isn't one of them. A quest for equity has our legal system deal not with facts but with opinions on facts. Defending counsel fight to defend accused they know to be guilty, while prosecuting counsel go all out to secure a conviction although possibly suspecting the innocence of an accused. Caught in the crossfire, truth perishes.

Our travels through the history of the Old Bailey reveal that it has done harm as well as good. Macaulay was unable to suggest an alternative, and neither can anyone today. What we have isn't good – but it's as good as we'll ever get.

SELECT BIBLIOGRAPHY

Caswell, J.D., *A Lance for Liberty* (Harrap & Co. Ltd, 1961)

Vanstone, Charles, *A Man in Plain Clothes* (John Long, 1961)

Rose, Lionel, *Crime and Punishment* (B.T. Batsford, 1977)

de la Torre, Lilian, *Elizabeth is Missing* (Michael Joseph, 1947)

Rude, George, *Hanoverian London 1714–1808* (Secker & Warburg, 1971)

Billett, Michael, *Highwaymen and Outlaws* (Arms and Armour Press, 1971)

Montgomery Hyde, H., *Judge Jeffreys* (Harrap & Co. Ltd, 1948)

Cole, J.A., *Law Haw-Haw* (Faber & Faber, 1964)

Barker, Dudley, *Lord Darling's Famous Cases* (Hutchinson, 1936)

Lang, Gordon, *Mr Justice Avory* (Herbert Jenkins Ltd, 1935)

Montgomery Hyde, H., *Norman Birkett* (Hamish Hamilton, 1964)

Adam, Harvey Lee, *Old Days at the Old Bailey* (Sampson Low, Marston & Co. Ltd, n.d.)

Van der Elst, Violet, *On the Gallows* (Doge Press, 1937)

Hancock, Robert, *Ruth Ellis: The Last Woman to be Hanged* (Weidenfeld & Nicholson, 1963 and 1985)

Sixty Famous Trials (Daily Express Publication, 1938)

McKnight, S., *Stagecoach and Highwayman* (Wayland Publishers, 1973)

Griffiths, Arthur, *The Chronicles of Newgate* (Bracken Books, 1987)

Gattey, Charles Nelson, *The Incredible Mrs Van der Elst* (Leslie Frewin, 1972)

Marjoribanks, Edward, *The Life of Sir Edward Marshall Hall KC* (Kessinger publishing London, 1929)

The Newgate Calendar (New Edition, London, 1960)

O'Donnell, Bernard, *The Old Bailey and its Trials* (Burke Publishing Co. Ltd, 1950)

Lord Russell of Liverpool, *Though the Heavens Fall* (Cassell & Co. Ltd, 1956)

Bechhofer Roberts, C.E. (ed.), *The Old Bailey Trials Series* (Jarrolds, 1946)

INDEX